GW00599300

THE
WHOLE
STORY

THE WHOLE STORY

Investigating Sexual Crime: Truth, Lies, and the Path to Justice

PATRICK TIDMARSH

JONATHAN CAPE

LONDON

3 5 7 9 10 8 6 4 2

Jonathan Cape, an imprint of Vintage, is part of the Penguin Random House
group of companies whose addresses can be found at
global.penguinrandomhouse.com.

Penguin
Random House
UK

First published by Jonathan Cape in 2021

penguin.co.uk/vintage

A CIP catalogue record for this book is available from the British Library

ISBN 9781787331037

Typeset in 12.25/16 pt Bulmer MT Std
by Integra Software Services Pvt. Ltd, Pondicherry

Printed and bound in Great Britain by Clays Ltd, Elcograf S.p.A.

The authorised representative in the EEA is Penguin Random House Ireland,
Morrison Chambers, 32 Nassau Street, Dublin D02 YH68

Penguin Random House is committed to a sustainable future for
our business, our readers and our planet. This book is made from
Forest Stewardship Council® certified paper.

MIX
Paper from
responsible sources
FSC® C018179

for Jacqueline

Contents

Introduction

Every sex offender I worked with taught me something. After a time, each conversation reconfirmed an understanding of how they see the world, and the effect they have on everyone around them. The patterns of offender action and victim reaction, whether they targeted adults or children, repeated over and over again. What offenders taught me, most importantly of all, was how to listen to victims.

We all know someone who has been sexually abused in childhood or raped as an adult. You probably know several people, whether you realise it or not. Perhaps you are a survivor yourself. When that person you know was abused or raped, whether it happened once or over a long period, they almost certainly kept it to themselves, at least for a time. Even with recent increases in reporting rates, only about half of adult rape victims will ever tell anyone, even their best friend.[1] Only about 5 per cent of victims will tell the authorities at the time of the offence.[2] Children are the least likely to tell anyone straight away.[3] Many people think that, if something bad happened to them, they would immediately tell the authorities and seek justice, but that isn't what victims of sexual crime usually do.

A fourteen-year-old girl and her sixteen-year-old boyfriend were in their local park, in the early hours of the morning. After going to a party, they were hanging out for a while before going home, when a group of young men came by. The boyfriend reported that he was physically assaulted and ran for help.

The girl reported that she was raped and sexually assaulted, by several of the men. The following day a colleague of mine, and the senior investigator on the case, was being interviewed about the matter by a local radio station. The broadcaster asked if he would answer the many texts being sent in by listeners, to which he agreed. The broadcaster then read out a text which asked, 'What's a fourteen-year-old girl doing out at that time of the morning?'

My colleague expressed his amazement at the question and, when asked what amazed him, suggested to the listening audience that the first question should have been, 'What's a group of men doing raping a fourteen-year-old girl?'

So why *wasn't* that the first question? Why would that listener focus on the actions of a teenage girl, rather than the adult offenders? Was their real question, 'Please tell me that can't happen to my daughter?' Did the world seem safer to that person if they could believe that the girl had somehow brought it on herself? Whatever the reason, their reaction drew them away from where the real responsibility lay. The girl later withdrew her complaint. We should all wonder why.

We might feel as if we know a lot more about sexual offending than we have ever done before. You probably hear something about it almost every day, as stories of sexual harassment, sexual assault, rape, and child sexual abuse are everywhere. We also seem more prepared to listen now, with inquiries leading us to many uncomfortable truths. The foundations of institution and family have been shaken, as we have dared to give them a critical look. What was previously too hard to believe is now almost commonplace. Even the rich and powerful have had their attitudes and behaviour exposed ... and still most victims do not come forward.

When the senior British politician Harriet Harman published her memoir,[4] she described the sexual harassment she had experienced in her university days. A lecturer, she said, had threatened a diminished grade unless she had sex with him, and guaranteed an A grade if she did. In the publicity around the book she was invariably asked, 'Why has it taken you so long to come forward?' and, 'Why didn't you say anything at the time?' In the interviews I heard or read, no one asked how she had coped, or even sympathised with her predicament. There was little open inquiry, just challenge, suspicion, and doubt.

How we listen to victims and how we ask questions matters. It isn't wrong to question how a victim reacted, but they aren't the most important questions, they shouldn't be the first questions and, when they are asked, it needs to be done with care. When we don't interview victims properly, don't *listen* to them, three things happen: we *sound* as though we doubt them, they will *think* we don't believe them, and we won't get the *whole story* of what happened.

So why don't more victims come forward? The answer is all of us. Our attitudes and what we believe about these crimes, the questions we ask, and what we think we know. It influences everything: who tells, how cases are investigated, who gets their day in court, the way we treat victims when they do get to court, and who gets held accountable for their actions. Think about the last time you heard the story of an alleged sexual offence. What did your mind do when you heard it? Was it deciding what happened ... filling in the blanks ... deciding who was telling the truth and who wasn't, even though you didn't know all the facts ... hadn't heard the whole story? I still find myself doing it and, after more than thirty years listening to these stories, I really ought to know better. It's the old teachings that make us do it, judgments we were taught as children, subsequently reinforced over time, and hard to get out of our heads. Take this case, for example, of a kind all too common in reports to police.

A woman goes for a massage. She works in geriatric care, so massages are a regular part of coping with the physical and mental stresses of her work. When she can't get a booking with her usual masseuse, she opts to try a new clinic that has just opened nearby. Her first impression of the masseur is that he is professional and polite, so it is a slight surprise when he instructs her to remove all her clothing, something she has not been asked to do before. Her alarm is minor, however, and his suggestion that the oil may damage her underwear allows a reasonable explanation for the instruction. She dismisses her concern. Her next anxiety is raised by him not leaving the room so that she may disrobe. He merely turns away to type into his computer. This too is new, so she is unsure how to respond. How might he react if she asked him to leave? It would be awkward and embarrassing, which is not the tone she wants at the beginning of a massage. She also puts her doubt aside when he turns to ask her a question as she is undressing, because he only looks in her eyes ... and when he doesn't replace the covering towels properly, because it's probably just a mistake ... and when his hands stray close to her nipples. Her brain deals with each alarm individually, not seeing the behaviour as an offender's pattern of manipulation. Why would she? Who goes for a massage imagining the masseur might be a sex offender?

After the abuse, a prolonged act of digital rape during which she lies frozen on the massage table, he doesn't make eye contact. At the end of the ordeal, he says 'How was that?', and she can't believe the words out of her mouth. 'Fine, thanks.' She is shocked and confused, even paying on the way out without complaint. Asked by the receptionist if she has had a good experience she answers, 'Yes, thanks.' Unsure whether to go to the police, she decides to 'just put it behind her'. In the weeks that follow she is barely able to sleep or eat, her brain full of conflict. She worries people will think she was asking for it. She doesn't understand why she didn't stop him. Blame and shame swirl around her head for days. Two weeks after the assault she drives into the car park at her work and cannot get out of the car. Unable to control her sobbing, and a rising sense of panic, she decides to get some help. Despite the urgings of her sister, she does not go to the police. There is just too much shame and blame from the voices in her head. Some of them are our voices, raising questions, suggesting judgment. Some are old voices from her childhood and adolescence, and some are imagined voices from the justice system she expects to encounter. Reviewing what happened, she sees only her actions and not his. She doesn't know that a specialist sexual crime investigator (if she gets to tell her story to one, and if they're any good) would immediately see the pattern of the offender's behaviour, understand her reactions without judgment, and be able effectively to investigate her case.

It is not just adults who are trapped by offenders' behaviour and the voices in their heads. It happens to children too, as in this case.

A fourteen-year-old girl is sitting in her bedroom. It is evening time, on a school night, and her mother is out at work. Her brothers, both older and younger, are in bed. She puts on lingerie, goes downstairs, and knocks on her father's bedroom door. As she enters the room he says, 'What are you doing here?', before she initiates sex.

As we read those lines, many of us might wonder why she went to his room in the first place, or why she put on lingerie and initiated sex. Some of us might assume she had been groomed, because that word is common these days, but I wonder how many of us would know how that happened. And did you wonder why most of your questions were about her, and not him? Even though offending begins with offenders, we reserve most of our questions, and doubts, for victims.

I have told this story a lot, over the years. It comes from one of the first men I ever listened to, when I was working in a sex offender treatment programme in the early 1990s. I've told it to all sorts of people, and they all ask similar questions. Hardly anyone asks about him, at least at first. What he did, how he did it, why he did it, how he silenced her, how he kept it from his wife (if he did), and so on. In almost every group I speak to, most people also give the daughter some of the responsibility for what happened, because she initiated it, didn't she? Remarkably, there are usually a few that say she is more responsible than him. Until they hear the whole story.

In treatment, the offender in this story told me everything he did and what he thought about it. He gradually disclosed how he had manipulated her from the age of six, how he groomed her to come to his room and 'initiate' sexual acts, and how he made her keep the secret. In his distorted thinking he had always blamed her, even though she was only a child. He began to understand how he had lied to himself about what he was doing, preferring to believe she was enjoying it as much as him, and that they were the acts of a loving father. He slowly demonstrated all the tactics he had used to hide the abuse from his wife and family. Eventually, he acknowledged that all the responsibility was his.

We have come so far in our response to offenders and offending, but there are some critical things still holding us back. Some of them are in our judgments and our questions, and others are in the systems we have created to make justice, as in this case, told to me by a prosecutor colleague, as he wrestled with the frustration of his day in court.

A ten-year-old boy is sitting looking at a screen in a room that connects, via video-link, to a court room. He is about to give evidence against his uncle, who has been sexually abusing him for several years. The boy has already given his evidence to the court, carefully laid out by the prosecutor. The boy knows the prosecutor well now, and he trusts him.

Then it is the turn of the defence. She seems polite, but the questions are more difficult, more complicated. Sometimes she asks two questions in the same sentence and he doesn't understand what she's asking. There is not much the prosecutor can do to help, and the boy feels as if he is on his own.

She keeps going on about the things he got wrong, particularly the dates and times. On and on about them, mostly memories he is less clear about. She keeps going back and forward, back and forward. While never crossing the line, she keeps testing him, because the law requires that his evidence be tested. And he begins to get confused and flustered.

'It is possible, is it not, that you were mistaken about that time?'

'Yes.'

'And if you were mistaken about where you were on that day, then you may have been mistaken about other times, isn't that right?'

'Yes.'

'In fact, I put it to you that your story is full of fabrications, isn't it?'

He doesn't really know what fabrications are, but he knows he has to answer. He feels stupid and begins to weaken. 'Yes.'

'Untruths.'

'Yes.'

Defence seizes the opportunity, as she's been in this position before.

'You have said a number of things that aren't true, haven't you?'

'Yes.'

'It is possible then, is it not, that everything you have said here today is untrue?'

Confused and bewildered, he gives in. 'Yes.'

Case dismissed.

A short time later the prosecutor, who has absolutely no doubt that the little boy has told the truth about the abuse, makes his way across to the building where the boy gave his evidence. The boy rushes up to him. 'I lied! I lied!' he cries, sobbing uncontrollably.

'What did you lie about?' the prosecutor asks.

'I told the lady that he didn't do those things, but he did do them … he *did* do them!' A while later the prosecutor, a veteran of this field of work, took an extended break from sexual offence cases, although he has since returned. I don't know how the boy is doing.

It is not always like this, but I can recall so many cases where this was the result, that it seems like the norm rather than the exception. A defence barrister once told me it was 'like shooting fish in a barrel'. When researchers ask court officials and the legal fraternity if they would advise parents and children to seek redress through the adversarial system, if they experienced sexual abuse, many warn against it.'[5]

Our attitudes, our questions, the way we listen, and the system we have created to hear these stories, are what victims fear. We may think that matters have improved in recent times, but is that so? In a time when a man who openly boasts of sexually assaulting women was elected to the US presidency, and who publicly criticises any complainant who raises their voice, how safe is it to come forward with stories of sexual harassment and assault? It is not widely known but, in the last thirty years, across the developed world, conviction rates for sex offences have *gone down*.[6]

And yet, as I started writing, a movie mogul fell, followed by a stream of others. A TV star was, after decades of sexually abusing women, sentenced to prison. Stories are pouring out about them, most notably about how long people have known, and tolerated, their behaviour. Questions have been asked of victims, but mostly with compassion, in attempts to understand. A few have said the victims were 'asking for it', attention-seeking, or looking for money, but most have not. Two cardinals of the Roman Catholic church have been found guilty of sexually abusing children, although one was later acquitted after multiple appeals. They are, by far, the highest-profile clerics to face charges. Some have said it was a 'witch hunt', or a conspiracy against the church, but most have not.

There are so many stories now, from so many walks of life. Is it possible that we will see that the man who runs the movie studio is the same as the man who runs the supermarket, works in the pet shop, the HR department, or the paediatric ward? Will we all finally realise how endemic this behaviour is in our communities?

It is too early to tell if the impact of #MeToo, and a raft of royal commissions, will produce long-term changes. In the past, these fallen figures were all too easily dismissed as isolated cases. Is that changing, or will most of these men still attend clinics for their 'sex addiction' and return unchallenged to their former lives? If charges are laid, how many will face trial? Looking at the number of current cases that don't make it to court, where trials are collapsing, or charges being dropped, there remain serious doubts.

Even though these issues are getting a lot of attention, it can also be hard to get free and open debate about sexual crime in our communities. I was giving a talk at a conference last year, discussing the breadth of scientific evidence about how sexual offending occurs, and particularly victims' reactions, when a woman asked a question. She had recently been in numerous conversations where the assembled company had debated issues of sexual politics and sexual crime. There were always voices, she said, demanding to know what all the fuss was about, challenging the feminist thinking and the 'man-blaming'. It was getting out of hand, they cried, and it was hard for men to navigate these uncertain times. She asked what her response could be to these voices. I suggested she could begin with a few statistics and see how the conversation goes from there:[7]

- 95 per cent of sexual offenders are male.
- At least 30 per cent of female sexual offenders co-offend with a male.

- 80 per cent of rape, sexual assault and child sexual abuse victims are female.
- One in five girls will be sexually abused in childhood, as well as one in twelve boys.
- One in six women will be sexually assaulted or raped as adults.
- Women are far more likely to be victims of sexual harassment than men.
- Violence and sexual violence are the number one 'burden of disease' issue for women.
- Only one in eight women will report rape or sexual assault, mostly owing to a fear of community judgment and our culture of victim-blaming.
- Up until 2015/16, fewer than two in ten sexual crimes reported to police were heard in court. In the last twelve months that number has *gone down significantly*.
- Sexual crimes have some of the lowest conviction rates of all interpersonal crime. These rates have also declined in the last thirty years.
- The chance of a rapist going to prison for his crime is less than 1 per cent. Fewer than 2 per cent will face any consequence at all.

These facts are backed up by decades of research, all pointing us to a problem with the structure of our relationships, a problem overwhelmingly driven by men. It is not that this is not happening to men too, because it is, although most of their abusers are also male.

It does feel harder for men these days, knowing our words and actions are more likely to be scrutinised. Like most men, I don't think I'm 'toxic', but I recognise the values I was expected to embrace growing up, messages that prepare young, white men for a lifetime of privilege, entitlement and dominance, rather than equality and respect. Like the woman at the conference, I am regularly challenged about whether the current climate has 'gone too far'. If it had, one might expect significant increases in prosecutions and convictions, but evidence suggests the opposite. Prevalence rates also remain high, suggesting a decline in sexual offending is also some way off. To make matters worse, wherever you look, around the criminal justice systems designed to provide protections and guidance, there are major flaws.

After two decades working with sex offenders, in prisons and in the community, I started working for the police in 2007, on a short-term contract. A colleague and I had been employed to develop a new specialist training course for sexual crime investigators. I had no intention of staying for longer than the two years of my contract. My colleague Mark, who joined at the same time, felt the same. He was there to improve police investigators' response to children and other vulnerable victims, while my focus was on helping them to understand the dynamics of sexual crime and the behaviour of offenders. Our goal was to improve the experience complainants had of police investigators and to make forensic investigations, particularly interviews with complainants and suspects, more effective. When we arrived, we spent time looking at policing and the court system, only to find problems and issues everywhere. We decided any real reform would take twenty to thirty years: an enormous task to which we could contribute only a tiny part. After a year, they asked us if we wanted to go on full-time, ongoing contracts, and we both said yes, immediately. Recently, I asked Mark why he decided to stay, when that had not been his original intention. He said, 'Because it isn't fair.' Once you see that unfairness, it is impossible to look away.

We know so much about offenders now, but so little of that knowledge has impacted on our culture and justice systems. Ironically, the way I learnt the myths and misconceptions of sexual crime came from listening to offenders. This book is about what they told me, as well as the testimonies of hundreds of victims and professionals I have worked with over the last thirty years. Through all their stories, I will describe how we currently respond to sexual crime, and what we now know about victims, offenders, trauma, memory, and healing. I will map out how police investigate sexual crime, including how we train them to interview complainants and suspects, before laying out how the courts understand and prosecute these offences. Finally, I will discuss some of the many positive projects and practices going on around the world, arguing for how we could do so much better.

We are all shapers of community attitudes and values, all fact-finders, and potential jurors. The better we understand these crimes, and particularly the effect they have on survivors, the more victims will come forward, the better sexual offending will be investigated, and the more tangible the promise of justice might become. Imagine what would happen, for example, if everybody in the justice system, from investigators to jurors, approached each story with an open mind, free of myths and misconception. As with every change, it must start with us.

Author's note

It is not possible to write about sexual crime without describing some of the worst aspects of human behaviour. The stories are distressing and can be deeply upsetting, particularly if these issues have touched your life personally. Even though my involvement has mostly been professional, there were still many I could not bear to write about. My motivation in telling these stories is to lay out, as clearly as possible, what is known about sexual offending and offenders, to inform current debates, and advocate for change.

There are things we all need to know and there's a lot of misinformation. I also realise that, like many people, I would not know it was misinformation if I had not spent so long listening to offenders and survivors. I grew up with the same messages, values, and misconceptions as everybody else. I am also a man, white, able-bodied, employed, and do not live in an institution – putting me in the least likely group to experience sexual abuse. I asked a colleague if some people might see me writing a book about sexual offending as a problem, because I am a man. Her advice was, 'We'll never get anywhere if we see sexual violence as a women's subject. Men need to be able to talk about these subjects, and, perhaps more importantly, to listen.'

The subjects of rape, sexual assault and child sexual abuse are laden with emotions and sensitivities. It is hard to write what needs to be said without causing upset and offence, so I want to explain the rules I have set for myself, in writing this book.

First, if you are a survivor, I want you to know that I am going to use the word 'victim' a lot, when describing the abuses, which will upset some. You may not like the word 'survivor' either, feeling it ties your future life too closely to the abuse you wish to leave behind. I respect that. When describing someone reporting a crime to police, I will use the term 'complainant', as that is the term used by investigators. None of these words is meant to define anyone or their experience, but only to clarify each aspect of the process, for readers who have not experienced abuse, or the justice system.

Pronouns are important, but I am not using the word 'they'. I mean no disrespect to anyone who uses 'they' to identify themselves. You will, instead, see the word 'he' used for offenders, and 'she' for survivor/victims. It is partly a writing shorthand, but it also reflects the statistics of sexual offending. I don't mean to minimise the fact that women offend, men can be raped, and that there are abuses in LGBTQIA⁺ relationships. However, sexual offending is overwhelmingly a gendered crime, perpetrated by men against women and children, where 95 per cent of offenders are male and 80 per cent of victims are female. Of the 20 per cent who are male, the majority will be abused as children.[1] Next, I am going to use the words 'child molester' in this book, instead of paedophile. There is an academic reason, that paedophile is only a sub-category of men who abuse children (which it is), but that is not my main reason. The original Greek word means 'child lover', and I can't bring myself to use it.

It is not possible to cover all inequalities and vulnerabilities equally, so I have predominantly focused on the core problem, of men's behaviour towards women and children. I am acutely aware that there are wider injustices and other groups who face abuse. Any inequality breeds further vulnerability, and vulnerability is what abusers are looking for. Groups outside the dominant norms will also face increased pressures in reporting, have greater trouble accessing the system, be less likely to have their cases heard, and have poorer court outcomes. This is so for, among others, young people and children in care, people of colour, the LGBTQIA+ community, the elderly, indigenous peoples, migrant groups, those without financial resources, people with mental health issues, as well as those subject to criminal justice orders or in prison. Anyone wanting to understand the relatively recent term of 'intersectionality' need look no further than sexual offending, where overlapping inequalities and vulnerabilities greatly increase both the risk of trauma and abuse, and reduced access to justice.

It would also be impossible, in the scope of this book, to cover all the intricacies of each country's criminal justice system. Every jurisdiction is different, but there are essential similarities, which common features I have tried to address here. Most of the stories and examples, but by no means all, are from the UK, US, or Australia, as these are the countries in which I have done most work. There are a lot of references and statistics, to demonstrate the evidence base for all the ideas presented. In all these contentious debates and emotive issues, it is imperative that you can fact check each topic. Where there is controversy, or the evidence is equivocal, I have tried to express that.

Lastly, I have changed names and details to de-identify the stories, except those that have already been published in print or online. Everything I describe in this book happened to someone. While the stories have been deconstructed to protect identities, I have tried to maintain their essential truths. They have been told to me by offenders, survivors, family members, and investigators over the last thirty years, and are as relevant today as the day I heard them.

Part I

Victims

There is a woman who comes to talk on our training courses, a survivor of child sexual abuse, perpetrated by her older brother over many years. She talks eloquently about her experience, of the struggle to get her mother to take the abuse seriously, and the rejection by her family when she disclosed. She describes visits to the doctor, who never asked why she had gynaecological issues so young, and the two trials she went through in her search for justice. She catalogues the inadequacies of the investigative and court processes and her experience of reporting to the police, from whom, at the second attempt, she eventually received a good service.

And she talks about shame. Shame about acts she didn't understand. Shame about the secret she was made to keep. Shame for taking the sweets, the toys, and the magazines. Shame about the stories she made up about her first kiss and her 'first time', because she couldn't say, 'It was my brother.' Most of all, the shame of feeling responsible, a feeling forced on her first by her brother, then reinforced by her mother and other family members. The justice system finally placed that responsibility where it truly lay, although most of her family still refused to accept the verdict.

Shame and blame are often a part of our response, too, with phrases like 'asking for it' still in common parlance. An exhibition in Molenbeek, Belgium, asked the question, 'What were you wearing?'[1] The exhibition shows the clothes that women and children were wearing when they were sexually assaulted. It has been followed by similar exhibitions in Japan and the US. Anything and everything are hanging in these exhibitions, from school dresses, office clothes and uniforms, to casual wear, sportswear, and evening outfits. Clothes that show the lie, in a thousand assorted colours.

The work I find most satisfying, if it doesn't sound odd to put it like that, are the historical child sexual abuse cases. The therapeutic nature of a good police response is evident here, perhaps more than in any other type of case. After years of fear, anxiety, and silence, to be listened to, and have one's story thoroughly investigated, can do wonders for a survivor's mental health. I have also known many survivors credit the investigator who first heard their story as the most important person on their road to recovery.

A couple of years ago one of our young detectives took a report from a man in his fifties, of abuse when he was a teenager. Newly trained, she recognised in his story the pattern of an extra-familial child molester. By the time the case went to court she had found fourteen other victims. Two of them were brothers, who had never previously spoken to each other, let alone police, about the abuse. Even when they did report they were reluctant to sign their statements. They had suppressed the stories, in part, because they had been introduced to the man by their sister, and they didn't want to upset her, or make her feel guilty. What struck me most about the brothers was the loneliness and isolation they had suffered for so many years, unable even to talk to each other, despite their shared experience. Feeling shame for the acts they were made to perform, for unwanted ejaculations at an abuser's touch, and for not telling anyone about it, they had suffered in silence for over thirty years. The investigator asked the brothers if they would meet with their sister, finally to tell her what had happened. After the resulting court case the offender went to prison and fifteen boys saw justice done. For those two brothers, finally released from shame and fear, the catharsis of telling the secret to each other, and reuniting with their sister, meant most of all.

Abuse does not define victims, but without our help and support it may have a longer lasting impact than it should, and life after abuse may only be surviving rather than thriving. Post-traumatic growth[2] describes a process long recognised, where recovery from trauma can leave people with a deeper understanding of themselves and their relationships, which may never have come about had they not needed to recover from terrible circumstances. It doesn't mean the abuse wasn't traumatic, or was a positive experience in any way, just that when the process of recovery is handled well, by the survivor and their community, it can lead to a positive outcome.

I first registered this phenomenon, quite by accident, many years ago. I was talking to a participant in a training day I had been a part of, as we all had a drink at the end of the day. As we got chatting, he told me of a terrible recent experience, while on holiday overseas with his wife and young child. He had become ill and been told he required urgent surgery and would not be able to return home for it, so severe was the problem. He was terrified, trying to cope with the diagnosis, the fear of surgery, and the prospect of a long recovery in a country he did not know and whose language he did not speak. To make matters worse, the hospital system only had a few nurses and didn't provide food, so his wife had to deal with everything except his immediate medical care.

I was riveted by his story. He and his family had got through it, but it had taken a toll, the pain and fear still etched into his face. He found he couldn't concentrate at work, his mind repeatedly drawn back to the hospital, and he wasn't even sure he cared about his work anymore. He was also experiencing, he said, a different way of seeing the world, as well as a calmness and sense of peace he could not explain. I just listened and asked the occasional question, initially unsure of what to say, but the more he talked, the more I realised what extraordinary insights he now had. He had to give a presentation the following week and was worried that his concentration would let him down and he would fall silent. 'They'll wait,' I said, 'because you understand the world now in a way that we don't, and we want to hear it.' He seemed surprised, and he thought about it for a while. (Incidentally, I'm not professing any therapeutic skill here, as I was brand new to the therapy business and was just trying to help him feel better. I think a few pints of Guinness also helped both of us dig into the depths and details of his story.) The more we talked, the more I kept seeing how this terrible experience also offered gifts, and that he now understood the world in a way many of us would envy.

The next day he came in and sought me out, telling me that he had gone home and told his wife all about the conversation, that they had talked through their experience for many hours. They had each been caught in their own worlds after the trauma, unable to comprehend what had happened to them. They had focused on their daughter, he explained, and tried to put the experience behind them. They had now resolved, he said, not to do that anymore, but to appreciate the changes and new insights that had been forced on them. Years later, when I was reading about the notion of post-traumatic growth, that memory popped into my head. Whether someone has experienced fear and pain in a foreign land, or the trauma of abuse, they have things to teach us about the worlds they've been subjected to, and how to survive and thrive after the abuse is finished, or the immediate trauma is over.

One survivor, who teaches on our course, talks about having to decide how she introduces herself when she is giving presentations. She is a successful career woman with strong professional credentials, as well as a survivor of sexual abuse. She has noticed, over the years, that when she mentions being a victim people's attitudes toward her change, and she feels that her standing is diminished. Whatever is prompting that response, it is something we need to change.

When Mark and I started in policing we noticed our investigators, rather than being focused on victims, concentrated on getting a confession from the suspect, and getting both a successful prosecution and a significant punishment for the offender. None of these things happened very often which, in a police service that focused on results, made sexual crime cases unpopular with investigators. There was little focus on victim welfare, or any perceived benefit for victims from the investigative process. The investigation model we introduced is centred on understanding the offending relationships and the process of an investigation, rather than the outcome. It creates practices that are more therapeutic for victims, as well as more effective forensically. The most important element is teaching investigators how to listen to complainants' stories. As Baroness Stern's 2010 review of the UK justice system's response to rape and sexual assault concluded, being listened to is inherently therapeutic.[3] Listening also tells us just how common these abuses are.

1

How much is this happening?

One day, training detectives, a young female investigator was looking at the statistics of how many people are sexually abused, both adults and children. She had a sceptical look on her face and said out loud, 'Nah. That can't be right.' That weekend she went home for dinner with her family. She told them about the training, about the figures, and her scepticism. In the silence after her comments her mother said, 'Well, it happened to me.' This was news that nobody around the table had heard before. When the young detective came back to training on the Monday morning, she was a changed woman.

We are all cynical about statistics, but the prevalence of rape, sexual assault, and child sexual abuse has now been analysed for over forty years, and the numbers haven't changed much. There is no need for exaggeration either, as the conservative figures are bad enough. Academics also agree under-counting, rather than over counting, is a problem for research conducted in this field.

As things currently stand, across the developed world, only about 5 per cent of victims tell someone straight away when they have been abused.[1] Of those who stay silent, many will stay silent forever. UK figures, in 2013, showed that between 430,000 and 517,000 people, mostly women, experienced sexual assault, and between 60,000 and 95,000 experienced rape.[2] Of those *total* numbers, approximately 54,000 reported sexual assault to police, and 15,670 reported rape. Averaged over a three-year period, the figures showed that fewer than one in five reported sexual assaults made it to court, where just over 50 per cent of those that did resulted in a conviction. In cases of rape, 2,901 reports made it to court, where only 1,070 resulted in a conviction. The 2017 survey[3] showed the estimate of sexual crime had risen to 646,000 sexual assaults, and rape estimates to approximately 120,000. Of these estimates, police recorded 80,001 sexual assault reports and 41,186 reports of rape. While case attrition rates have remained unchanged for some time, and conviction rates have been in steady decline for decades, the latest figures show charging rates in the UK have plummeted in recent times, particularly for rape.[4]

Between 15 per cent and 20 per cent of adult women will experience rape or sexual assault in their adult lifetime (after the age of fifteen).[5] Young women, between the ages of eighteen and twenty-five, are most at risk.[6] In any given year, approximately 2.5 per cent of the adult female population will experience rape or sexual assault, and one of those women almost certainly lives near you.[7] You may also know her abuser, because he is likely to be a partner or ex-partner.[8] The offending will usually take place in her home, the offender's home, or other premises known to her.

In childhood, approximately one in five girls, and one in twelve boys, will be sexually abused.[9] This represents about three girls and one boy for every classroom of children, of all ages, in every school, all over the world. Most of the abuse will take place before they are eleven years old.[10] These figures are conservative. Researchers agree that child sexual abuse is 'a global problem of considerable extent',[11] and, 'relatively common in the general population'.[12]

In the UK, between 2013 and 2017, reports of child sexual abuse to police more than doubled, from 24,085 to 53,496.[13] These numbers represent a fraction of what is really going on in homes across the country. The sexual abuse of children is happening in your neighbourhood, possibly in your street, to children that you know. You probably know the abuser here too. Until relatively recently, most messages about preventing child sexual abuse were about 'stranger danger'. While this is important, it makes up only a small percentage of abuse perpetrated on children. Like adults, children are usually abused in their own home, the home of the perpetrator, or another place they know, by people who claim to love them.[14]

The sexual assault and rape of men is, contrary to popular opinion, relatively common. It has been studied with far less frequency than the sexual abuse of women, but nonetheless there are reliable figures about how often it is happening. Approximately 4 to 5 per cent of men report that they have been sexually assaulted in adulthood (after the age of fifteen),[15] a small proportion of which is at the hands of women. In any given year, 0.5 per cent of the male population will report that they have been sexually assaulted.[16] Like women, they are unlikely to report the abuse to the authorities.

The sexual abuse of boys is also far more common than generally believed,[17] with most abuse perpetrated by men and older boys.[18] Although girls are sexually abused at much higher rates, some research suggests abuse of boys is proportionately more likely to involve penetration.[19] There is also evidence that boys are less likely to report than girls.[20] This may, in part, be explained by the double standard sometimes applied in sexual abuse cases, where the abuse is perpetrated by a woman. There is a repeated myth that boys are always happy to have sex, even when quite young and the women decades older than them. Research suggests the opposite: that the sexual abuse of boys, by women, can have long-lasting psychological effects.[21] Although most sexual offending is perpetrated by men, with about 5 per cent of sexual offending perpetrated by female offenders,[22] there is research that suggests the rate of women offenders may be higher, and is under-recognised and under-reported.[23] They are more likely to offend with men than male sex offenders are[24] and, when sexually abusing children, at least a third of female offenders will co-offend with men, or be coerced into offending by men.[25]

A significant proportion of sexual abuse experienced by children is perpetrated by other children and young people. At least 30 per cent of all offending against children is thought to be perpetrated by other young people.[26] As with adult perpetration, a significant majority of the children and young people doing the abusing are male. I have a colleague who works with young people with sexually abusive behaviours. Her service has seen a rise in referrals of girls in recent years, so they now make up about 20 per cent of the clients.[27] Most other programmes have also seen a rise, although nowhere near as steep as hers. I asked her why she thought the rise had occurred and she replied that, as with most kinds of sexual offending, we only saw it when we started looking. Hopefully, both research and therapeutic practice will continue to tell us what other factors we need to be aware of.

Offenders target vulnerability, so the more vulnerable the group or individual, the higher the risk of abuse. Being young has inherent vulnerabilities, so it will come as no surprise that young people are the most targeted of all groups. Over the Internet, thirteen- to seventeen-year-old girls, closely followed by boys of the same age, are the most targeted.[28] In public space, eighteen- to twenty-five-year-old young women are most at risk.[29]

People with disabilities are at greater risk than those without, as are people with mental health problems, or intellectual disability. Both research studies and police data suggest that having a disability more than doubles the risk of abuse.[30] Offenders are aware that people suffering a cognitive or physical impairment, or a mental health issue, are less able to report. They are also the least likely victim group to have their cases heard in court, and twice as likely to have their reports deemed by investigators to be false.[31]

Indigenous peoples, minority, and migrant communities, are also over-represented in the statistics of abuse.[32] Gay and bisexual men report higher levels of sexual victimisation than heterosexual men, and bisexual women more than lesbian or heterosexual women.[33] Economic disadvantage is also a significant risk factor.[34]

Alcohol and drugs are commonly present in cases of sexual assault and rape, particularly alcohol. Even when it comes to so-called 'drink-spiking', it is usually spiked with extra alcohol, rather than prescription medication or other drugs.[35] That does happen, of course, but alcohol is the main culprit and, whether self-administered or not, alcohol is incapacitating and leads to misjudgments and confusion. For offenders, it creates a vulnerability they can exploit.

This book is about sexual crime, not relationship and family violence, but it is important to recognise the connections. The extent of violence in our homes and relationships is staggering, with the police force in my area typically recording six times more reports of violence than of sexual crime.[36]

In the UK, according to the Home Office, 'There are some 2.4 million victims of domestic abuse a year aged sixteen to seventy-four (two-thirds of whom are women) and more than one in ten of all offences recorded by the police are domestic abuse-related.'[37] I heard one senior police officer, in Australia, estimate that family violence and sexual abuse make up more than 50 per cent of all police work. Research shows victims of family violence are seven times more likely to die when rape and sexual assault are part of the abusive relationship, with sexual abuse the strongest individual predictor of worsening violence.[38] Studies also suggest that children growing up in a violent home are often more than just witnesses to violence and are at significant risk of violence themselves.[39] They are also much more likely to be sexually abused than children who grow up in a home without violence.[40]

Some research says that sexual offending is beginning to decline, including studies by the well-respected child sexual abuse researcher, David Finkelhor, who has been writing about this field for decades.[41] The National Society for the Prevention of Cruelty to Children (NSPCC) says a report of child sexual abuse, in the UK, is made every eight minutes, and that police figures show sexual abuse against children is on the rise.[42]

2

The aftermath

A woman goes for a night out with her husband. There is an 80s dance night at the local pub and everybody is going. It's a fun night, with lots of drinking and loud music, and she hasn't had a good dance in ages. Her husband fades early, as he's been putting in long hours at a new job and he doesn't like crowds. She knows a lot of the people there and she's having fun, so she tells him she'll stay for a while. After a few drinks she wants to let her hair down a bit, so she dances with a few of the guys. She is friends with their wives, and it's all good fun. A song comes on she loves, and she goes for it. Carried away, she lets slip to her new dance partner that she thinks dancing can be better than sex. It's a silly comment, and not like her really. He replies that he will show her how good sex can be if she likes. He puts it crudely, too, telling her what he'd like to do and to which bit of her. The fun goes out of everything and, at the end of the dance, she makes her excuses.

She tries to get back in the party mood but now, wherever she goes, he keeps trying to be in her company. She wants to go home, but it's a long wait for a taxi, so she decides to walk. Ten minutes later a car pulls up, and there he is. He grabs her between the legs, saying he knows she wants it as much as he does. She says she does not. He doesn't listen.

When she gets home later, she goes straight to the shower. As she climbs into bed with her husband, she wakes him up. Desperate to erase the events of the last hour, she wraps herself around him and they make love. She just wants it all to be normal, like it never happened.

She tries to forget, but then the text messages start. She doesn't know how he got her number. Don't tell my wife, she wouldn't understand, and I've got kids. He is writing as though it was an affair. Then the insomnia starts, and the days where it is a struggle to leave the house. She has horrible dreams where she's floating away in a strong current. There is a rope, but she can't reach it. She goes to the GP, and asks for pills, but doesn't tell the doctor the real story.

Months later she tells her best friend. The next summer, when they're away from home at a friend's wedding, she tells her husband. She has been so terrified of how he'd react, but he shows nothing but love. He is angry, but also supportive of her.

She tells the police everything she can remember, including her stupid comment, the drinking, and the flirting. She details how he followed her and how she said no, time and again. The police are supportive too. They believe her, but they know what his defence counsel will do when it gets to trial. Carefully, they will prompt the jury to think that she gave mixed signals, was maybe even 'asking for it'. They know juries can fall for that, especially when they're mostly male. She feels the police and prosecution have done everything they can and is grateful for their support, but she believes them when they say her prospects are no better than 50–50. They are right. A not guilty verdict is delivered.

Women and men who experience this kind of assault can suffer a range of debilitating after-effects: PTSD symptoms, depression and anxiety disorders, and substance abuse problems.[1] There is evidence that they are likely to need higher rates of medical care, like hospitalisation, or persistent GP visits, for years after the original trauma.[2] Relationship violence, sexual assault, and rape are the biggest contributors to the burden of disease in women worldwide,[3] as well as a significant factor in homelessness for women.[4]

A thirteen-year-old girl came home from school. She had just got an 'A' on a maths test and texted her parents to let them know. When she walked in the door, her father was there to greet her. He congratulated her and gave her a hug. It was not a 'Well done' hug, but one that came with the signal that he wanted 'special time' with her later. There are other signals, so small that anyone watching wouldn't notice, all denoting how she must behave towards him. She tried everything, when she was little, to get her mother to notice, but has long since given up trying. Her father told her it would ruin everything if she knew, and that they would *both* be kicked out, so she decided to just keep handling it until she can leave home. The years roll on. Every time her mother goes out … 'Special time'. One day she can't take it anymore and starts an argument, before storming off to stay with a friend. When her friend's mother asks what's wrong, she drops a hint. Met with understanding and kindness, the rest of the story comes out. Before long, after emotional conversations, she and her mother go to the police. Her father, frantically calling both their phones, suspects what is happening.

So far, during the first sixteen years of her life, she has had to understand how to live in multiple worlds, and she's had to work out how to do that by herself. All the different rules, even for the weird worlds. She has kept the secret, a constant anxiety. Constant. All the while she missed the way life was meant to go and how kids are supposed to learn. She realised it sometimes too, when she saw the way some of her friends were with their dads. She never had the chance to explore at her own time and pace, because everything she learnt was skewed by his lens, his view. A view she would struggle to get out of her mind.

Research suggests the most severe effects come from abuse by those closest to us: the younger it starts, the closer the relationship, the longer it goes on for, how frequently it occurs, and the more the abuse involves penetration, the harder it will be for victims to recover, survive, and thrive once the abuse stops.[5] Compared to a girl who has not had to endure this kind of childhood, she will be more likely to suffer from depression, anxiety and other mental health problems. The penetrative abuse she suffers has been linked to later development of psychotic and schizophrenic disorders.[6] She will be far more likely to suffer from eating disorders, to self-harm, or commit suicide. She will be much more likely to have drug and alcohol problems, or to die of an overdose.[7] She will find it hard to trust, to believe in touch, intimacy, or kindness. Although most child sexual abuse victims will recover and avoid abusive men in adult relationships, victims are more likely to have a future partner who is violent, or sexually abusive, than those who grew up without sexual abuse.[8] It isn't a case of picking the wrong kind of man, as some might say, but the other way around. Abusers will, both consciously and unconsciously, seek her out.

A police colleague and I got into a discussion with a defence barrister about the nature of harm caused by sexual offending. He was defending, literally and figuratively, a couple who had groomed a fourteen-year-old girl into making pornographic films with them. The girl had been in the care system for some time and had a previous history of abuse. Given those facts, he said, 'I can't see where the harm is being done.' How wrong he is, as it must surely have compounded any trauma from earlier years, further breaching her connection to people and community. The most important phase, for the long-term recovery prospects of anyone who discloses, is the period immediately after disclosure. Disbelief is devastating,[9] chaos or inaction nearly as bad. Listening, prioritising safety, removal of the offender, support, and reassurance, are a good start.

The justice system provided little or no satisfaction in either of these stories. Fortunately, the people around them did all the right things: listening, support without judgment, placing responsibility where it belonged, the right kind of help, time and space to recover. Love.

In both these stories there were also other people to tell, to help recovery, acknowledge what happened, and offer support. Research is clear that healing from the psychological, physical, and emotional impacts starts with positive reactions and support on disclosure. Victims need to be able to tell their story, have community acknowledgement of the wrong done to them, and be sustained by strong social networks.[10] For those who never disclose, or receive a negative reaction, these pillars to recovery are not present. As the trauma expert Judith Herman expresses it, 'The core experiences of psychological trauma are disempowerment and disconnection from others. Recovery, therefore, is based upon empowerment of the survivor and the creation of new connections.'[11]

Listening is the beginning of reconnection with community. Every victim needs to tell their story without fear or shame, and we must hear them without judgment. Without a path for recovery being laid down, suffering continues long after the abuse itself has stopped.

3

Fight/Flight/Freeze/Surrender

There are only four ways people can react to sexual offending. They can fight back, run away, freeze with indecision, or surrender to their abuser. When we think about these possible reactions, what do we want people to do?

Every time I ask people that question, whether it's training police investigators or talking to groups who have nothing to do with the criminal justice system, they say the same thing. We want them to fight back or, if not, at least run away. Despite what we might wish, however, they hardly ever do. It is reasonably common that people freeze, but far and away the most common response is to submit to offenders' demands. Some people do fight back, of course, so let's start with them.

Several years ago, a detective colleague of mine was grabbed from behind as she got out of her car and walked to her front door. The man put his arm around her throat and tried to drag her into the neighbour's garden. His intent was clear. She immediately tried to free herself and fought him off as hard as she could. As she struggled, he hit her repeatedly in the head, and she struggled even harder. After what seemed to her like hours, but was probably only a matter of seconds, he gave up and ran away. She didn't react like that because she was a policewoman. She fought back because her brain reacted to the alarm before she could think. In her career she had been confronted by violence, or the threat of violence, on hundreds of occasions, and had never reacted with aggression before. When there's time to think, we do not fight.

Another woman was out jogging near her home, on a path popular with runners and cyclists. She ran there every day. A male cyclist approached her from the front and, as he passed, she felt a violent blow to the side of her head. She fell to the ground, physically and mentally stunned. He dragged her to a secluded area, off the path, pushed her down and began to rape her. After a short while, he complained that her clothing was bothering him. He lay down and told her to take her tracksuit pants off and 'get on top', which she did. When he was finished, he got on his bike and rode off. Only then did she put her clothes back on and run for help.

Later, when decisions were being made about whether to prosecute this case, the focus turned to her reaction. Would a jury be able to understand why she did not run away when she had the chance, and would that cast doubt in their mind about whether she was telling the truth? Would the prosecution need an expert to explain it? In our adversarial system, defence lawyers play on a jury's lack of knowledge and suggest that victims' behaviour is questionable. And think about it: what do you want her to do? If she can't fight back, then run away at the first opportunity and get help, right? Me too, but that rarely happens, except on television. The real problem with this thinking is that we have a way of turning what we would *like* to happen into what we think people *should* do.

There is compelling scientific evidence that, under conditions of trauma, our brains are incapable of functioning in their usual way. Decision-making is scrambled, and logic is hard to find. As one traumatic memory expert put it, 'Trauma shocks the brain, stuns the mind, and freezes the body.'[1] This can continue for some time, and will affect everything victims do afterwards: whether they choose to tell someone, the way they tell their story, and how they remember the event. Going over cases in my mind, I can only remember a few occasions when people have reacted by running away. It usually happens when someone interrupts the offence in some way, or there is a clear path to safety. When there is any doubt about that path, people will not run.

The scientific explanation for these reactions is that people who are surprised, and who have little time to think, often react instinctively, in a fight-or-flight response.[2] When people have time to think, this reaction is much less likely. When we have time to consider the risks and weigh up the options, our most common reaction is to do nothing. Most victims have plenty of time to think.

One evening, about fifteen years ago, I was travelling home from a football match on the train. At first the carriage was rowdy, full of supporters and people who had spent the day in town. As we got further out the numbers dwindled. There were two people sitting opposite me and, on the other side of the aisle, a woman and man, seated next to each other. The woman across the aisle was no more than three feet away from me. After a few more stops the man got off. As the train pulled away from the station, the woman who had been sitting beside him turned to us with a look of shock and bewilderment on her face. We all noticed immediately and one of us said, 'Are you OK?' She blurted out that he had been groping her from the moment he sat down, maybe ten minutes before. At first, she thought he was just getting comfortable in his seat. Then, when she realised that she was the subject of his attention, she froze. Her shock was two-fold: that someone would do this to her, and that she hadn't done anything to stop him. Even though we were all right there, she said nothing to bring attention to her plight, which is a common response.

I have a friend, who is also a colleague in the police, and works in the sexual crime area. She is young, fit, and does power lifting. She did our specialist sexual crimes investigator training but wasn't entirely convinced about the teachings on victim reactions. One evening, only a couple of years ago, she was travelling home on the train. It was busy, so she had to stand, and a man stood behind her. He began to touch her sexually and she froze for a few moments, before moving to the other side of the train. He followed her, once again positioning himself behind her and sexually assaulting her, and she froze again. As the train pulled into the next station another man got off. As he walked past, he said, 'Good luck with him!' pointing to the man behind her. He had witnessed the whole thing and done nothing.

She stayed on the train until her stop and, as she got there, her police training finally kicked in and she ran for help. There were two officers at her station, and she got them to take the man's name and make a report. It never went to court, because the CCTV was 'inconclusive', and no witnesses came forward. Her word was not enough, even with CCTV pictures to back it up. Like the other woman, on the football train, my friend could not understand why she had done nothing. Even though she knew from her police training that most people freeze, she never thought that is what *she* would do. Her experience also demonstrates how lonely people feel in these circumstances, even though there were others around who could have, and should have, helped.

The scientific term for freeze behaviour is tonic immobility.[3] It is a biologically programmed response to threat that has been the subject of much research, including in sexual crime victims. My friend and colleague now, unfortunately, has experienced tonic immobility first-hand. She is now an even stronger advocate for victims of sexual crime.

Perhaps the response we find least comfortable occurs when victims surrender to the abuse. Maybe it reminds us of our own fragility and helplessness, when we see it reflected in the behaviour of another. Whether provoked by violence, or the coercions and manipulations of grooming, surrender is by far the most common response to sexual abuse, as shown in these four cases.

A woman was woken from sleep in the early hours of the morning by a man standing at the foot of her bed, holding a knife. Her son, a strapping young man in his early twenties, was asleep in the room next door. The woman said, 'If you put down the knife, you can have what you want.' He did, and that is what happened, after which he left, and she woke her son and called the police. Faced with a weapon, and the desire to protect her son, she chose to surrender rather than risk the consequences.

Several years ago, a serial offender was attacking women, and 'attack' is an appropriate word here, as he grabbed victims from behind and pushed them to the ground, before attempting to rape them. On most occasions, the women fought him off or screamed for help. Within a few months he had changed his tactics, targeting bars and clubs, and attempting to form a relationship with women as they left these premises. He would pretend to be lost, or looking for another bar and, as the women talked to him, he would walk closer, no hint of threat in his voice. One of his victims described him as looking like someone who had just come out of a club, rather than someone who appeared threatening. She said the first inkling she had that there was danger was when his hand stopped her closing the car door. Then, in a calm voice, he told her to move to the passenger seat and, without knowing why, she complied, as she then did with each of his further demands.

A mother of two would hear her husband whisper in her ear, every Friday night, 'Go and get ready.' What had begun as sulking and withdrawal when his wishes weren't followed, progressed to verbal abuse and ridicule. Occasionally there was physical abuse, mostly choking and holding down, to show his physical dominance. When the verbal abuse was transferred towards the children, she succumbed completely. Attuned to the abuse and the abuser, and trapped by her instinct to protect, she wasn't sure who she was anymore. She complied with his request, and the indignities that followed.

A fifteen-year-old girl had lost touch with her mother, who was struggling with drug and alcohol addiction. Her biological father was long absent. The only constant in her life was a stepfather who was, for the most part, kind and loving. He provided a home and a routine. When she went to his bed they cuddled and talked. She knew that he would also expect sex, because she was used to it, and afraid of further rejection and loneliness.

I am always uncomfortable with the word 'surrender' because it sounds like giving up, which is not a fair representation of this survival strategy. There are always acts of resistance, as in this case: two of my detective colleagues, who have become good friends over the years, went to visit a man in his late forties, who lived in a remote country cottage. They had gone there because of a school photo, brought into their police unit by another man, who reported historical sexual abuse by a teacher at his boarding school, in the 1980s. When he showed them the photo they asked if he knew of any classmates who had also been abused. He began to mark which other boys had been abused and, by the time he had finished, only two faces remained unmarked. The man they were visiting was not one of those two.

As usual, as they approached the cottage, they came up with a cover story in case someone else answered the door. Knocking on doors after decades is a delicate business, requiring tact, skill, and empathy. One of them would usually stay in the car, as most victim/survivors, particularly men, find it easier to show emotion as privately as possible. At the first knock, there was no answer. At the second knock she heard a whistle, and turned to see a man, standing by a small garden shed. As she walked over, she could tell that he knew they were police. He averted his eyes as she got closer. 'I reckon I know why you're here,' he said.

'OK', she replied, 'and how do you feel about that?'

There was a long pause, before his knees buckled and he collapsed to the floor, his face wracked with pain and his eyes streaming tears. My friend said all she could think, in that moment, was not to cry herself. She knelt down, maintaining a safe and respectful distance, quietly explaining who they were and why they were there. He said he didn't know what to do or say, so she told him where they'd be staying in town, and that they would wait for him to get in touch.

Two days later he knocked on their motel door, surprised to find they were still there. She explained that this was their work, and that they knew these matters could not be rushed.

Over the next many hours, he detailed a string of abuses, of him and others. He described how helpless he felt, being so far from home, at the mercy of an all-powerful figure. His parents had sacrificed so much to send him to the school, he explained, that he couldn't bring himself to tell them what was happening. Despite his parents no longer being alive, after failed relationships and problems with alcohol, he still hadn't told a soul.

He remembered every boy in the class and put marks next to the names of all the same boys the first man had nominated. He also told them, without realising they already knew, that nine of the boys in the picture were now dead. Six of them had died at their own hand. 'What about the two who don't have crosses?' they asked.

'They punched him when he tried it, and he gave up,' was the reply. Extraordinary resistance from two boys, who would only have been nine or ten at the time.

There are many types of resistance, each requiring its own kind of courage. I have often been struck by the strategies that adults and children use to avoid or survive abuse, like the women who wear sanitary pads all the time, so when their abusive husbands grab them between the legs, they have a plausible reason to avoid further sexual contact. There were the sisters, and sometimes brothers, who took it in turns to go to their father's bed, basing the decision on which of them felt most able to bear it. There are children who pretend to be asleep, women who pretend to faint, boys who initiate abuse to protect their younger siblings. The list goes on and on.

There is another range of more involuntary strategies, where victims remove themselves from the reality of their situation. If you have ever found yourself lost in a movie, or so engrossed in a book that you didn't realise how many hours had flown by, then the experience of dissociation will be familiar, meaning a dis-association from identity, time, memory and place.

I heard a trauma trainer once describe dissociation as 'the spectrum of strategies for not knowing something', which neatly summarises the breadth of reactions that victims can experience. Many describe a process of being outside themselves, looking down on what is happening or taking themselves to another world. While this helps them survive the abuse, problems arise when they return to their lives and relationships. At one end of the spectrum is the phenomenon of Dissociative Identity Disorder (DID),[4] once known as Multiple Personality Disorder, where distinct personalities exist within the same person, regularly taking control of their behaviour. These personalities are known as alters and are a psychological protection mechanism from the effects of trauma. The development of DID is strongly associated with child sexual abuse and early childhood trauma.[5] In a 2019 Australian case,[6] a victim of sexual abuse was allowed to give a victim impact statement in the voice of her alters, each having a different expression of the trauma she had suffered.

All survival strategies carry a toll. Whatever ways victims survive the acts themselves, the fabric of relationships and trust is torn, emotions become hard to navigate, and the rules of everyday life carry less meaning. No surprise, then, that sexual abuse survivors often have issues with mental health, drug, and alcohol issues, and are also more likely to have trouble with the law. We will see later how this can cost them dearly when it comes to seeking justice.

4

Truth and lies

When someone walks into a police station to report a crime, police manuals will inform investigators that their first job is to establish whether a crime has been committed. The instruction is supposed to help them ascertain what has happened, so that they know how to apply the law and investigate the allegation. Somehow, though, in the investigation of sexual crime, this instruction has traditionally been interpreted to mean, 'Before you do anything else, check if she's lying.'

If the complainant is a child, or has a cognitive impairment, their evidence will usually be video-recorded. When the cameras are turned on, investigators will run a process we call 'truth and lies'. Every police force has a version, and the main intention of the process is to test the complainant's understanding of the concept of truth. Up until very recently, in my home state of Victoria in Australia, they were asked if they understood what a lie is, followed by a question about what truth is. The next question involved responding to a supposition put to them (the interviewer would hold up a pen but say it was a bunch of flowers, for example, to test if they could articulate the lie). Then, typically, they would be asked if they knew what would happen to someone who told a lie. It was argued that these were necessary tests of comprehension, better asked before time was wasted. on someone whose understanding was uncertain and who may pose a credibility problem in court. Here, too, there was the historical legacy of disbelieving women and children.

After years of lobbying, we are now able to use the much simpler, 'And is everything you've told me today the truth?' at the *end* of the interview, as would happen when any witness/complainant was asked to attest to the veracity of their statement. The final catalyst for change came from the introduction of intermediaries,[1] whose role is to assist children, and adults with cognitive impairments or disabilities, to tell their story. They have helped significantly to improve the quality of forensic interviews with vulnerable people.

I was listening to the *Today* programme a few years ago, as a senior official from the Crown Prosecution Service was interviewed. The prosecutor was there to talk about the rise in reports of sexual assault and rape being prosecuted by her office. In the allotted time to discuss the subject, the interviewer chose two areas to focus on: did the rise in these cases mean that other types of cases were not getting enough attention, and what evidence was there that the young women's stories were not fuelled by alcohol and regret? In short, were these cases important, and were the women lying? If you listen to interviews about rape and sexual assault these questions are usually asked, particularly the one about false reporting.

The seventeenth-century Chief Justice of England, Lord Hale, famously wrote that rape was an easy accusation to make, a hard one to prove, and an even harder one to defend. This view has been remarkably persistent over the centuries, being argued in courts well into the twenty-first century,[2] although it turns out only one of his assertions is true. If rape were an easy accusation to make, then more than one in eight women would report it. If it were hard to defend, then rape wouldn't have such high case attrition and low conviction rates. Those conviction rates, however, also show that he was right about one thing. In our criminal justice systems, particularly the adversarial ones, rape and sexual assault are awfully hard to prove. Several centuries later, in 2020, his namesake Baroness Brenda Hale, the former President of the UK Supreme Court, expressed the view that prosecuting rape has not got any easier.[3]

It is not only women who have had a hard time persuading the legal system of their truthfulness. Children have fared little better. As recently as 2009, an article in a prestigious law journal questioned the veracity of children's evidence, describing them as malicious, and as capable as adults of lying about sexual offending.[4] In fact, children hardly ever lie about sexual offending.[5]

The notion of women and children as liars has persisted into modern times, across the wider community, as well as in policing.[6] Asked to nominate a figure for the false reporting of sexual crime, most people place it higher, even considerably higher, than empirical evidence suggests. One young police officer, in training, put the adult false report figure at 100 per cent. That is, he believed every single woman reporting rape or sexual assault was lying. When asked how he came across such an incredible idea, he said, 'My sergeant says he's never had a real one.' In a recent lecture, to university students, one of them suggested the number was 85 per cent. He could not remember where he had learnt that figure.

In a way, I got a job in policing because of investigators' beliefs about false reporting. The Victorian Law Reform Commission, in Australia, produced a report detailing the failings in institutional responses to sexual crime. The police came in for significant criticism, particularly in respect of their attitudes towards victims. Detectives who were interviewed for the report believed that the rate of false reporting was between 40 per cent and 50 per cent, considerably higher than the actual figure.[7] They also believed that false reporting was even more common in country areas, which says a lot about how difficult it is to report in communities where everybody knows each other, and local men from all walks of life socialise together. Police forces in rural areas have also, traditionally, been overwhelmingly male. Interestingly, the uniformed police working in this field, usually women, put the figure lower. However, their figure was still much higher than the evidence suggests. Why was there such disparity between what investigators believed and the reality? Alongside the attitudes we all grow up with, they got it from police lore, handed down from generation to generation – from that sergeant to his new recruits, for example. They come from the ideas we all receive about how rapes and sexual assaults happen and how victims will react, so much of which has been profoundly wrong. They come from the domination of the justice system by men and the hyper-masculinity of traditional police forces, where crimes of violence and sexual violence against women were ignored, or relegated to second-class investigative status. And they come from language like 'regrettable sex': words used in policing to describe the woman who wakes up in the morning and, realising she has made a mistake, then reports what happened as rape, to cover her tracks and absolve herself of blame. Of course, this does happen now and then, but it is far less common than many believe.[8]

One of the problems in policing is that, when false reports do happen, they have a profoundly negative impact. Some of this is understandable, as investigators often feel duped, even betrayed, by someone they had put their faith in. Then there's frustration at the obvious waste of police time when there are always too many cases to investigate. The false report stories are widely circulated too, increasing the negative effect on both investigators and the wider police culture, reconfirming negative assumptions and beliefs about victims' stories. False reports, when they do occur, can also have a devastating impact on the accused person. There are serious consequences for false reporting, and rightly so, but they are seldom used. In policing culture, part of the reason police believe the false reporting figure to be higher than research suggests, is because they don't believe the official figure. They know it minimises the number of cases that could have been prosecuted. Not having a credible figure allows sceptics to set their own figure as high as they like. Having said that, false reporting should not concern us nearly as much as the high rates of non-reporting sexual crimes, and the small percentage of cases that are prosecuted or result in convictions (known as case attrition). These are, statistically and culturally much, much bigger issues.

There are other words, official words, that have shaped the debate about false reports. All police forces allocate a reason for the end of an investigation, logging it into their data systems with a word or phrase. In the UK, it is called 'no criming'.[9] This phrase is supposed to denote that it could not be established that a crime took place, and that the case was closed. It can be interpreted in different ways, however. Could it mean that a crime was not committed, or that investigators could not detect a crime? Could it mean they believed the complainant, but couldn't find enough evidence to support a prosecution, or that they didn't believe her and thought she was lying? A cynical person might think it means that a 'no crime' case will not be recorded as a negative on police crime statistics? A more generous interpretation might be that the case was just too hard to solve, too time-consuming, or a potential drain on an over-worked detective service. This lack of clarity about the meaning of key words and phrases, and how they should be interpreted, is a common theme throughout policing and the justice system.

Another phrase used by police is 'brief not authorised'. When a case is concluded, the investigator will submit a 'brief of evidence' to a senior colleague, who will then determine whether it should be sent to the prosecution service. The brief will include a recommendation from the investigator as to whether the senior officer should authorise it for prosecution. Sometimes investigators write extensive reasons for their recommendations, but often they do not. Sometimes there are codes that replace a full explanation, like 'complaint withdrawn' (CPWD) or 'victim withdrawal'. All police forces have codes or phrases like these for when a complainant decides they don't want to proceed with the investigation. Police have always been suspicious of people who report abuse and then change their mind.

There is an important caveat here, as withdrawn complaints do not always mean the system isn't working. Some complainants are satisfied just to make a report, or that the offender has been spoken to by the police. Issues arise, however, when there is a difference between complainants' expectations of the process, and the system's ability to meet those expectations.

Once complainants have given their evidence to police, the investigator will explain what will happen next and how their case might progress through the system, a process we call the 'options talk'. When victims know what they are up against they can change their mind, and understandably so. This hasn't stopped CPWD becoming a euphemism in many police forces for false report. Historically, options talks have also been a process where investigators, who were reluctant to proceed with cases they believed they couldn't win, would manipulate complainants into withdrawing. For the victim, this only adds insult to injury: the system didn't want your case, persuaded you to go away, and then insinuated you were a liar when you did.

There are other catch-all phrases like 'no further police action' (NFPA), which indicates that the investigator felt there was nothing else they could do, and the case was concluded. While not as damning as CPWD, this phrase still conveys the sense that the story lacked substance or merit. Then there is 'no offence detected' (NOD), a phrase destined to be interpreted in different ways, depending on the reader. Does it mean that the case was historical, witnesses were unable to be found, and nothing could be substantiated? Or does it mean that forensic evidence could not determine whether a sexual act had taken place? It is often interpreted as 'nothing really happened'. 'Insufficient evidence', as the noted conclusion of a case, is perhaps the clearest of them so far. Anyone reading the case notes, however, may still not be sure whether 'insufficient' meant that evidence was hard to find, wasn't enough to persuade a jury, or was not there in the first place.

Even when a case does go to trial, the prospect of the victim being seen to be lying doesn't go away. If the defendant is found not guilty, reactions can be swift and vicious. For example, a celebrated Australian Rules footballer was accused of rape. The case went to court and he was acquitted. As soon as the trial was over, social media sites lit up. There was a strain of commentary, from both men and women, calling the complainant out for being a liar, along with comments about what consequences she should receive for her lies.[10] Trials conclude with a decision based on whether a case was proven Beyond Reasonable Doubt. Occasionally that means she was lying, but mostly it means the prosecution couldn't eradicate every doubt.

The lack of clear language and practice has led to the belief that false reporting is significantly higher than it is. According to the best available evidence, the false report figure for sexual crime is between 2 per cent and 10 per cent of cases – probably around 5 per cent.[11] This includes all complaints that are thought to be false, for a variety of reasons, both malicious and not.

When I started training police officers it was one of the most contentious subjects that came up. There were arguments, sometimes lengthy, and occasionally quite hostile. Tempers were tested, and it was very hard work. On one occasion, I got so angry that I insisted the training group replicate a piece of research on false reporting carried out with sexual crime investigators.[12] This research looked at all the cases of rape investigated over a three-year period. First, they looked at cases resulting in a prosecution for false reporting, which had occurred in fewer than 1 per cent of cases. Then, to get over the statistical scepticism of police officers, they asked the original investigators to list any others where they had suspicions about the veracity of the complaint, or the complainant, irrespective of whether they could prove it. The final figure came to just over 10 per cent. So, even if the investigators were right in all their suspicions and, given the widespread myths about victim behaviour and the lack of specialist knowledge and training at that time, that is *highly* unlikely, they still only reached 10 per cent. I went to the seminar where the results were delivered. Even though it was their own work and their own views, some police investigators still didn't believe the figures. When we replicated this research in the training room, we got everyone to add up all the sexual crime cases they had worked on and follow the same process that the researchers had. The final figure, on that first occasion, came to about 3 per cent. Even though the classroom exercise began as an act of desperation and anger it became so successful that, in subsequent training, whenever there was a difficult group, we used the same exercise. We *never* got a figure above 10 per cent. Now, after ten years of specialist training, we rarely have an argument about the 5 per cent figure, because training and knowledge can change police lore, as it can with community attitudes. Most police forces still have a long way to go.

There are a few common types of false report. The most common type isn't really a false report at all, although it can be misconstrued as such by inexperienced investigators. Victims often tell part of their story to test the reaction of the investigator, only to add, subtract, or change details at a later stage. Given what they have come to talk about, and the crippling fear, self-blame, and shame that victims often suffer, this is hardly surprising. It can, however, lead investigators to lose faith in both the story and the storyteller.

There are reports by women, and sometimes men, with significant mental health problems, who continue to report acts of abuse that cannot have taken place as described. Sometimes these are attempted reports of real events, either contemporary or historical, sometimes an expression of past traumas, and sometimes delusions.

There are reports by young women who, when they tell a friend of participating in an act they found unpleasant or distressing, get talked into going to the police. Once they have told their friend, they can feel obliged to report it as a crime. Sometimes a complainant is caught out cheating by their partner, only to invent a scenario to show their behaviour was non-consensual. Again, once told, these stories are hard to back away from, and often go further than the cheater had anticipated. Finally, sometimes the stories are made up and malicious, to punish another or gain advantage of some kind. This last cohort is only a small percentage of total false reports.

There is also a persistent belief that women frequently make up stories about ex-partners sexually abusing their children during child custody disputes. There isn't a wide body of research on this subject, but what research there is says that this notion too is incorrect, and that the real figure of false reporting in these circumstances is about 12 per cent.[13] Here, too, not all claims of abuse are malicious, but the result of misunderstandings or misinformation in the middle of fractured relationships. A child might come back from a weekend visit with a rash around the groin area, for example. Stress and conflict might lead nappy rash to be mistaken for evidence of abuse, and authorities become involved. Research also found, importantly, that the false reports were from both sides of the custody battles, not just from mothers. The percentage of false reports directly from children was very low.

Dylan Farrow, the daughter of Mia Farrow, gave an interview about sexual abuse by her ex-parent, the filmmaker Woody

Allen.[14] In it she reiterated an allegation she had made twenty years previously and asked the question, 'How is this crazy story of me being brainwashed and coached more believable than what I'm saying about being sexually assaulted by my father?' Good question.

5

Myths and misconceptions

A few years ago, my colleague Mark and I ran a training session for senior judges. The judges' clerks, all up-and-coming young lawyers, were also present. The bulk of the session was on current scientific understandings of sexual offending, including a broad range of misconceptions. In the question time at the end a young woman put her hand up. 'Do you think that these myths and misconceptions have largely come about because of patriarchy and misogyny?' she asked, which was a gutsy question given the assembled company, of very senior, and mostly male, judges. She was looking at Mark when she asked, and he said, 'Yes'. She looked over to me and I said, 'Yes'. Then, in coincidental harmony, obviously feeling we needed to emphasise the point, we both said, 'Yes' again. There was a ripple of laughter, followed by a short silence during which, I can only guess, we all considered what that said about the system we all worked in.

The dynamics of sexual offending have now been the subject of significant scientific inquiry, mostly by criminologists, social scientists, and forensic psychologists, for over forty years. Although much of the evidence gathered refutes commonly held views, many myths and misconceptions persist. I began this book by saying that we, as societies and communities, represent the biggest barrier to, as well as the greatest prospect of, change. Each misconception we hold becomes a part of the problem, affecting attitudes, stopping victims from reporting, and impacting decision-makers and factfinders. This lack of knowledge provides the architecture of current failures to provide justice. Change starts with new knowledge, and attitudes can quickly follow suit.

It is extraordinary how many things we believe that are contrary to available evidence. A 2011 study in Ireland[1] looked at beliefs about rape and sexual assault in the general population. Participants were presented with twenty myths about rape and the researchers found, as McGee and her colleagues put it, 'Ten of the twenty rape-supportive beliefs were endorsed by *at least* 20 per cent of the sample' (my emphasis). Some myths were believed by 40 per cent of participants. It is little wonder that adversarial justice provides so few convictions, if 50 per cent of false beliefs may have the support of at least one in five jurors.

Some misconceptions occur because of the many and varied ways we interpret words that describe abuse, particularly the word rape. In the UK, non-penile penetration is called sexual assault by penetration,[2] but other countries have laws where any act of penetration is considered rape. Running 'respect and responsibility' training for professional football clubs,[3] ten years or so ago, I was surprised to learn how many participants thought that rape only related to penetration with a penis. They didn't know that where they played and worked, in Australia, penetration with fingers, objects, or tongues is classified as rape in almost every state and territory.[4] Even victims of rape don't necessarily connect the word to their experience. If you ask people, when conducting surveys, whether they have ever been raped, you get a smaller response than one might expect. If you ask them if they have ever had an unwanted sexual experience, and then describe the elements of rape, responses are much higher. I recently read an article about the Roman Polanski case, where another filmmaker said the case was not rape, but only 'statutory rape'. The girl (aged thirteen) had been 'down with it', he said, so it was just her age that made it rape.[5] He went on to explain his view that the word rape should only be used for violent acts, where people were physically assaulted and thrown down against their will. These views may explain, in part, why reporting rates are low.

There are just as many misconceptions about the sexual abuse of children. A 2010 study,[6] looking at the beliefs and attitudes of jurors in child sexual abuse trials, found 119 separate misconceptions about child sexual abuse. They were clustered in four key themes: denial of the extent of abuse, minimisations or exaggerations of the harm posed by child sexual abuse, stereotypes about perpetrator characteristics, and minimisations of blame attributed to perpetrators. A 2009 Australian study of 659 people found that fewer than half of the participants could provide accurate responses to two-thirds of the questions about misconceptions of child sexual abuse.[7] One can only imagine how many trials are influenced by those beliefs.

There are several key sets of broader misconceptions, each with a body of research that disputes them. One of the most damaging, and most often used by defence barristers to undermine a jury's confidence in the complainant, is the belief that people will report immediately when they have been offended against.[8] Even now, when some jurisdictions have directions (given by the trial judge) that a delay in reporting should not be seen to diminish the veracity of the complaint, defence will still insinuate that the delay is suspicious.

How victims behave when they do report is also the subject of misconception. Common sense may suggest that a person who has experienced a traumatic event would be highly emotional when they spoke about it, but that would be wrong. Victims present in a variety of ways, from aloof and detached, to calm, focused and rational, right through to distraught and barely able to speak.[9] One senior investigator described a case to me about these types of assumption. One of her junior investigators phoned to tell her that he was on his way to the scene of an alleged home invasion rape, in an affluent suburb, which had purportedly taken place that morning. The inexperienced detective was already sceptical, as these kinds of crimes are rare, and he had not experienced one before. She instructed him to put scepticism aside and investigate the complaint. When he arrived, the victim told him what had happened, quietly and calmly. Confused further by her demeanour, he became convinced she was lying, and even wanted to charge her with false reporting. The senior officer refused the request, and it was just as well she did, as the offender's DNA showed up in a series of other sexual assaults.

In conversation with a very senior judge, who is a strong advocate for our work and for other reforms, we started discussing a case that had recently been overturned on appeal. One of the points of contention in this case of historical child sexual abuse centred on offending that was alleged to have taken place while the offender's adult partner was nearby. The judges did not feel an offender would behave like that, therefore undermining their belief in the credibility of the victim's account. We discussed how offending in close proximity to other adults is common in child sexual abuse cases, and a tactic often used to silence victims.[10] She acknowledged that it was disappointing those judges didn't know that. She also said that education of judiciary might ensure that the next time such a subject came up one of the judges (there are usually three in such matters) might say, 'Oh, that's typical in these cases,' which would be the end of any doubt.

Sometimes people are confused as to why victims remain in a relationship with the perpetrator.[11] This is based on the notion that, if something bad happened to you, not only would you report it, but you would immediately leave the situation in which it happened. As we have seen, it is much more complicated than that.

We also get a lot of cases where women have met a man, and had consensual sex with him, only to be raped in the aftermath as he expected to be able to have sex again whenever he wished. I never cease to be amazed at the number of people in training sessions who, when faced with such a scenario, don't classify it as rape. 'What did she expect?', they sometimes say, or, 'She'd already said "Yes" – how is he supposed to know?' I am not only talking about our police investigators here, but people from all professions and backgrounds.

It is still a common expectation that victims of rape will suffer injury during the offence, but they seldom do.[12] This misconception is based on the notion that all victims will physically resist their attacker which, as we have seen, they don't. As soon as you understand grooming, and the fact that most people are abused by people they know, this misconception begins to seem foolish. If the abuse occurs once a victim has surrendered to the act, then injury is unlikely. Relationship and grooming are not the only reasons this is a falsity, however, as offenders may also work hard to ensure the victim 'enjoys' the experience. This is true in some types of adult sexual assault, and particularly in child sexual abuse cases. Offenders do so for a variety of reasons, perhaps to lessen their feelings of guilt, to persuade themselves that the act is one of love rather than abuse, or to demonstrate their perceived sexual prowess, for example. I worked with a rapist once, in a prison treatment programme, who insisted that the women he raped always had orgasms. When he was challenged, by other offenders in the group, that the women had only faked orgasm to get him to desist and leave, he was incandescent with fury. They persisted, however, until he was forced to admit that this was a possibility. The other offenders did all the work, and I just acted as a referee, in what was an incisive deconstruction of a long-held set of distorted thinking. It was very satisfying to watch.

Despite the obvious cognitive distortions of that rapist, it is surprisingly common for victims of assault to experience some arousal, erections, and even orgasms during abusive acts. One can only imagine how devastating and confusing this must be, and how hard it would be to discuss those aspects of the abuse. The reason for this phenomenon is that our bodies can react physiologically, despite what is happening in our thoughts and feelings. Males, for example, may experience erection and ejaculation when anally penetrated, because of the physical stimulation, while feeling nothing but revulsion for the act and the perpetrator.[13] The dissonance between mind and body can have a very damaging effect on their mental health.

Once misconceptions are challenged, it is also extraordinary how far accurate and up-to-date knowledge can take you. New Zealand courts conducted an experiment, educating jurors about child sexual abuse cases before they took part in trials. The educational sessions were non-case specific, providing knowledge of typical offender behaviours, victim reactions, memory issues and so on. Studies of the subsequent trials showed that defence counsels made significantly fewer attempts to draw on misconceptions as a part of their strategy.[14]

One of the most important projects I have worked on, with colleagues from the Australian Institute of Family Studies, was a resource for court officials and police, documenting the current literature on child sexual abuse, rape, and sexual assault. It focuses on the myths and misconceptions that are most damaging in sexual offence trials and examines the science that refutes them. We have produced a follow-up document, focusing on adult rape and sexual assault, for the Australian Institute of Criminology.[15] Both of these are aimed at fact-finders throughout the justice system, but we also hope they might influence wider public opinion.

We have found that the most effective method of teaching detectives to understand sexual crime is to start with understanding offenders. In one of the first sessions of the course, we ask about cases that have confused or frustrated them, and the ones they choose almost always focus on misunderstanding the behaviour of victims. The next session is the introduction of our new methodology, with its focus on offending, and beginning with the offenders. During this session we frequently see moments of recognition and understanding, as they see the connection between offender behaviour and victim reaction. There is often a palpable feeling of relief in the room, as investigators begin to see how offending works and how they might better investigate it. Our training has also resulted in a significant reduction in victim-blaming attitudes,[16] which have traditionally been so prevalent in police forces around the world,[17] although not necessarily at higher rates than the rest of the community.[18] To test the effectiveness of training, we designed research to inform us if what we were doing was effective, particularly attitudes towards victims. Investigators in training were given twelve scenarios (taken from real cases and de-identified), which were administered before and after training. They were given to them again after twelve months of work in the field (there were two sets of similar scenarios, counter-balanced, which they were randomly assigned at every time period). Two scenarios depict cases that would not be authorised, two cases that would, and eight cases that were ambiguous and harder to interpret. These ambiguous cases included different types of so-called 'counter-intuitive victim behaviour'. Our research showed that by the end of training negative attitudes towards victims reduced by over two-thirds. Even more importantly, there was only a small rise in judgments of the ambiguous scenarios after twelve months in the field, showing that the training changes were robust enough to withstand the pressures of the wider police culture. I have included the statistical breakdown of results in the references[19] for those of you who want to check the numbers.

If we can change attitudes and beliefs in the conservative and male-dominated cultures of police forces, there is no reason why we cannot do it everywhere. The science determining fact from fiction gets clearer every year, so it's up to all of us to pass on that knowledge. While so many myths and misconceptions persist the justice system will continue, in effect, to be rigged.

Part II

Offenders and offending

Sexual offending has probably affected all our lives, whether we realise it or not. I didn't understand quite how much of my life had been affected by sexual offending until relatively recently. I was giving a radio interview, talking about work we had been doing with specialist sexual crime investigators. My then eighty-seven-year-old mother was visiting at the time. She, and my wife Jacqui were listening. I told the story of the woman who was sexually assaulted during a massage, explaining why she had reacted to the assault in ways that people listening might not have expected. It was a live interview, and during the broadcast a woman rang in and talked about how the same thing had happened to her, many years before. She explained how she had never told anyone because she didn't think she would be believed, and that she felt guilty for not doing anything to stop him. She felt bad, she said, that she had never told anyone, and spoke about how it had affected her life since. She broke down several times, but she got to the end of her story.

As she was talking my mother turned to Jacqui and said, 'That happened to me, too.' In the fifty years since, she had never told anyone. When I got home, Jacqui took me aside and told me what had happened. When I sat down with my mother, she said his actions had shocked and confused her. Later, she wondered if it had happened because of something about her. The physiotherapist had come recommended by a friend, which raised other questions in her mind. Did her friend know? Why did she recommend him? With so many doubts, so much confusion and self-blame, she had decided, as so many victims do, not to tell anyone.

I am also aware that I was lucky to avoid being abused by one of my teachers at school. He took an interest in me and made himself a part of my life. He used to take me plane spotting and came to one of my birthday parties. I was at boarding school so that was unusual, but in those days nobody thought twice. 'What a lovely man,' they said. 'What a committed teacher.' I remember some of his grooming, including stories about his relationships and sex life. There were questions about whether I liked boys or girls, if I had kissed anyone, or had sex yet. I remember spending hours in his study, which was right next to one of the dormitories, listening to music. He would always play the Moody Blues, and to this day I can't hear that music without immediately thinking of him. I liked him, and he seemed to understand me at a time when school was difficult. Now I know, of course, what was really going on. Thankfully, I do not know why, it never progressed to abuse in a physical sense. I heard that it did later with another boy, for which he went to prison.

I also remember, from that time, how I first learned about sex and consent. As you may imagine, at an all-male British boarding school in the 1970s, my formal sexual education was not progressive. It was, apart from information about the biological functions, non-existent. There was no discussion of relationships, consent, respect, fun, boundaries or what was normal. I am English, too, so any discussion of sex at home would have been far too embarrassing. The key message I picked up at school was, 'Go as far as you can until she says

"Stop" or pushes your hand away.' I don't remember where it came from; we just seemed to know it. And then there were the lessons we learned from pornography, with pictures of smiling, naked women, alongside stories of athletic male prowess which I was later to learn were highly improbable. When it comes to educating young men and women about relationships and sex I wonder how much has changed. When I was working with young people who commit sexual offences one of the most striking things was that, despite their behaviour, they knew very little about sex. Perhaps less surprisingly, they knew even less about relationships.

The first time I remember hearing about sexual offending was listening to my mother, who was talking to her friends about someone they all knew. Their friend had been walking along a roadside underpass when a man had grabbed her and tried to 'do things'. I vividly recall them describing how she had said to him, 'You do know that Jesus loves you, don't you?,' and that the man had run off. I remember thinking how clever that was.

School and university provided other abusive experiences. The teacher I described was the first, although I did not see it as abuse at the time. Then there was the older boy at school who said he wanted to rape me. I didn't know what he meant, but I avoided him. There was the older student friend at university, who kept telling me what he wanted to do to me whenever he got drunk. There was a man in the toilets, at a gig, who pushed me against the wall and tried to kiss me, which was the most frightening. Looking for the toilets, I had asked him where they were, and he had either mistaken my meaning or seen an opportunity. The toilets were in the basement, down a steep, narrow staircase, and as I got to the bottom of the stairs to leave, he was coming down. I remember feeling fear, without quite knowing why and, as we passed in the narrow space, he pushed me to the wall and leaned forward. I turned my head. He was a lot bigger than me and he held me there for what seemed like ages but was probably only a second or two, before he grunted and let me go. Those are the ones I remember, which I put down to being unlucky, or that there was something about me that attracted that sort of behaviour. I didn't realise that it happened to boys quite a lot, as well as to men. Neither did I know until later, when I started working in treatment programmes and with victim groups, that it is much worse for girls and women.

When I started working with sexual offenders, and listening to their stories every day, I was disturbed by what they told me. In the late 1980s, I was working in prisons with a theatre company called Geese Theatre. We started the company as an offshoot of an American group, putting on plays and improvisations about prison life, running theatre and drama therapy workshops as a part of rehabilitation programmes. Geese regularly ran workshops at a community-based treatment centre for men who sexually abused children, where I then started working. I co-ran a group every day for three hours, for eight to ten men, all of whom were there because they had sexually abused children, but a few had also raped adults. Some of the men had been in prison for their crimes, and some had not. Some of them had come to change and some had not, but they all had a story to tell about why they were there. Sometimes their stories were just full of lies, but the longer the men went through treatment, and the more some of them wanted to change, the more direct and honest they often became about their behaviour. As a therapist, you also get better at spotting truth, half-truth, self-deception, and outright lies.

Even though I'd had some experience when I had come with the theatre company, I was shocked at how different the stories were from what I was expecting, because offender understanding, back in the 1980s, was not much more than, 'Don't take sweets from strangers.' Perhaps I was still thinking about the man in the underpass, or the guy at the gig. The stories I was hearing were different because, whether they offended their own children or other peoples', there always seemed to be a relationship. We now call that relationship grooming, but it was a new word back then. There was guile and manipulation, of victims and those around them, secrecy and pressure, threats and bribes, the creation of confusion, anxiety, and fear. Some behaviours were deliberate and conscious, while others seemed instinctive. Most of it was devastatingly effective because, in story after story, no one was telling on them, at least not for long periods of time. I lost count of the times their offending had come to light 'by accident'.

We were working on grooming in group one day. One of the men said that in his grooming process he tried to get the children to *think* like him. He tried to get them to believe that it wasn't abuse, or that they wanted or deserved it in some way. It sounded terrible, but I realised how he had formed this twisted logic.

The next man along said that he went further, trying to get the children *to be* like him, which was hard to hear. How terrible for a child to be subject to such an orchestrated onslaught on their sense of self. A British study in 2015 found that the average length of the relationship between child and abuser was seven years.[1]

Another man in group said that he had a 'rule of three', and my heart sank. Rule 1: Get them to do what you want them to do. Rule 2: Do and say things to minimise them telling on you. Rule 3: In whatever way you can, get them to *feel responsible*. No wonder nobody told on them.

It wasn't that the stories became commonplace after a while, but they did become familiar. Whether abusing children or adults, these men were using the same kinds of manipulations, the same masks, lies, and subterfuge. Sometimes the behaviour came with accompanying physical violence; always, it came with confusion, secrecy, threat, and fear. With those early realisations about abusive relationships, one thing became crystal clear to me. Offending begins with offenders.

6

Offending begins with offenders

I sometimes use an exercise, when training police investigators, which can make them feel decidedly uncomfortable. We ask them to think like sex offenders and imagine certain scenarios. For example, they may assume the role of a teacher and football coach who moves to a country town, and who wants to abuse boys. Then, in small groups, they try to work out how he will behave, mapping out his entire grooming strategy: the boy, his family, the club, the school, and the town. As we run it in the latter stages of training, they are usually quite good at it, which can freak some of them out. Most offenders' processes, however, are corruptions of deceptive behaviours we all use from time to time. For example, as offenders must hide their behaviour, and gain the trust of victims, they are adept at using masks to obscure their real intention. While not having the same sinister motivation, we all use masks in everyday life, to present our best side, or to fit in to new environments. When you understand what offenders do, how they do it, and the masks they wear, it is much easier to investigate sexual crimes, and to design processes and practices that can make communities safer, particularly for children.

Although different grooming methods are used in adult and child cases, the same principles apply: create a relationship of power, control and/or authority over the intended victim, then move the relationship to a sexualised frame. Grooming is present in every offence, however quickly it occurs. The relationship formed, however long, holds the key to understanding the abuse itself. Even when there is a minimal timeframe between first contact and abuse, there is always an element of power and control, where offenders attempt to overwhelm any resistance. Typically, there is a significant timeframe over which control and sexualisation takes place, which is the process commonly understood to be grooming.[1]

The question we get asked most often in training is, 'How can you tell if a particular behaviour is grooming?' During our course, inevitably, a participant will offer one of the trainers a sweet, or a coffee, and there will be someone who immediately accuses them of grooming. The joke, stale as it is, is part of investigators working through what they think and feel about grooming, and how it differs from what they do in their own lives, to relate to people, or get others to think well of them.

The answer to the question, 'How can you tell it's grooming?', is *what happens next*. Grooming is progressively defined by each action, becoming clearer and clearer with each subsequent action. There are patterns, and the more you know about grooming, the easier they are to spot.

Grooming has two distinct, and connected, phases. To help our investigators understand it, we call them 'grooming 1' and 'grooming 2'. Grooming 1 is the phase of non-sexual grooming, and it is the *most important* part, providing evidence that can make all the difference when a case goes to court. Such evidence will explain what later took place and why victims behaved as they did. There may be witnesses to certain elements of the process, even if they did not know about the offending itself. The offender's grooming process also tells us what kind of relationship he believed he had with the victim. It will show what he thought and felt about his offending, and how he justified it, which will be useful to investigators in police interviews, and to therapists who may later work with him in treatment. The more that is known about him, the better victims may also be helped on their road to recovery.

In casual dating circumstances, the problem is that grooming 1 looks a lot like the usual courtship rituals. There will be signs, though, like these:

- He won't let her pay for any of the drinks;
- insists that she put her number in his phone;
- doesn't acknowledge her friend or the group she's with;
- on occasion even takes her phone and wallet;
- will not respect any boundaries she tries to put in place;
- will use pressure tactics (perhaps to get her to go on to a new venue, go back to his place, or to ditch her friends).

Sometimes, however, paying for the drinks is just a nice gesture, and being attentive is just enthusiasm, which is part of the problem, because it can be hard to tell one from another. This will all be more complicated, of course, when alcohol or drugs are involved.

There are clear connections between abuse patterns in sexual offending and relationship violence. Victims will typically describe periods of good times, including consensual sex, followed by periods of violence, abuse, and rape. Grooming 1 tactics used by offenders who are violent in relationships are designed to make her feel responsible for his moods, to become focused on him and his needs, to diminish her sense of self, and destroy her ability to think and act independently. The term for grooming, commonly used in cases of relationship violence, is *coercive control*.[2]

Similar tactics will be used in sexual harassment cases. Sometimes, for example, the power of seniority at work is used in an aggressive, entitled way. At other times it is more subtle, like an offer to move into the 'inner circle' which is hard to resist. Next may come the suggestion of closeness in the relationship, the giving and taking of confidences, perhaps physical touch. All this before anything sexual is made explicit.

In cases of *intra-familial* child sexual abuse, grooming 1 often involves creating a different environment and different rules when the non-offending parent isn't around. Offenders usually work on creating divisions between their intended victim and other family members, typically their mother. These processes gradually leave the victim feeling confused, disconnected, and aware that they are expected to behave differently under these changed circumstances. This process was first described by Roland Summit, only as recently as 1983, in his paper, 'The child abuse accommodation syndrome'.[3]

In *extra-familial* cases, offenders place as much focus on getting the child's family to trust and value him as they do on gaining the confidence of the child themselves. The intention is to be allowed more and more access to the child, away from the care and attention of any protective adult.

The second phase of grooming (grooming 2), in all types of sexual offending, is much more obvious. Once offenders have created a position of power, control, or authority over their intended victim, they begin to sexualise the relationship. This process can be fast and aggressive, but some offenders may wait months, or even years, before they move to this phase.

Once offending begins, offenders continue both grooming 1 and 2, particularly tactics that increase victims' feelings of responsibility. A typical example of such a tactic might be a child molester praising a boy for having an erection during the abuse, even though he had done all he could to ensure that happened, like showing the boy pornography. He may also suggest to the boy that this shows he might be gay, implying that he must have wanted sex with the offender all along. The boys in these situations are unaware that their body is responding against their will. If you masturbate a penis it will usually become erect, whatever the circumstances, and anal penetration may also produce this effect.[4] The resulting confusion, shame and guilt will, in many cases, lead to the child's continued silence. If they were going to tell someone, how would a child find the words to explain?

It is important to know that grooming occurs *before* any offending, *during* the offending itself, and *between* offences. It will also, in most cases of both adult sexual assault and child abuse, occur *after* the direct abuse has stopped, to ensure continued silence. For example, rapists often bombard victims with text messages after the offence. Sometimes messages are simply threatening. At other times they may tell her how 'hot' she was the night before, or how they cannot wait to see her again – messages completely at odds with her experience of the abusive behaviour. Whether or not these tactics are deliberate, they create distress and confusion. Unfortunately, such messages can also be used by defence counsel to suggest the relationship was consensual, so investigators and prosecutors need to be wise to the phenomenon.

Offenders look for vulnerability and, if they cannot find it, try to manufacture it. I have worked with men and boys of all levels of intelligence and each one of them knew, or had worked out, how to exploit opportunities presented to them. Most of them had also developed ways to create opportunities when none was immediately available. For example, in two adult cases from a couple of years ago, the vulnerability was around employment.

One young woman, who was the sole money earner in her family due to illnesses suffered by her parents, reported harassment and abuse by her boss. The manager of the food outlet where she worked regularly made sexually suggestive comments, complimented her on her appearance, and joked about wanting to do various sexual things to her. She put up with it for months, only going to the police when he started touching her. During the six weeks it took her to complete her statement, she remained working at the shop. The investigator in the case struggled to see why she would do that and worried what a jury might make of it. Why would anyone put up with that? Eventually he understood that both the distress caused by the abuse, and the economic hardship experienced by her family, left her conflicted, confused, and unable to act decisively. He made sure her statement explained the complexity of her situation.

In a related case, a young woman who had been unemployed for two years finally got a job at, of all places, an employment agency. In their earliest encounters, her new boss made it clear that she had potential, which was music to her ears after so long out of the workforce. Unemployment had taken a toll on her self-confidence. The boss also advocated staff awareness sessions, in which colleagues shared experiences of their own struggles. He explained that the sessions would help them to understand the needs of the people they were trying to help. She shared stories of a tough family life, and abuse at the hands of a former partner. Her boss complimented her honesty, and they began to discuss each other's lives and relationships more frequently, outside the session times. Over time she was promoted to the position of, in his words, 'unofficial leader' of her group, with the implicit prospect of future advancement.

Suddenly, there were special private meetings, work sessions out of hours, and 'I shouldn't really be telling you this' discussions about her colleagues and their problems. When, after several months of this, she was called in to the office on 'an urgent matter', she was unaware that she and her boss were the only ones in the building. When he used this carefully crafted opportunity to assault her, she was shocked. Unlike the woman in the food shop, she had not seen it coming. As he began his sexual advances, she was utterly confused and frozen into inaction.

Child sex offenders find or create vulnerability in similar ways. In one case a Roman Catholic priest, working in a boarding school, organised to have his office directly opposite the telephone that boys used to call home. He could glean which child was unhappy, lonely, or homesick. He used this information to 'comfort' the boys, as he saw it. In another case, a man in our treatment group described, through role play, his typical pattern of abusive behaviour. He would seek out the single-parent groups in his area, where he would then befriend one of the mothers who had boys and start a relationship with her. He would always maintain a sexual relationship with the mother, albeit a limited one, despite having no sexual interest in adult women. Then, of course, he would go through the typical patterns of isolation and abuse.

Not all offenders set about their grooming in a conscious, deliberate way. Sometimes it is more opportunistic than that, or a circumstance that evolves over time, before the offender sees an opportunity. A typical opportunistic offence might involve a group of friends and acquaintances, with vulnerability created by alcohol or drugs. Rape may not have been the offender's deliberate intention at the beginning of the night, but he was prepared to take the opportunity when it arose. Even in these cases there will be an element of grooming 1 and 2 before the offence, perhaps topping up the drink of an already drunk person, 'accidentally' missing the last train home, or offering to 'look after' the drunk woman in question. Grooming is still there, just in a shortened form.

So, except in cases where violence is the sole strategy of the offender, the process *always* goes like this. First there is the *non-sexual* grooming (1), followed by the *sexual* grooming (2). These two processes are then used together until the offending starts. The abuse itself then acts as a third element of grooming, because offenders will make sure victims feel responsible. All three processes, together, are designed to maintain the abuse, silence victims, and make the offender feel OK about what he is doing. The last element is important, because one of the things that most surprised me, when I first started working with sex offenders, was how much they wanted to be thought of as good people, even though they knew that what they were doing was wrong.

As we discussed previously, approximately 5 per cent of sexual offences are committed by women,[5] and they are much more likely to have a co-offender than male offenders, with at least 30 per cent of all female offenders co-offending with a man.[6] They tend to target children, often related to them, or in a caregiver setting.[7] Female offenders are more likely to have experienced abuse in childhood than both non-offending females and male offenders,[8] and appear to have more complex reasons for offending than their male counterparts.[9] Female sex offenders are far less likely to reoffend than males, with rates of approximately 2 per cent.[10] Recidivism is usually linked to a broader criminal history, rather than a dominant focus on the sexual abuse of children.[11] Recidivism rates for male sexual offenders are between 10 per cent and 15 per cent.[12] Importantly, however, when it comes to grooming, they can use the same strategies as men. One typical female offender type, the 'teacher-lover' offender,[13] will use similar tactics to male child molesters. She will target boys in their early teens, or even younger, building trust with them and their families. All the time, like male offenders, she will be persuading herself that it is a mutual relationship. Although such offenders are usually in their late twenties or early thirties, in the last such case I worked on the woman was forty-nine, and the boy was twelve.

Adolescents commit a significant proportion of all sexual offences, comprising between 15 per cent and 20 per cent of all arrests for sexual crimes, and approximately a third of all sexual crimes against children.[14] Research shows that about 4–5 per cent of boys and 1 per cent of girls admit to coercing someone into a sexual act.[15] Early studies of adult offenders showed at least half admitted beginning their abusing in adolescence,[16] but the results may have been influenced by researchers focusing on known offenders, in prison or on parole, who may not have been representative of most sexual offenders. This led to some incorrect assumptions about what proportion of adult sexual offenders began abusing in adolescence, and that adolescents who began offending would probably continue into adulthood. Adolescents can be persistent in their offending during their adolescence, however, and may continue into adulthood (estimates range between 2 per cent and 20 per cent, with higher non-sexual reoffending rates estimated at 40–50 per cent).[17] Most offender types will desist from sexual offending, however, as they enter adulthood. Again, non-sexual reoffending is more likely to continue. Importantly, adolescents are likely to benefit from early intervention, further limiting potential reoffending.[18]

When it comes to grooming, adolescents certainly understand the power of manipulation as well as adult offenders, although most of their strategies are more simplistic. Bribes and threats are the most common, but they are sometimes more devious. One fourteen-year-old boy, in our treatment programme, wished to abuse his younger sisters. He was often left in charge of both his sisters and his two younger brothers. To make sure neither the girls nor boys told on him, he made the younger boys perform sexual acts with the girls. Somehow, he realised that this would ensure their silence.

The Internet gives offenders another medium with which to access and manipulate potential victims, with teenage girls and boys the most common target. You might have read about such cases and wondered why a fourteen-year-old girl, or boy, would travel far from home to meet up with a forty-year-old man for sex? First, they were probably unaware of his real age, and that his primary intention was sexual. In the modern age, it is easy to create fake profiles and pretend to be someone or something that you're not. Also, offenders are adept at persuading people that they have what that person wants or needs. In training, we often ask, 'When you were fifteen, what did you most want?' The answers come flooding in: freedom, money, things I knew I wasn't supposed to have (like alcohol, cigarettes, or drugs), stuff (particularly mobile phones, the must-have accessory), the time and space to do what I wanted, when I wanted to, and to have fun.

The next set of answers is just as important: attention, acceptance, to be listened to and valued, to have someone to confide in, and to be treated like an adult. Even though it is a false promise, offenders will offer all these things.

In trials and media reports, victims are often accused of having a misguided loyalty towards the offender, language which potentially places some responsibility for that loyalty with the victim. But any loyalty shown to the offender has been crafted by him, often carefully built over considerable time. There have been many cases, over the years, that have brought this home to me, like this one.

A woman in her early twenties reported sexual abuse by her stepfather, that she said had been going on since she was twelve years old. She had been living with him until a few months previously and they were still having sex. She finally decided to go to the police when her stepfather asked her to move out, which he had done because he wanted his new girlfriend to move in. The investigator in the case, who had not yet attended specialist training, was confused about some critical aspects of her statement. Now she was an adult, he wondered, why didn't she report earlier, and why was she still having sex with him? He also thought that defence counsel would just say she was making it up, jealous of the new girlfriend and angry at being asked to leave.

The answers to all these questions, as usual, lay in the early stages of their relationship. His grooming 1 had started almost as soon as he joined the family, when she was about six years old. Whenever there was conflict between her and her mother, he would side with the girl, who then reciprocated when there was conflict in the adult relationship. When he moved out of the family home, as he did on several occasions before the final split, she went with him. These schisms fractured the relationships with both her mother and her siblings. He became the one constant presence in her life, also telling her that she was his 'soulmate', but that they couldn't be together publicly because 'the world wouldn't understand'. As she was six when it started, the decision to keep the secret was made at that time. She thought they loved each other, that he had always been on her side, and she on his. She felt guilty at 'the affair' (his words) she was having behind her mother's back. These messages kept her attached to him well into her twenties. Victims' behaviour should be understood from the entirety of the grooming process, and the age they are when it begins, not by the timing of their disclosure. It was only the manner of his rejection, when being told to move out, that gave her clarity about his avowed love for her, and which created the impetus finally to disclose.

How is someone made to feel responsible for their own abuse? It is, like many of the concepts here, a phenomenon you're probably already familiar with, albeit in different contexts: guilt-tripping, positioning people to see a situation in a certain way, active or passive aggression to insist someone conforms. If you have ever experienced 'gaslighting', where someone deliberately acts in a way that makes you doubt your thoughts and feelings, then you are familiar with the principle. These are all tactics offenders have adopted for their grooming processes. It is easier with children, as they are so much more vulnerable to the views and beliefs of adults, but it happens to adults too. Grooming and coercive control create a feeling of responsibility, often exacerbated by isolation and silence. Maybe you have had a relationship go through a bad patch, only to be told by the other party that it was all your fault. Perhaps you also believed them, stewed over it for ages, until you talked to a friend who gave you some perspective. Offenders do not want friends, or perspective, as they want to be the only ones who can be relied on. Mostly, this process is done over time, with a mixture of coercive and love-bombing tactics, although sometimes the process is quicker and more obviously brutal. Once we all understand grooming, it is so much easier to understand offending relationships, and to place responsibility with offenders.

The next question we are often asked is, 'Why do they do it?'

7

Why do they do it?

When I say, in police training, that I am about to talk about the theory of sexual offending behaviour, I can see the eyes in the room begin to glaze over. Theory is important, however, as it helps us understand the motivation of offenders, the differences in the way they offend, and the effect of different offence patterns on victims. When it comes to investigators, theory also informs how they should approach offenders, including clear messages to do so without judgment, which is not easy. The job of an investigator, in interviewing suspects, is to get them to talk. Judgment leads to shame, and shame leads to silence. There's evidence that sexual offence suspects are the quickest of all offender groups to perceive hostility in their interviewer.[1] This is hardly surprising, given the personality types of the offenders, and their knowledge about how police and the community feel about their behaviour.

In one training session, after all the information on child molester thinking was presented, I asked, 'So, do you understand this man?', and there was silence. At the back of the room, an older detective was staring at me. He looked furious. I asked him what was going on and he said, coldly, 'I will never understand him.' He was clearly angry that I had even asked him such a question. 'I'm not asking you to identify with him,' I explained, 'I'm asking if you can understand how he sees the world.' He just repeated himself, which left me with a dilemma. How would we tell him that he was not suited to this kind of investigative work?

The culture in policing, as in the wider community, is to show contempt and hostility towards offenders. When I first got the job with police, I met the culture of loathing regularly. I have heard it in almost every policing culture I've visited. However, in most offices someone would say something like, 'You should talk to So-and-So, because he/she is really good with them,' so I would go and talk to them. What they had worked out was that you get better results if you treat offenders with respect, irrespective of their crime. One of them explained their approach as, 'You've got to leave them with a bit of dignity.' However uncomfortable it may be to do so, if we are truly to help victims, as specialist sexual crime investigators, then feelings must be put to one side.

The way we begin, in training, is through understanding how offenders justify their behaviour, the technical term for which is cognitive distortions, or distorted thinking. Distorted thinking is the glue that holds their world view together. Whenever something comes along that might give them pause for thought, distorted thinking will paper over the cracks. We have all seen plenty of examples of such distorted thinking in recent times. How is it possible, for example, to be accused of sexual assault and harassment by at least twenty women (and counting),[2] as well as being recorded saying that you have kissed women without them wanting you to, and grabbed them by the 'pussy' without consent, and yet say, 'No one respects women more than me'?

An offender I worked with once did a role play on his grooming behaviour, which was a regular exercise that all group members participated in. He worked on it so hard that he didn't stop to consider what he was enacting. As a part of the exercise, he was required to pause regularly, to tell the other group members what he was thinking or feeling during important moments. I often used the exercise to help new members get over a problem that offenders often exhibit in the early stages of treatment. If you said to a new group member, 'Tell us how your offending started,' they would usually say, 'I don't know ... *it just happened.*' Offending *never* just happens. This man had begun treatment in such a way, convinced that his daughter had wanted the relationship as much as him. As he began to demonstrate the manipulations he had performed, to gain his daughter's compliance and maintain the secrecy, it was clear to everyone what had taken place. As the role play finished, he sat down and there was a long silence. Finally, he said, 'She didn't have any choice at all, did she?', and there was silence again. Then, suddenly, and violently, he punched himself in the face, almost as if he were trying to drive the thought out of his head. He was too late, though, as it was already there, and his distorted thinking was beginning to crack.

Distorted thinking is just as prevalent with adolescents who offend, albeit a bit more basic. A colleague in the States told me of a group programme for young people who had sexually offended that had an innovative strategy for dealing with distortions. When members of the group felt that one of their number was not being truthful, they would begin to raise their feet, to keep them out of the imaginary bullshit. It was very effective, by all accounts, as the boys had come up with the strategy themselves, to encourage honesty within their group.

Sometimes, offenders try not to think at all. In our programme for adolescents, we ran lots of exercises to help boys see how they were deceiving themselves. In one we would ask them whether they ever looked into the eyes of the people they were abusing, and they would say 'No'. We then asked, 'Why not?', and they told us that they did not want to see what was there. To the question, 'What would you have seen if you'd looked?' they could catalogue a range of things: fear, hatred, disgust, shock, etc. They knew what was there, and the impact of their behaviour, but sometimes bullshitting means pretending you didn't see, or did not know.

The problem with cognitive distortions is particularly acute when they cluster together to form attitudes and beliefs. We use a model called implicit theory (IT) to show how this can happen, a process first explored in child molesters by Ward and Keenan.[3] The concept of IT derives from the notion that human beings, particularly children, are acting as scientists in the way they explore the world, developing an understanding of their own beliefs, needs and wants. Early researchers defined the exploratory process as 'theory of mind',[4] suggesting that it helped children create theories and beliefs about how to navigate the world, supported by ways of thinking. Those working with sex offenders noticed that they often held a lot of views that distorted the nature of relationships and sex, using them to justify their offending. When they looked at how this distorted thinking hung together, the idea for using implicit theory to understand them came about. The method has now been used to explore the theories and world views of child molesters, rapists,[5] perpetrators of relationship violence,[6] and men who are violent in other situations.[7]

The first implicit theory studies, looking at child molesters, found that they held five key theories about the way the world works. The five theories they isolated were:

- Dangerous world
- Entitlement
- Uncontrollability
- Nature of harm
- Children as sexual objects

Dangerous world refers to the way child molesters perceive the adult world to be a hostile and dangerous place, both psychologically and emotionally. They find it hard to navigate adult relationships, and struggle with intimacy, closeness, adult friendships etc. It's why they say things like, 'Children understand me, and I understand them,' as they feel safe in relationships they can control. This is not to say that all child molesters will look unsuccessful in the adult world – far from it. They can be married, hold a range of jobs, appear to be the pillars of their community, and have a range of friends ... but they will not *feel* successful. One case we worked on illustrated this perfectly, as the suspect ran a successful business, had a large house in an affluent suburb, a 'trophy' wife, and children at private school. He was also targeting 13/14-year-old girls on the Internet.

Entitlement is more straightforward. In the early days of working in offender treatment I had some Roman Catholic clergymen in my group. We were running a session exploring how each group member started to offend when one priest said, as best as I can remember it, 'I gave my life to the church and to the community. I had to be available to them 24/7 and

I had no life of my own.' Then he said something I will never forget, 'So, I felt I was entitled to a little bit back.' That *little bit* was sexually abusing his parishioners' children. He said it in such an offhand way that even other offenders in the group were shocked.

There is an important qualification here, distinguishing male and female sex offenders, because a sense of entitlement to abuse is the only implicit theory that does not show up in female offenders' core justifications for abuse. Even though female offenders have suffered higher rates of abuse, both in childhood and as adults, than their male counterparts, they don't feel entitled to do it to anyone else.[8] There is also research suggesting that, although the implicit theories are similar for male and female offenders, the content of their pro-offending thinking is different. For example, female offenders focus more on hostile and dangerous males, rather than perceive their entire world to be dangerous,[9] and they do not generalise children as sexual objects.

Uncontrollability is a commonly held notion across a range of transgressors. It wasn't my fault, because … (insert justification here) – e.g. I couldn't help it, I'd been drinking/watching porn/I was lonely etc. In psychological terms, offenders place the locus of control for their behaviour outside themselves, but it just means they will not take responsibility for their actions. If you take these first three: *Dangerous world*, *Entitlement* and *Uncontrollability*, you get the basis for a range of problem behaviours. It is the last two elements of sexual objectification and minimising the harm done, sitting on these first three theories, that add the critical risks for abusing children.

Offenders are adept at minimising the effects of their behaviour and the *Nature of harm* caused. They justify what they do by persuading themselves that it is not that bad, or that it's the victim's responsibility. People often ask, 'Does that mean he doesn't know what he is doing, or he knows and he's suppressing that knowledge?' It is usually the latter, but sometimes it is hard to tell. There was one man in treatment who had been sexually abused by his father from an early age, including being loaned out to his father's friends for abuse. When this abuse upset him, he turned to his father for comfort and reassurance. To make him feel better, his father masturbated him. As is common with children growing up in this kind of environment, he began to abuse younger children in his early teens and was arrested for it in his early twenties. When he went to prison, he was regularly assaulted because, when asked what he was in for, he was unaware of what would happen if he told the truth. One of my colleagues asked him what went through his mind after he was assaulted by the other inmates. He replied, 'I thought ... well, if that's the adult world, you can keep it.' All the violence had done was confirm that the adult world was a dangerous place – one of many reasons why aggression and retribution alone can be counter-productive when dealing with sex offenders.

Obviously, men who sexually abuse children see *Children as sexual objects* and potential sexual partners, despite clear community messages that this behaviour is unacceptable. But how clear are those messages? In online pornography, the biggest sub-category is 'Teens'. Some of this might be because the biggest consumers of pornography are teenage boys and young men, but that is not the only reason. Depicting young bodies sells, and it drives the belief that teenage bodies, particularly girls' bodies, should be available for sex. The legal pornography industry is worth tens, even hundreds, of billions.[10] Pornography commonly offers the fantasy of teenage bodies, made to look as young as possible. They may be depicted playing with dolls, their hair in bunches, naked and in sexual poses, even having sex with older people, and no one is breaking any law. (They are breaking the law in some countries, of course, where all pornography is illegal). Once the laws are broken, we get into the realm of child exploitation material (CEM), where what is on offer online is almost limitless, and heartbreaking. It is estimated that, last year, the CEM industry was worth around US$10 billion.[11] There are, at any one time, approximately 100,000 online sites offering child exploitation material.[12]

There are also sexualising pressures on teens and 'tweens. Campaigns that lobby for children to be free of such pressures, whatever part of the political and religious spectrum they come from, regularly highlight the sale of sexualised images and products to children, the eroticisation of children in advertising, and the marketing of age-inappropriate products. So how clear are our messages that the sexualities of children and adults are entirely separate? Those using sexual depictions of children and young people may say, at the very least, 'I'm not the only one who's doing it.'

Having begun with child molesters, researchers[13] went on to look at the similarities and differences between child molesters and rapists in terms of implicit theories. Rapists also struggle in adult relationships, so it is no surprise that *Dangerous world* is present here too. Researchers found a belief that 'Women are unknowable', leading to an automatic association between their relationship failures and victim-blaming attitudes.

They also found few differences in rapists' sense of *Entitlement* to behave as they did, compared to male child molesters. Entitlement is a common thread through all sexually abusive behaviour, from harassers to child molesters. Beliefs in male rights and privileges, closely tied to victim-blaming attitudes, are at the core of this thinking, including as a justification for violence.

There were some differences with child molesters when it comes to *Uncontrollability*, with rapists reporting more clearly that their sexual thoughts and feelings felt beyond their control. These justifications are often wrapped up in phrases like, 'She got me horny. What was I supposed to do?' and so forth. Rapists are far less likely than child molesters to worry about whether others see them as good people, so have fewer justifications about the *Nature of Harm* they cause. How many times, lately, have you heard the phrase, 'Mr X believed all sexual relations were consensual' – well, of course he does. Rapists typically convince themselves that the behaviour was consensual. If the justification is not that it was consensual, they will construct it as deserved.

Obviously, *women* replace *children* as the dominant vehicle of objectification for rapists, although some will hold these views about children as well. The objectification of women might sound like, 'I knew when she came in what she wanted.' The intent of such thinking is to place responsibility on the victim, confirm their justification for the abuse, and allow a sense of inevitability about their behaviour.

Whenever we were working with a sex offender who held these views, it was important to work through where their beliefs came from, and when their offending began. While offenders' early years are often critical for the development of problems, the start of offending can come much later. There are four critical ages when sexual offending can *begin*.[14] The first is in *early adolescence*, around the age of puberty. Typically, they target younger children in their family, extended family, or local neighbourhood. Some will continue to offend against younger children as they get older, some will offend in their peer groups, and some will desist.

The next age is *late adolescence*. These young men, usually sixteen to nineteen years old, typically offend peer-age girls in their school and friendship groups. These sexual assaults are much more likely to feature alcohol or drugs. Some of these young men desist, but others may keep offending.

The most common age to *begin* offending, which may seem surprising, is in *middle age* (usually defined somewhere between forty and fifty-five years old).[15] This doesn't mean that the traits and behaviours weren't present earlier, but rather that the factors leading to abusing did not reach a critical point until middle age. The precipitating factors for offending increased, the protective factors diminished, or both.

The last group is smaller, described as offenders at the *end of their working lives*. Colloquially, they are known as 'grandad offenders'[16] and, typically, they abuse young children. Here too, the risk factors may have been present from an early age.

While offending can be present at any age, these typical *starting points* are revealing: early adolescence, late adolescence, middle age, and the end of a working life, all of which are significant change moments in the lives of boys and men.

I have generalised here, about typical target groups, as there are many variations of offender targeting, including offending across gender and over wide age ranges. When I began working with sex offenders it was assumed that they were likely to be specialist in their interests. This turned out to be largely untrue, as research now shows sex offenders are much more likely to be generalists than specialists.[17] Research continues to clarify the parameters of other types of sex offending. For example, many indecent exposers will never progress to sexual assault, some offenders who use CEM will only use abusive digital images, whereas others will use CEM *and* abuse the children outside the online world. Some rapists and child molesters will stay with one age group, but most are capable of offending children of all ages, or even adults. They do not necessarily stay with one gender, either. Offenders may prefer to abuse girls or boys, but abuse both. Even with adult rapists, there are those that will abuse both men and women.

In training, we are repeatedly asked, *how many sex offenders are victims themselves?* I think we find it easier to understand why someone would do something so awful, if we can see it as learned behaviour. The answer is much more complicated, of course, and, like a lot of research in this field, difficult to pin down definitively. Looking at data from a range of programmes related to ours, we found out that each programme believed between 40 per cent and 50 per cent[18] of the adolescents they worked with had been sexually abused themselves, which rate is significantly higher than the general population. It meant, however, that 50–60 per cent were not victims of sexual abuse. We found that family violence, physical abuse, being bullied, isolation from peers, and pornography use, were all more highly represented in their backgrounds than sexual abuse. So, the behaviour *is* learned, but from a variety of abusive and destructive places.

Definitive figures for adult offenders are also difficult to find. Both rapists and child molesters have much higher rates of physical abuse, family violence and neglect in their childhoods than the general population. There is also a clear link between sexual abuse and later offending in both rapists and child molesters, although child molester rates are the highest.[19] None of this excuses sex offending behaviour, of course, and most people living with sexual trauma in their past do not go on to sexually abuse others.

8

When young people commit sexual offences

In early 1993, when I was asked to start a treatment programme for adolescents who were sexually offending, we were trying to think of a name for the programme. At the time, the programme was voluntary, so we had to be careful. Who would want to send their kid to the Sex Offender Programme? It wouldn't be long before most programmes were compulsory, but we didn't know that then. So, we opted for MAPPS, Male Adolescent Programme for Positive Sexuality: both a description of what we did, and a guide for their futures. I am glad we started with something positive, focused on their age and our goal, rather than their offence.[1]

Early work with offending adolescents borrowed methods from the adult field, which had been around for longer. It did not take us long to figure out that a lot of those methods did not work with young people. In the adult world, getting abusers to see themselves as offenders may make sense, but when you are working with adolescents the focus is on who they are going to become. If you get them to say they are offenders, you are imprinting the notion that they should think of themselves as offenders. Believe it or not, with such troubled young people, many would rather identify with something, even being a sex offender, than not be able to identify with anything. It is a clear sign of how lost and empty these boys often feel. More and more, as we went on learning about our work, we realised the focus should be on their adolescence, first and foremost, as the sex offending was symptomatic of wider problems. It was important for us to address their offending, because it was very damaging to others, but not to let it define them. One psychiatrist described our approach as, 'You gotta love 'em, but you gotta watch 'em,' which sounded about right. You cannot help people change if you do not treat them with care and respect, but you also can't help them if you're naïve about the risks they pose. There has been a lot of hype about adolescent sexual offending, and it's irritating that every time a media outlet runs a story about the issue it is billed as an 'explosive revelation', an 'exclusive story', breaking one of the 'last taboos'. People have been working with these boys for over thirty years now.

Adolescents commit at least 30 per cent of all offences against children.[2] They also commit a significant percentage of the assaults against their peers, particularly in later adolescence, totalling approximately 15–20 per cent of all sexual offence reports.[3] While most will desist from their offending as they move into adulthood, they are unlikely to stop, without intervention, during adolescence. Some will continue to offend sexually into adulthood, and a bigger percentage will continue to offend non-sexually,[4] but most will stop.[5]

We made a training tape of twelve adolescents from the programme being asked the same question: *While you were offending, did you think you could have stopped on your own?* It is a leading question, I know, but all twelve answered, 'No'.

So, what makes it so hard to stop?

We used to run a whole range of exercises getting kids to work out why they were offending. One said, 'Because it makes me feel good here, here, and here.' He pointed to his head, his guts, and his groin. Thinking about offending and planning it, getting apprehensive and excited, followed by sexual arousal, is a dangerous mixture.

Another, in a written exercise asking them to list their top three reasons for offending, put: Fun, Power, Excitement.

Sometimes their motivations come from an obvious place but are nonetheless shocking. One of my clients had an extensive history of abuse at home. He had been taken into care, only to be abused by the son of the carer. When they sent him to respite care, on the occasional weekend, he was abused by one of those carers too. A relentless barrage of abuse throughout his childhood. He was sixteen by the time he got to us, had done a lot of offending himself, and was one of the highest-risk clients we ever had. Working through the development of his own offending, we came to a critical juncture. His offending had escalated significantly after the respite carer abuse. When I asked him why, he said that was the time he decided the world was made up of only two kinds of people, and the latest abuse had confirmed for him which he wanted to be. I asked what the two categories were. 'Fuck, or be fucked,' was the reply.

The boys I saw in treatment tended to come from similar backgrounds. Most of them had experienced significant abuse or neglect,[6] and family violence and physical abuse were common in their backgrounds. They often had problems at school, were isolated from their peers, were frequently bullied, and often bullied others, too. The most common coping mechanisms were excessive pornography use and masturbation to offending fantasies. Adolescence itself is a risky phase, of course, being an extended period of rapid change and development, pivotal to the formation of adult attitudes, behaviours, and ideals. Puberty is particularly important for the development of sexuality, and an adolescent who is sexually abused around the age of puberty is at twelve times greater risk of committing sexual offences.[7] Abuse before or after that period, while also damaging in many ways, carries a much smaller risk of later offending. The most effective preventative measure is early intervention. Identify young people with problem behaviours, as early as possible, and get help for them and their families. Consequences, yes, but proportionate ones, that encourage change as well as providing a deterrent.

Sometimes, even when positive processes are put in place, the system gets in its own way. I was asked, many years ago, to talk to our local Legal Aid office about our work at MAPPS. Until that point, we had taken the view that the young people at MAPPS should be encouraged to report all their offending behaviour. We believed that the boys should make reparation by relieving victims of the burden of coming forward, and that every secret they kept left a thread back to offending. We felt the approach had merit, and several boys had gone back to court, having reported themselves for further abuses. None of them had received an additional sentence, and although one had a conviction recorded against him, it was rescinded on appeal. In short, we believed the courts had seen the disclosures as acts of contrition, and signs of the positive impact of therapeutic intervention. Legal Aid did not see it that way, arguing that the practice was irresponsible and detrimental to the kids' futures. As time went by, we began to feel they were right too, and the more we prioritise punishment over early intervention, the more right they are.

Sometimes the attention brought to adolescent offending seems to work the other way, and someone suggests it is just another moral panic. In case you get into one of those discussions, it may help to know that there is a lot of good research to suggest our attention is warranted. There are also lots of good guidelines, which will list what behaviours may be of concern, like some of these:

- The victim is two or more years younger than the abusing child
- Coercive behaviour described by the younger child (usually simple threats or bribes)
- A preoccupation with being in the presence of the younger child
- Persistent sexualised language or behaviours
- Refusal to accept redirection when challenged about problem behaviours

And so on. There is a difference between a child who always has a hand down his pants and a child who is a danger to others. We know a lot more about it now, and there are good resources available to help professionals, and parents, decide.

Incidentally, language is important when talking about young people: children under ten are now called 'children with problem sexual behaviours'; older children are said to have 'sexually abusive behaviours'.[8] No child under eighteen should be called a sex offender, because they do not have an adult identity yet. The softer language doesn't stop them being held accountable, and it's better for the young people and the long-term prospect of change.

My favourite ever commentary about MAPPS and adolescent treatment came from a policeman, one of the regular professional visitors to the programme, who came to find out about adolescent sex offending and how to tackle it. He was an old-school uniformed officer, dragged along to our programme by a younger and more broad-minded colleague, and he looked decidedly unimpressed when he arrived. At the end of group, which was always three hours, with a dinner break in the middle, he came up to say goodbye. 'Well,' he said, 'I thought you were all going to be a bunch of soft cocks, but that was really good.' We met his comment with stunned silence. Later, when the staff team gathered to debrief, we fell about laughing. He had obviously thought that we would sit around sympathising with the boys, singing 'Kumbaya' and braiding their hair. Perhaps, like most visitors, he was shocked by the direct way treatment works, and the boys' ability openly to discuss their abusive behaviour, and the challenges of change.

Not all kids respond to treatment. Sometimes this is because the damage done to them is already too severe, and sometimes because the offending has taken hold, or both. We used to call the first group 'tick the box' kids. It is a terrible phrase, I know, and it looks even worse as I write it down. What we meant was a child who had experienced every kind of trauma: physical abuse, neglect, sexual abuse, family violence and familial breakdown. They were nearly always deemed too difficult to last in mainstream schools and were usually in the care system. They often had a history of offending that stretched back several years and included lots of non-sexual offending, sometimes including sinister elements like killing animals.

One boy, by the time he got to us at sixteen, had already been in eighteen separate care placements. He was so practised at surviving in new environments, and so well camouflaged, he was almost impossible to reach. I had an extraordinary session with him one day which, as I was relatively new to working with adolescents at that time, was something of a revelation. He started by being quite jovial and convivial, before going silent as the discussion turned to why he was there. After sulking for a while, he became more hostile, threatening violence and throwing small things around the room. Common enough behaviour so far. Then he took it up a notch, threatening to harm me and burn the programme down if I continued, standing up and leaning into my space, hoping I would rise to confront him. That level of threat did not come along very often, and he was a big boy, whose history I was aware of, so I took him seriously. I waited for him to calm, tried to help him understand his emotion and manage it. Teenagers can also be unpredictable, lacking an awareness of consequences, so trouble comes quickly. Then, suddenly, he was calm and convivial again, until we got back to matters at hand. Then he sulked, before getting angry again ... you get the picture. That was his repertoire, and in a later session he told me that one of those strategies usually worked, so he was not sure what else to do if they did not. He did not trust anyone, or anything, for obvious reasons. Unfortunately, we didn't have him for long, and a couple of sessions a week is nowhere near enough for a boy like him, so we were never really able to help him. He would be almost forty now and, if he is not in prison, he will be offending.

With boys like him, that you know are going to reoffend if they get the opportunity, all we can do is pass on everything we know about them to the next people in line, which is usually the police or child protection. In the early days, passing on such information was controversial, although now, quite rightly, you would get into trouble if you didn't. Treatment programmes operate under a system of limited confidentiality, so known risk to others, or knowledge of a victim, must be shared and the public protected. It is not like confession.

How do you tell the difference between who will and who will not reoffend? Well, whatever anyone tells you, it is sometimes little more than educated guesswork. There are some good risk assessment tools,[9] and clinical judgment comes with time. It also helps if you are part of a team, because groups tend to make better judgments than individuals, but it can be a nerve-wracking business. The stakes are high, and people can get hurt if you are wrong.

On the wall at MAPPS, we had a handwritten poster. It had three words to remind us what adolescents needed to help them change: Connection, Experience, Simplicity. Make them feel a part of community, of something better, but hold them accountable for their actions. Give them experiences to help them understand the harm they have done, but also focus on what future, positive relationships can be like. And don't over-complicate it.

9

Monsters or men?

Sex offenders are frequently described as monsters. But they aren't monsters, they're men. One of the reasons it has taken us so long to understand both sexual offenders and other abusive men, is that we have been looking for monsters. This language leads us away from understanding how some men come to behave in this way and, just as importantly, why other men do not.

The first time you hear a child say she loved her dad, who was sexually abusing her, the inadequacy of the word monster begins to crack. The first time you hear a woman say he was a good husband and father, apart from the abuse, the narrative gets more complicated. If you're a child watching TV, and a report comes on about the monsters abusing our kids, but you were being abused by a man who says he loves you, buys you gifts, and makes you believe you initiated the abuse, what would you think? If you were having sex with a partner, who didn't stop when it was clear you were no longer actively consenting, would you automatically see them as a monster? Monster language stops us understanding sexual crime and stops victims from reporting abusers.

When we made some educational films, for use in our training programmes, an experienced actor was chosen to play the role of the child molester, a character who was sexually abusing his teenage daughter. In rehearsal, he started playing him like a theatrical villain. 'He's not Dr Evil,' I teased him.

'He was Mr Average, and you'd never have picked him out of a line-up as a sex offender.' He became less and less villainous, until he finally looked and sounded like the man next door, because that is who most of these men are.

Sometimes the hysteria around sexual offending can border on the ridiculous. One newspaper headline, trumpeting the shock of a kindergarten child touching another's genitals, described him as 'Boy, 4, sex fiend'.[1] There's little doubt that someone needed to help that child (and his family), and programmes that help under-tens with sexual behaviour problems are increasingly common, but instead of writing about the real problems that show up in our communities, when children are seen to be acting in a sexually problematic way, all the newspaper could do was create a mythical new monster.

Sex offenders, particularly those who abuse children, have become modern-day pariahs. To a certain extent this is inevitable, as they prey on the weak and the vulnerable, demanding our wrath and our condemnation. They have also become the whipping boys of every politician who wants to appear tough on crime, with moves to public registers, limits to allowable residence, and longer and longer sentences. These measures may be popular, but not only is there little evidence of their effectiveness, in preventing crime or reducing recidivism, but they may even be counter-productive.[2] Have we become so angry and vengeful that we have lost sight of the bigger picture?

The history of criminal justice systems that prioritise punishment is littered with failures. There was Scared Straight,[3] a system that took high-risk youths into jails, to be lectured by long-term prisoners, and only made the young people identify with the men they met. Then there was Short, Sharp Shock,[4] a system brought in under Thatcherism to 'get tough on youth crime' and instil discipline, which created highly compliant, military-style prisoners. It was so disconnected from the young people's community reality, however, that it only succeeded in making fitter and healthier young offenders, having no effect on recidivism whatsoever. The 'tough on crime' notion is still so attractive that it is often suggested by politicians, despite being consistently evaluated as ineffective.

It is easy to be angry and to emphasise punishment, but it has little impact on offending and, even more importantly, on reoffending. As the criminologist John Braithwaite put it, 'Societies that are forgiving and respectful, while taking crime seriously, have low crime rates; societies that degrade and humiliate criminals have higher crime rates.'[5] It is hard to find clear indicators of such processes, but looking at recidivism figures can prove illuminating. In the UK, where the imprisonment rate is 140 people per 100,000 of population, the overall reoffending rate is 59 per cent within two years. In Norway, where the imprisonment rate is less than half the UK figure, the recidivism rate, over the same time frame, is 20 per cent.[6] It is important to use caution with such figures, of course, because the disparity may be due to a range of factors, such as community supports, access to treatment in prison, or to community drug, alcohol, or mental health services. It is indicative, however, of the ineffectiveness of simple punishment as a community safety measure. Braithwaite advocated for a process he called 'reintegrative shaming', using shame to challenge and then reconnect offenders with community. It drew a lot of criticism for its focus on shame, but it is the 'reintegration' element that is the most radical here, in the context of dealing with sexual offenders.

In the early days of treating sexual offenders, programmes were criticised for 'nonce bashing',[7] meaning that the style and tenor of therapeutic programmes was seen by some as too aggressive. Some of that criticism may have been fair, as the struggle to get people to take treatment programmes seriously often meant selling them as hardline alternatives to prison. Subsequent research has clearly demonstrated that, in the most effective programmes, positive relationships with staff and compassionate treatment processes, coupled with effective methodology for challenging offending, produces the best results.[8] As one practitioner/academic put it, 'Society may baulk at the idea of sexual offenders being treated as anything less than monsters; however, the vast majority of research indicates that the more you acknowledge offenders' human aspects, the better they do.'[9]

In Norway, the premise of the criminal justice system is that, once offenders have been punished, they will return to be everyone's neighbour. The principles they follow emphasise reducing recidivism risks while offenders are in the system and supporting them on their return to the community. This may be why their recidivism rate is the lowest of any country in Europe.[10] Whether you agree with the Norwegian thinking or not, it is certainly true that almost all sexual offenders who are imprisoned will be released back to our communities. Recent figures show that, although the length of sentences continues to rise in the UK, the average is still only five years,[11] so they aren't out of our communities for long.

There are also more unknown sex offenders in our communities than those that are known about, with 80 per cent of sex offence reports involving suspects previously unknown to police.[12] So, why are most of our efforts to reduce offending predicated on known offenders? We have also become so focused on them that some of our supervision systems are inefficient. For example, those that manage offender registers are usually expected to remain vigilant of all offenders' classifications, even those considered low-risk, as it has become so difficult to make the arguments that a low level of risk means he is unlikely to reoffend, or that most offenders will desist from offending.[13] As there are never enough resources to go around, this inevitably means that offenders who present a greater danger have less time spent on their monitoring and supervision. Importantly, even the highest-risk offenders have large reductions in reoffending risk over time.[14]

Restrictions placed on where offenders can live have led to an increase in homelessness, a factor likely to increase reoffending risk. In 2015, the California Supreme Court found residency laws to be unconstitutional,[15] due to unaffordable alternative housing options. At the time, the number of registered sex offenders who were homeless, and living on the streets, had climbed to over 6,000.[16] They also noted several other consequences of the hardline residency laws, exacerbated by increased homelessness, including restrictions on rehabilitative services, and increased difficulties for law enforcement officers trying to monitor and rehabilitate offenders. This point was reinforced by figures published by the California Sex Offender Management Board in 2016, stating that reoffending by homeless offenders on probation was 19.2 per cent, and 32 per cent for those who were homeless and on parole from prison. As only 6 per cent of registered offenders were homeless at that time, they concluded, 'These numbers indicate that homelessness is a significant factor in the risk of reoffence.'[17]

It is not that registration is a bad idea, as research shows it can have a small deterrent effect on men contemplating offending, and also that registers assist police by providing useful intelligence.[18] We need to be realistic, however, as they are not the panacea we might want them to be. Public registers, which publish images and addresses of known offenders, are even less effective, and can have a counter-productive effect on community safety. They can drive offenders underground, away from contact with authorities, diminishing the possibility of offenders reintegrating into society and elevating risk factors for reoffending. They also appear to have little effect on diminishing public anxiety about offenders, one of the strongest drivers for setting them up in the first place.[19]

There are always going to be some offenders that law enforcement needs to keep an eye on. Police now use registers proactively, to target and track high-risk offenders. I worked with a man, in the late 1980s, who had abused many children and was one of the first really high-risk offenders I encountered. He had been sexually abused by his father at an early age and further abused by a friend of his father's. This man then went on to introduce him to other men, who also abused him. As is common in these cases, he then began sexually abusing younger children himself, in his early teens, setting him on a lifetime path of abuse. In one sense, he never really had a chance, so comprehensively had his childhood been defined by abuse. His father, by contrast, never faced any consequences. Despite the best efforts of the treatment programme, he made little progress and was unlikely to do so. I felt sorry for him, but men like him need to be incarcerated, or face the highest level of supervision, if we are to keep the community safe. I have worked with numerous men, and a few teenagers, for whom the same would hold true.

I suspect many of us would be comfortable with the notion that some offenders should be permanently removed from our communities, but it does not happen very often. Many offenders found guilty of sexual offences will only be subject to a community-based order. The best bets we have for community safety measures, if removal from society is only a temporary option, are treatment, monitoring, supervision, and community reintegration. So, what are these processes, and how do they work?

Sex offender treatment is a collective term for a series of measures designed to understand and minimise an offender's risk to the community, and to prepare him for a non-offending life back in the community. The process of risk assessment[20] is designed to determine what risk an offender poses of reoffending, and what prospects there are of successful community reintegration. There are two main kinds of risk assessment, called static and dynamic. Static risk assessment looks at all past behaviours and other risk factors, before determining an overall risk score. Static assessments are broadly indicative of future risks, as past behaviour is a reasonable guide to future behaviour. Critics point out, however, that they leave no room for alterations to circumstance or attitude, consigning offenders to a future without the prospect of change. Dynamic assessments are more rigorous and time-consuming, requiring regular updates on critical areas of risk and need. Emphasis will be placed on acute risks,[21] which are those most closely related to an offending relapse. The two most important risk factors for future offending are an attraction to deviant sexuality and anti-social attitudes, neither of which is easy to shift.[22] Dynamic assessments are more expensive, requiring skilled assessors to maintain the process. Importantly, they are also reliant on regular, positive communications between the assessor and the assessed. All medium and high-risk offenders would benefit from such assessments, but they are not foolproof, as with all the measures described here. What all risk assessments should achieve, irrespective of the part they play in predicting reoffending, is the development of an in-depth understanding of each offender, which may be used by community monitors, police, and other relevant agencies.

I cannot tell you how many times I've heard both adult offenders and offending adolescents tell me that prison was easier than treatment. This is because prison, awful and dull as it is, requires no self-reflection, only survival. It is an ineffective punishment, as many decades of research has shown. Treatment,[23] on the other hand, requires offenders to confront their actions, their distorted thinking, and the effect of their behaviour on others, as well as attempting to develop strategies for a non-offending life. It doesn't always work, of course, particularly if the treatment is poorly targeted, as a recent review of the UK's prison Sex Offender Treatment Programme (SOTP) showed.[24] Cost-benefit analyses have regularly shown, however, that appropriate interventions with offenders, particularly young people who are offending, provide benefits that far outweigh the costs.[25] Treatment programmes are now a common feature of corrections systems across the developed world, and play an important part in reducing reoffending, when properly targeted.[26]

Most treatment programmes follow similar methodology these days, using cognitive behavioural therapies as the base. It is also increasingly common for justice systems to utilise processes like the Risk and Responsivity model,[27]or the Good Lives Model of rehabilitation.[28] These models focus on enhancing offenders' well-being, as well as holding them accountable for their actions, and helping them to manage their risks.

The most effective treatment programmes continue monitoring and supervision for a period after treatment has concluded, particularly after release from prison. Most jurisdictions will continue contact via another agency, such as probation, while offenders attempt to develop a non-offending lifestyle. There are also variants on the community panel model, where offenders are required to report to a group of professionals and volunteers, tasked with assisting them to maintain an offence-free life. Sex offender registers also require regular reporting to law enforcement, and subject offenders to random tests and checks.

A colleague once joked that if we were serious about reducing offending, we should all adopt a sex offender and help them to reintegrate into the community. As it turns out, there are models that mirror her suggestion, to a certain extent. Circles of Support and Accountability (COSAs)[29] are an extension of the supervision and monitoring models, aligned with the Good Lives Model of community safety and offender reintegration. What they provide, as the title suggests, is a level of support and community connection to balance the monitoring and supervision processes. The idea is that offenders are encouraged to use the network, to develop community connections, and are also held to account when the network itself sees concerns. The UK versions are called Multi-Agency Public Protection Arrangements, or MAPPAs, and have been in place since 2004.[30] The UK model is primarily run by police, and probation, but allows public representatives to question processes put in place for offenders.

When I tell the story, from the very beginning of the book, of the girl who has been groomed by her father to go to his room and initiate sexual acts, there is often discussion of what should happen to the father. Unsurprisingly, the replies are mostly punitive. When I tell them the rest of the story – that his wife left him, that he was prevented from seeing his children unless they chose to contact him when they were adults, that he had to move to another town and struggled to gain employment, make friends, or engage in any new relationships – the mood barely changes. Their reaction is understandable and, when I first heard his story, and thought about the damage he inflicted on his daughter and family, I probably felt similarly. But – and it is an important but – every one of those consequences also raises his risk of reoffending, leaving him disconnected and adrift. When we discuss that in training even police officers, some of the most cynical people I have ever met, reluctantly acknowledge that we must do something about those risks.

The appalling behaviour of sexual offenders stirs anger and condemnation in all of us, and consequences for their crimes are a vital element of any justice system. However, the next time you hear a politician call for harsher penalties, we must ask them what else they are going to do to make our communities safer. We should enquire what they are doing to increase reporting and improve community understanding of sexual crime. We should insist on improvements to the justice system, and demand they put money into prevention and early intervention, particularly for young people. And we should call for an end to seeing offenders as monsters rather than men, so we may continue to discover the drivers of this very human behaviour.

10

The continuum

There is a continuum of misogynistic and sexually abusive language, attitudes, and behaviour throughout our culture, which forms the bedrock of sexual offending. The elements that allow harassment are the building blocks of rape and sexual abuse. For every Harvey Weinstein and Jimmy Saville, there are thousands of other Harveys and Jimmys. For every rape there are many more sexual assaults, and considerably more instances of sexual harassment. There are key factors that turn up in the theory books to explain where offending comes from and how it is all linked, through culture, situation, and individual pathology.

Stop Violence Against Women, an international body, publishes figures on sexual harassment in numerous countries around the world.[1] It found rates were high in countries as diverse as South Africa, Japan, the US, Armenia, Australia, the Czech Republic, Poland, and Belarus. Most of the research is about the harassment of women, but it also indicated that harassment happens to men much more frequently than previously thought.

There is a wide range of other sexually abusive behaviours that affect our lives. In 2013, the Australian Centre for the Study of Sexual Assault (ACSSA) wrote a report stating that it was important to see *all* sexually abusive behaviour as part of a continuum.[2] The report went on to catalogue the statistics of some of the so-called minor offending, referring to surveys conducted by the Australian Bureau of Statistics, cataloguing the experiences of Australian adults. At the time, the Australian population was approximately 22 million. The Personal Safety Survey (2005) showed that, since the age of fifteen:

- 32.5 per cent of women (one in three) and 11.7 per cent of men (one in eight) had experienced inappropriate comments about their body or sex life
- 1.9 million women and 737,000 men experienced unwanted sexual touching
- One in three women (31.5 per cent) and one in seven men (13.7 per cent) experienced obscene phone calls
- 23.6 per cent of women and 8.6 per cent of men experienced indecent exposure
- 19.1 per cent of women and 9.1 per cent of men had been stalked. Two-thirds of all victims were stalked by someone known to them (ABS, 2006a)[3]

The survey gets repeated every five years or so, but the figures show only minor variations. The 2016 survey[4] found, for example, that one in five women (18 per cent or 1.7 million) and one in twenty men (4.7 per cent or 428,800) experienced sexual violence since the age of fifteen. They also stated that the proportion of women experiencing sexual violence (over the previous twelve-month period) had remained steady between 2005 and 2016 (1.6 per cent in 2005 compared to 1.8 per cent in 2016). A 2017 report by the Australian Institute for Family Studies[5] concluded that the prevalence rate for child sexual abuse of boys was 1.4–7.5 per cent for penetrative abuse and 5.2–12 per cent for non-penetrative abuse, while girls had prevalence rates of 4–12 per cent for penetrative abuse and 14–26.8 per cent for non-penetrative abuse. In short, statistics show that we have *yet to make a significant impact* on any of these problems.

It is not always easy to put statistics in context unless we see the human impact. There are several tram lines, in an area of Melbourne, that pass a cluster of all-girls schools. A police colleague described how many cases emanated from those tram lines, and how they need to give 'special warnings' to the girls in those schools. There would hardly be a girl, in any of those schools, that had not seen an adult man expose himself by the time they left school. One of my daughters was subject to this kind of behaviour too, when she was at pony club. The offender jumped out in front of her, on a woodland path, masturbating. He said, 'I want to come in your mouth.' She was twelve.

A poll of 600 women in Paris found that every single one of them had experienced sexually harassing behaviour while on the Metro subway system.[6] Over half the women said it had happened to them before they were eighteen. Many of the women had not registered the behaviour as abusive until they were asked about it by researchers, because they had become so used to it. In the year of the survey, of the many thousands of offences, only 203 were reported to police and 152 arrests made. Recent research shows that sexual harassment is just as prevalent on the London Underground and, despite a 42 per cent rise in reports over the last four years (from 844 to 1,206),[7] 90 per cent of abuses still go unreported.[8]

I was giving a lecture to students on a university criminology course. The lecture was on the way the justice system responds to sexual offending, and in the first hour we had been discussing consent and sexual assault. Two young women came over, in the break, to tell me about their experiences. One described being out on the previous weekend and having a young man grab her face and move his close to hers. They did not know each other, nor had any previous interaction that he could have construed as permission to behave in such a way. He then told her how attractive he thought she was. The young women then went on to tell me how often they are grabbed on the bottom, on their breasts, and occasionally between their legs. Sadly, like the women of Paris, they had come to see this as normal behaviour. They had not fully realised until they started their course, they said, that what men do to them, on a persistent basis, are sexual offences. I told them that each of the grabs they described, should they have reported them to police, would have been investigated as a sexual assault. They seemed surprised.

If those young women had come to think of it as normal, then do young men think so too, and where might that belief have come from? When I was working with young people committing sexual offences, we regularly ran training for professionals in related fields. To illustrate some of the ideas that young men grow up with we used to show part of a documentary. We were trying to demonstrate problematic elements in the wider culture, and that sexual offending by adolescents is not just an anomaly from a few aberrant teenagers. Neither is it only occurring in some socio-economic or cultural groups. The documentary we showed was about an elite, all-boys private school.[9] In one of the episodes the boys were putting on a play, with girls from the local all-girls school, and two scenes have stuck in my memory. In one, a boy of about fifteen or sixteen was talking about the party they were going to have after the show. He was looking forward to it, particularly meeting up with a girl that he fancied. He said he was looking forward to 'getting her in a corner, all nice and vulnerable ... and then moving in for the kill'. In another section a girl of about the same age was asked about dating and relationships. She was very pretty and had obviously received a lot of attention. At one stage, she looked plaintively at the camera and said, 'Why do boys always pull your face around when they want to kiss you?' I think she even demonstrated the move as she said it. Now, I am not suggesting this is necessarily a bad thing, but *always*? As it happens, I know the answer to that question, or at least one of them. He does it because he does not know how to say, 'I'd really like to kiss you,' or words to that effect. He doesn't know because nobody has shown him how or told him that such words are important.

And then there's pornography. It was hard enough when the magazines were only full of nudity and ridiculous stories, but now typical viewing is what we used to describe as 'hardcore'. It will probably entail oral sex, followed by vaginal and then anal sex, after which the actress will perform oral sex again before the male actor ejaculates on her face. It is a long way from 'I'd really like to kiss you.' We started the programme working with adolescents who were sex offending in 1993, just before the Internet fully arrived. By the time I left, in 2007, every boy said that he used Internet pornography routinely.

Looking back, the culture I grew up in left me utterly unprepared to navigate sex and relationships, cued to play out scenarios that were unwittingly abusive. Try to go as far as you can until she lets you know it's not OK, and then stop. Then try again in case she didn't mean it. Sex as a struggle or even a fight, rather than a connection, a pleasure, and a joy. If you then add all the myths and misconceptions about how sex and sexual offending happen, and how women should behave, there are the ingredients for an undercurrent of hostility and abusiveness in our sexual relationships.

In all the subsequent years, I wonder how much has changed. Public commentary about sexual education can sometimes provoke aggressive reactions, particularly if the opinion connects a lack of sex education with sexual abuse, or dares to suggest our culture has a widespread problem with men's behaviour and sexual violence. I suspect, at some stage, this book will be criticised by commentators as a pile of nonsense, because such attacks now seem to be commonplace in public debate. But I wonder, will they threaten me with rape? Tell me that I should never have children? Say I am only writing this because no one will fuck me?

Online articles by women writers (maybe look up Laura Bates's social media, or Clementine Ford's), are accompanied by a plethora of aggressive comments underneath: 'You should be raped to death' … 'Sit on a knife so you can't have children' – that sort of stuff. It is vicious, vitriolic, violent – and sexual. Sexual violence, directed at women with words, is a part of our culture.

Long after the #MeToo movement began, a group of senior executives, from large UK companies and corporations, gathered for a President's Club charity dinner.[10] The event was men-only, except for 130 'hostesses', who had been instructed to wear high heels and short skirts. There were auctions for a night out at a strip club, and for getting plastic surgery for your wife to 'spice her up'. Allegations later surfaced of the hostesses being repeatedly asked for sex and harassed, alongside reports that some of them were 'groped'. These are the same powerful men who are supposed to create workplaces of equal opportunity, free of sexual harassment and abuse. Can you do that at work, and still grope and harass women in your spare time? Research into sexual harassment says that the first intervention, attempting to eradicate abuse in the workplace, 'should be aimed at altering the behaviour of top management in an organisation'.[11] The President's Club would seem to be a case in point.

There was a lot of negative reaction to the President's Club dinner, alongside calls for such events to become a thing of the past. Not everyone agrees. Letters to the *Financial Times* (which ran the original exposé of the event) critiqued the 'puritanism' inherent in any criticism of the event and expressed outrage at the violation of the *men's* civil liberties. One letter writer attacked any criticism as being 'overly sensitive', 'childish' and 'shallow zealous leftist hysteria'.[12] Research has routinely found that, like the women on the Paris Metro, most victims don't even see themselves as such, so enculturated have they become to the abusive behaviour.[13] Studies also suggest that very few sexual harassment victims report the abuse.[14]

Research has also been conducted to determine if some women are more sensitive to harassment than others, reporting even when it is relatively minor. One study, from 1993,[15] looked at whether there was a difference between women who reported and women who didn't. The study was testing this so-called sensitivity, seeing if reporters and non-reporters of sexual harassment were noticing different things, or had a different threshold for, or tolerance of, abuse. The study found that the ability to identify harassing behaviour was similar in both groups, whether they reported it or not.

Harassment may not be the same as rape and sexual assault, but the effects can be similar. Researchers have routinely found, over the years, that even relatively minor harassment can have a significant impact on the victim's work and home life, as well as their mental and physical health. The more severe or prolonged the harassment, the worse the effects.[16]

Many industries have, in recent times, begun to (or been forced to) acknowledge the sexual harassment and abuse within their ranks. The film industry, government, classical and popular music, theatre, gaming, industry start-ups, medicine, taxis, the pornography industry, television, the hospitality industry ... the list goes on and on. The police force where I worked called for an independent inquiry into its culture, specifically around sexual harassment and abuse.[17] The results were damning, with 40 per cent of women and 7 per cent of men reporting sexual harassment. Gay men were six times more likely to report harassment than men overall. Women reported that harassment was part of a wider culture of hostility towards them, and the review found evidence of widespread sexism, a high tolerance for sexualised behaviour and interactions in the workplace, and that sex discrimination and sexual harassment were widely regarded as 'non-events'. Other emergency services, as well as the military, have also been forced to acknowledge widespread problems. Any organisation that has not already acknowledged these abuses will do so eventually.

If the wider culture tolerates derogatory and sexualised language, harassment, and abuse, it is inevitable that our workplaces and institutions will replicate this culture. Conversely, our workplaces and institutions, bound by tighter rules of conduct, and greater openness to discussion, could also provide a platform for developing more positive relationships. Sexual harassment experiments have looked at whether men, with either high or low likelihood to sexually harass, would do so if provided with environments (created in complex role-play scenarios) where they were either actively encouraged, or discouraged, to act out abusively. The results showed that men with a low likelihood of harassing behaviour, determined by tests of their personalities and sexual attitudes, did not act abusively when placed in situations which would allow them to do so. Unsurprisingly, in such situations, men with a high likelihood did. However, when men with a high likelihood of harassment were presented with an environment where such behaviour was actively discouraged, they did so less frequently.[18]

When it comes to the links between individual offender pathology and all abusive behaviours, the connections become more obvious. Inadequacy in adult relationships, a sense of entitlement, and a refusal to take responsibility. Laying blame on victims, the capacity to see intended victims as sexual objects, and the ability to minimise any perceived harms from the abuse. These are all present in the individual pathology of sexual offenders, but who am I talking about? Is it a sexual harasser, a rapist, or a child molester? Early research into sexual offending suggested that men who abused children were unlikely to commit rape, and vice versa. They were thought to be separate, and specialist in their interests. A landmark study in 1985 found that, of about 600 child molesters who took part in the research, almost one in five admitted to raping adults, as well as sexually abusing children.[19]

Whether research has been done on rapists, child molesters, sexual harassers, or family violence perpetrators, it has found more similarities than differences. In the theory base we use in training, of how offenders believe the world works, several themes emerge. The ones that stand out most starkly are that offenders feel a sense of entitlement to behave the way they do, seeing those they abuse as objects rather than people, and convincing themselves that what they are doing is either harmless, or the abuse is deserved. They will also persuade themselves that they aren't responsible for their actions.[20] I have worked on many cases that show the intersections of abusive behaviours and raise these uncomfortable connections. Take this case, for example.

A senior manager in an emergency services call centre was well known for his extrovert personality and his lively 'banter'. He was described as having a great sense of humour, an antidote to the difficult work of the department, and the fact that his jokes were often sexual was overlooked. The women in the department, who were the majority, had a completely different impression of him than the men. They heard the jokes without finding them funny, although they knew to laugh along, as that was part of the workplace culture he had established. They also knew that his jokes marked a set of attitudes that he brought to bear on them in more personal ways. He often stood uncomfortably close behind female staff, even when they were dealing with distress calls. He would put a hand on their shoulder, offer neck rubs to 'relieve the tension', and ask questions about their sex lives. Some women had commented to management about his behaviour. When nothing changed, some staff left. Those who did not, or could not, developed ways to help protect each other from his advances. There were code words on emails, as alerts to his presence. New female staff were given a 'heads-up'. Wherever possible, diversions would be run, to draw his attention away from whichever woman he appeared to be targeting. Even with these tactics, over the two years he had been managing the service, several women had become the subject of repeated attention. Although they were visibly uncomfortable in his presence, and never offered him the slightest encouragement, he was oblivious to their signals. The women he targeted would experience their shift times being changed and being singled out to help on 'special projects'. They reported that, when alone in his office, he would say things like, 'It's so good we can finally be alone together,' put his arm around them, or kiss them. So, is he a sex offender or a sexual harasser?

Engineering a position of dominance, power, and control. Creating a culture that promotes abuse and minimises the chance of disclosure. Sexualised language. Moving the boundaries of touch to a sexualised plane. A lack of empathy. Missing a range of contrary messages, or translating them into an abusive, self-serving script. Assuming she feels the same as him. These are all elements that connect harassment and rape. Elements that would also be present if the victim were a child.

To those who would question how it is possible to draw a connection between all the relationship abuses in our culture, I would say, how can you *not*?

11

The Internet age

In one sense, sexual offending hasn't changed in forever. Offenders have always used the same targeting and grooming strategies, the same manipulations and deceptions. The arrival of the Internet has not changed the fundamentals, but it has changed the way some offenders operate. Where the sexual abuse of children is concerned, there are three key groups who use the Internet:[1] those wishing to groom children for abuse, those wishing to collect child abuse images, and those wishing to make a profit from child abuse images.

Before the Internet, child molesters who wanted to access children had to do so directly. Now, they often attempt to groom children online. One of my daughters was a big fan of the *Lord of the Rings* films. There were fantasy writing sites that grew up around the films, where aspiring writers could share their stories, discussing their interests in chat rooms. On one occasion, she met a 'friend' and began chatting. Within a few questions he had moved to a personal tone and began asking questions about boyfriends and sex. She came to tell me what was going on, proudly showing me her reply suggesting he was a 'sleaze bag' and should leave her alone. She was pleased with herself, and I was very relieved that she had come to tell me about it, but I could not help wondering what impact the experience had on her.

The other grooming tactic that has become increasingly common is the encouragement to show and share naked images.

Offenders often target teenagers with requests, accusing them of not being 'fun' if they do not comply. For many teenagers, not being seen as 'fun' is a terrible prospect. When they comply, the screenshots are then used to blackmail them, usually with demands for increasingly graphic sexual images, and then for sex.

These fears were uppermost in my mind when another of my daughters wanted a new laptop, as we disagreed about what sort she should get. It was about the time when every laptop started to come with a built-in camera. I was against a camera, as one of the hazards of this work is that you see risks everywhere. She, on the other hand, was desperate to have one. It was not only about connecting with her friends, but also fear of being the only one in her group who *didn't* have something. Every teenage generation has something like that but, in the moment, I had forgotten. I tried to explain the risks, asking her to imagine what the camera would see, if it were looking at her right then. She was in her room, so I described what I saw. I pointed out what the posters on her wall said about her interests, and how anyone could start a conversation with her about them. She was wearing her school jumper and I pointed out that anyone could tell where she went to school. I was on a roll, but had gone too far, too fast, as her face became riddled with anxiety. Eventually, we talked about it in a more measured way and I explained my anxieties more carefully, about who and what a camera might let into her life. She then expressed to me, with typical adolescent understatement, how it would be 'the end of the world' if she didn't have a camera in her laptop. We talked about rules for using it, she got the laptop with the camera, and the sky did not fall in. I am glad we had the conversations, though, even though I made a mess of the first one, as it really is the only way. Young people usually make smart decisions if we give them the right information. Fortunately, there are now lots of organisations that provide good information for parents and young people about negotiating the hazards of the online world.

At any one moment, across the world, many thousands of abusive images are being shared or downloaded. Over the course of a year, it will amount to many, many hundreds of millions.[2] One recent study suggested, conservatively, that 4 per cent of UK adults had accessed abusive images online.[3] It's hard to tell exactly how many offenders there are, because of the ways people can hide their identities, and create multiple accounts. The FBI estimates that, at any one time, 750,000 sexual offenders are using the Internet for nefarious purposes,[4] although the evidence for this claim is unclear. Police forces do not have the resources to go and find them all, as there are just too many. Having said that, law enforcement in this area has improved dramatically in recent times and is a lot better at keeping pace with technological advances.

Men are the biggest consumers of CEM.[5] The only women I have encountered using it have done so alongside a man. They may do so on their own, of course, just far less frequently. CEM offenders do it for a range of reasons: they are already abusing children and use it for justification and gratification, they are using it to groom children, are curious about abusing children and are using it as desensitisation before abuse, or they are indiscriminately searching online and impulsively click on more and more abusive imagery.

In the late 1990s, we had our first adolescent at MAPPS who had committed offences using the Internet. He had found a user group that shared images of child sexual abuse, which group he wanted to join (you can imagine his background). Members of the group were only allowed in if they brought new images to share with the others, which is typical of such 'closed user' groups. It means they can add to their gruesome collections, but it also ensures that all members take the same risk, thus maintaining everyone's continued silence. The boy filmed himself abusing his nieces and was then allowed access to the group. He told us that it had not occurred to him to abuse the girls until he came across the group, which may or may not have been true.

Research evidence is inconclusive about how much the use of CEM might be increasing the number of children being abused. While it might seem logical that someone who is searching for abusive images would be likely to be abusing children himself, it is not necessarily the case. Even if someone is masturbating to child sexual abuse images, with all the psychological and physiological reinforcement that behaviour brings, they still may not be abusing children in their 'real world'. Incidentally, I know the online image is real, and that children are being harmed in the production of it, I am just trying to draw a distinction between the realities of everyday life and the online world. One of the most common excuses CEM offenders give for their behaviour is that they do not see it as wrong, as the image is already out there. They use this distorted thinking because they want to preserve an image of themselves as a good person. They pretend that an image is a fantasy, rather than acknowledging the abusive and exploitative element, and that the abuse in the picture happened to a real child. Sometimes offenders even claim that the CEM is stopping them from abusing children. This could be a lie, to stop us finding the children they *are* abusing. It could be a lie because they know they are interested in moving to abuse. It may also be the truth, as there is a group of CEM offenders who only use the Internet for their sexual expression and are unable and/or unwilling to have any kind of sexual encounter, abusive or otherwise, in the real world.[6] The main user group of CEM comprises those who are also contact offenders.[7]

CEM is big business. The majority is created in Northern Europe, Russia, the US, and Canada.[8] There are also a variety of user-pays sites and systems, mostly for child sexual abuse. On such sites offenders typically pay to have children abused via a webcam service. These are often in the developing world, in countries like the Philippines.[9] One offender we arrested justified his use of such a site by claiming he provided a much-needed humanitarian boost for a poor family. As well as money, he sent schoolbooks and other items, to help pay for the children's education. Perhaps it helped him to sleep at night. The horrors are without limit. If you can imagine it, there is someone using the Web to find it, including abuses of women and children, and their torture and murder.

The Internet has also provided other avenues for sexual expression, which can also have pitfalls. Although sexting is not, technically, an Internet phenomenon, it is connected. The sharing of sexual images has become more common, although research has shown widely varying rates. A recent study, with a broad sample base, found 49 per cent of respondents aged between thirteen and twenty-five (most were thirteen to eighteen) reported sending nude images or videos of themselves. The highest rates were among respondents who identified as gay, with lesser rates among lesbian and bisexual respondents, and the lowest rates among those who identified as heterosexual. Despite alarm at the rise of this phenomenon, the research concluded that,

> findings suggest that most sexting occurs without negative consequences and within existing relationships. It also suggests most sexting occurs between a small number of sexting partners. The data also suggests that a significant number of young people engage in consensual sexting, but that only a small number do so frequently.[10]

There are studies that highlight the gendered nature of image sharing, suggesting that girls are much more likely to suffer negative consequences should the images be shared.[11] There are also concerns that young people may fall foul of the laws concerning the production and transmission of child abuse images if they 'sext', as the law has failed to keep up with technological advances and developments in young people's sexual behaviour.[12] We started to get young people referred to our programme for 'transmitting or distributing child abuse images'. What they had done was share naked pictures of their girlfriends with their mates and, because the girls were under sixteen, they were deemed to have committed an offence. While their behaviour was clearly wrong, and reprehensible, it is not child sexual abuse.

The sharing of sexual selfies is open to abuse and can have a devastating impact on the victim of such behaviour. Along with unwanted sharing of images, there is the more sinister phenomenon of 'revenge porn'. The term, unfortunately, trivialises the nature of the abuse, because it is not posted online for public titillation, but to hurt and cause distress. It is not always done for revenge, either, but to control, humiliate, or blackmail. It is a crime which, like most sexually abusive behaviour, is largely perpetrated by men against women.[13] Researchers have advocated for inclusion of sexual ethics in relationship education, to address such abuses,[14] with calls for the focus to be on the perpetrators' behaviour rather than the victims'.[15]

Technology has also given sexual offenders, stalkers, and relationship violence perpetrators a wider variety of ways to abuse, frighten, silence, and humiliate victims.[16] Creators of the technology haven't always thought through these issues beforehand, nor have they been quick to respond when abuses are pointed out to them. It is not that any of these issues was not present before, but the Internet has made them much more accessible. The Internet has also created a platform for myriad depictions of sex, particularly through pornography.

12

Pornography

When it comes to the visible expression of how we treat each other in sexual relationships, there is nothing more important, currently, than the availability of pornography, and its impact on our sexual attitudes, beliefs, and behaviour. We seem, however, to have a problem discussing it openly and honestly, and in deciding how we should help young people navigate it.

My goodness, we are watching a lot of porn. There are, as I write now, six pornography sites in the world's 100 most visited Internet sites.[1] PornHub is the most popular, at number 6 in the world. Last year, PornHub's site was visited 28.5 *billion* times.[2] In 2016, on PornHub alone, 91 *billion* videos were watched, which is about 12.5 for every person on the planet. On one site![3] The biggest user groups are eighteen- to thirty-year-olds,[4] and PornHub states that, last year, 26 per cent of visitors to its site were women.[5]

I typed the word 'porn' into my search engine, and it offered me over 43 million sites to choose from. The word sex yielded 34 million choices, so it is no surprise that the use of Internet pornography now accounts for an estimated 30 per cent of all Internet traffic.[6] One site offered me a choice of more than 40 million videos to watch. Just out of curiosity, to see what is happening to our sense of perspective, I typed 'food' into my search engine, which offered only 28 million options. 'Climate change' yielded a paltry 14 million.

Early research into the effects of pornography, in the 1970s, concentrated on whether it was good or bad. The opposing claims were that it was either a liberation from conservative sexual attitudes and a force for the emancipation of women, or a template for rape and the depiction of women's sexual oppression. The question everybody was asking, and one of the main reasons for including discussion of pornography here, was: Does pornography cause sexual violence?

Malamuth's 'confluence model'[7] describes two main pillars of sexual aggression: hostile masculinity (HM) and an attraction to impersonal sex (IS). Research continues to confirm the correlation between HM, IS and sexual aggression, emphasising its importance for men with other high-risk factors.[8] There is evidence of both moderating factors, such as individuals who show higher rates of empathy,[9] as well as factors that heighten risk, like increased use of alcohol by men with high HM and IS.[10]

Malamuth acknowledges that, for most men, pornography exposure is not associated with high levels of sexual aggression. However, his studies estimate that for men in the high-risk groups, which constitute approximately 7 per cent of his samples, those who were also frequent pornography users had sexual aggression levels four times higher than the infrequent consumers. Moderate risk groups also had elevated levels, with frequent consumption.[11]

Other researchers have been prepared to go further, suggesting that the effects are not limited to those in high-risk categories, with a 2015 study concluding,

As with all behaviour, sexual aggression is caused by a confluence of factors, and many pornography users are not sexually aggressive. However, the accumulated data leave little doubt that, on the average, individuals who consume pornography more frequently are more likely to hold attitudes conducive to sexual aggression and engage in actual acts of sexual aggression than individuals who do not consume pornography or consume pornography less frequently.[12]

There are also concerns about recent increases in violent pornographic imagery, suggesting that there has been a shift away from pornography depicting women as unwilling sex partners, who ultimately enjoy the experience, towards an even more worrying trend, depicting sexual dominance of women who appear willing throughout the experience. Their concern, obviously, is the normalisation of aggression and dominance within cultural sexual scripts.[13]

My friend and colleague, Maree Crabbe, works as an educator, teaching adults about the impact of pornography, particularly on young people. She also makes films, like *The Porn Factor*, to provoke wider discussion about this extraordinary cultural phenomenon. In one of her films, she interviews a male performer about his experience of the industry.[14] He talks about recent moves to more aggressive enactments, showing some discomfort about the things he is required to do, although he continues to do them. One scene he discusses involved five men, including him, who systematically penetrate and abuse a woman performer. She is slapped, pushed, choked, 'fish-hooked' (has her mouth forced wide open) and has her head trodden on, all while being relentlessly penetrated in every orifice. The actor was clear that, as in all similar scenes, the woman was required to show that she was enjoying it, and that the director would not have included any images to the contrary in the final cut. He also explained that these scenes are popular and sell well. The one he described won an industry award for 'best scene of the year'.

In Maree's film the rationale for the industry's move to more violent imagery is explained by a successful producer, who argues that porn needed to show a greater reality in its imagery, to improve the relationship with its target audience. His point is intercut with commentary from a woman performer, discussing what she does and does not do at work and at home, sexually speaking. Her conclusion is that any man who is doing to their partner, at home, what performers are doing to women on the set of pornographic films, should seek professional help. So, which of the two, the producer or the performer, has a better grip on reality?

The impact of trends in pornography was also brought home to me when I was listening to the representative of a major sexual assault centre present figures detailing the rise in choking injuries presenting at their service. Choking is now a common feature of mainstream pornography, where it was not a decade or so ago. Any forensic medical examiner will also tell you that questions of anal penetration are now compulsory when examining rape victims, so common is the behaviour. They also say that victims under thirty-five are far less likely to have pubic hair than older women. Both anal penetration and absence of pubic hair have also become common features of pornography in relatively recent times. These changes, and the observations of professionals in the sexual assault field, indicate how pornography may be shaping body image and sexual behaviours. As one feminist pornographer put it, 'Pornography is sex education ... whether you like it or not.'[15]

I have read many articles about the effect of pornography over the years, both scholarly and populist. Some argue passionately that pornography ruins marriages, *fosters* sexual violence and is creating generations of porn addicts. Others assure the reader that it is beneficial to health and well-being, enhances people's sex lives, and *reduces* sexual violence.[16] So, who to believe? I should also lay my cards on the table. I do not have a problem with depictions of sex and nudity, nor images of consensual sexual practice. I do believe there are problems with the context in which pornographic sex is depicted. It is not the sex or the nudity that causes problems, but the messages that come with it. We are not just watching sex here, but creating sexual politics, and constructing the sexual relationships of the future.

Pornographers are good salespeople. They were one of the first industries to move online, have constantly innovated with things like point-of-view (POV) technology and now virtual reality. They understand the addictive nature of their product, like the makers of alcohol, cigarettes, and fast food. Give people a dopamine hit and, when it begins to wear off, give them another. It offers endless apparent variety, so consumers stay hooked, all calibrated by the modern pheno-menon of computer algorithms.[17] Most of what is on offer in the mainstream pornographic tropes are young women, barely old enough to vote, who are the object of the films rather than the subject. Mainstream sites not only exploit performers by not paying for their work but also, despite their protestations of 'zero tolerance' for anything illegal, portray a staggering array of abusive acts. Performers are routinely slapped, choked, splattered, and pounded into submission. Some individual performers are lauded as 'stars', but the language used to describe women in porn is frequently vulgar and misogynistic. We would not put up with it anywhere else, would get fired from our jobs if we used the language at work. Somehow, though, we put on blinkers when we go online and choose what to masturbate to, so as not to notice, perhaps, that the film we are watching is advertised as 'cumslut whore gets slammed in every hole'.

Mainstream porn also has a way of redirecting all sexual expression back to the lowest common denominator. Take BDSM, for example. Devotees will explain that, at its heart, BDSM is an expression of trust and intimacy, using power and control as an erotic interplay. Even a cursory glance shows that mainstream porn uses BDSM quite differently, to show women being bound and penetrated. Pornographers have also taken over alternative words. If you type 'erotic' or 'love-making' into your search engine, you will be led to the main porn sites, to the core model. They are good not only at sales, but also at keeping away the competition. There are those trying to keep the lens wide, providing ethical guidelines for consumers, feminist standards for both production and consumption, and films that celebrate sex rather than commercialise it. Currently, the juggernaut of mainstream porn leaves these voices on the margins.

One researcher[18] summarised the arguments for the positive effects of pornography as increasing sexual pleasure, decreasing sexual repression, increasing sexual communication and openness, providing stress relief and emotional regulation, increasing sexual variation and experience, as well as the frequency of sex, and normalising alternative sexual practices. Alongside this list of potential benefits lurk some dangers, however, particularly with the moves to more aggressive content.

For example, neuroscience suggests that mirror neurons in our brain, vital in allowing us to copy and learn new skills, also drive the copying of sexual behaviours. Research shows that subjects exposed to sexual imagery have activations in their mirror neurons, creating a desire to 'take the place of' the actors in the videos they watch and 'reproduce' what they are doing.[19] Porn has clearly played a role in opening discussion about sex and pleasure, and broadening our repertoire of potentially enjoyable experiences but, as we watch, are we expressing ourselves freely, or playing out the scripts of pornographers?

In all the discussion about what effect the proliferation of porn is having, one thing is abundantly clear. It is having a significant impact on children and young people. Research shows that about *half* of under-sixteens have used pornography, with most beginning viewing before fourteen years old.[20] By the end of adolescence the numbers rise to more than 90 per cent of boys and 60 per cent of girls, and should now be seen as a normative experience of adolescence.[21] Young people between nineteen and thirty report regular usage, with young men being substantially more likely to do so (around 90 per cent) than young women (around 30 per cent).[22] Researchers mostly agree that pornography is having a significant impact on the way young people view sex, and sexuality, and can form a script for both bodily ideals (with particular effects on girls) and sexual practices.[23] There are some other alarming elements of current research, suggesting links to increased permissiveness and sexual risk-taking. For some young consumers, there are also strong connections with the development of sexually aggressive attitudes and behaviours towards women.[24]

There are also encouraging signs, however, that most young people are working out how to navigate the world of pornography. Some report positive effects on their sexual lives, although these more optimistic research studies tend to come from countries that have comprehensive sex education.[25] Young men, it should also be noted, report more positive effects than young women.[26] Many researchers, from a range of countries, agree that information on how to deal with pornography must be included in sex education, and that sessions should start before young people are likely to begin viewing it.[27] When young people are asked what kind of education they would like, they say the focus should be on them as sexual beings, rather than on reducing any negative outcomes of sex. One study suggested young people want educators to 'say everything'.[28]

We can probably all agree, I hope, that young people need some help navigating the online pornographic world, even if we cannot agree on how to go about it. What about the rest of us? At the end of a training day, a few years back, a young detective came up to me. I knew he wanted to ask about something personal, because he waited around until everyone else had left. He asked if it was OK that he was still masturbating to pornography, given that he was now working in the field of sexual crime. I was surprised by the question but admired his honesty. We talked it over thoroughly, including porn's addictive properties, feelings of double standards and hypocrisy, mood associations with his usage, and how pornography had affected our lives. It was a long conversation, and I enjoyed the discussion, as men do not talk to each other like that very often, more's the pity.

Subsequently, and discreetly, I have asked quite a few people what they thought my answer to his question should have been. They were people who work with victims or offenders, as well as those who do not, both male and female. The most common response, by far, was that my first response should have been, 'It depends what you're looking at.'

Pornography, with its cheap thrills and easy accessibility, is never going away. We do not have to use it, of course, and there are also sites helping people to give it up. If we do use it, however, there are decisions to make. What we watch will affect our desires and practices, whether we like it or not. It will affect our relationships. The more we use porn, the more that will be so. Occasional use may not cause problems for most people, but the imagery we choose still says something about the values we hold, as individuals and as a community. We must, at least, be critical consumers. We should consider the values inherent in any imagery we watch, and those of the people who made it. Recent moves by finance companies, prompted by lobbying from the National Center on Child Exploitation and a *New York Times* article, forced the biggest site, PornHub, to remove huge amounts of abusive content from their platform, and to review their policies on uploading content.[29] Other major sites soon followed suit. Whether you think Visa and Mastercard are the right people to be leading the fight against exploitation or not, it shows what lobbying and consumer power can do. As we continue to debate what we should or shouldn't watch, we must equip the next generations with the information they need to navigate pornography, and the effect it has on us.

Part III

Investigating sexual crime

After twenty years in offender treatment, I was ready for a change. At the time, a Law Reform Commission[1] had published a report on the way the criminal justice system dealt with sexual offences, which was heavily critical of all the agencies dealing with sexual offending. The police were criticised for lacking expertise in understanding sexual crime and disbelieving victims. The report suggested police did not have the confidence of the public. Two of us were then employed, by the police, to create a training programme that would address their shortcomings. One of us was to concentrate on the interviewing of children and other vulnerable victims, and the other on teaching investigators about sexual offenders, the dynamics of offending, and improving the interviewing of sexual offence suspects.

My colleague Mark and I set about understanding our new world and culture. Because the fundamentals of police investigations involve preparing victims' stories for court, we sat in on trials, which proved a rude awakening. Trial after trial I watched, as evidence I knew should be there did not get presented – parts of the story that would have been vital to explain what had happened. Why did she initiate things? Why didn't he tell his mother? Why did she stay in a relationship if he really did what she said? Time and again the relationship details were not there.

Cloistered in my world of offender treatment, I simply had not realised that the stories we were so familiar with had not made it into other important areas of the justice system. Police and prosecutors expressed many misconceptions and misunderstandings about offenders and victims. They were also acutely aware that the public, who sit on juries, struggle to understand these stories. They seemed to be afraid of juries and were only likely to send cases for trial that they thought would be easily won. When I looked at the statistics of how many cases reported to police went to court, I got the next shock, as it was only about two out of every ten.[2] Further research showed that it was similar all over the world, usually from assumptions about which cases would present a reasonable prospect of conviction. Despite recent advances in reporting and investigation, these figures have not changed that much,[3] or have even got worse.[4]

Police and court officials had all sorts of beliefs about how people behaved when they were offended against. Most importantly, they didn't know enough about offenders. After one particularly frustrating experience watching a trial, I returned to the office disheartened, and sought out Mark to vent my frustration. 'That trial was so unfair!' I exclaimed. 'The jury just didn't get to hear the whole story!'

We both paused, realising that phrase held the kernel of an idea, and I started writing down a plan.

It would have to start with the police, because if they understood how sex offending worked, could stop being judgmental, and investigate without their old assumptions and misconceptions, we might have a better starting point. If they could be taught how best to listen to victims and ask the right questions, then maybe we might be able to gather evidence in a more effective way. When Mark and I developed the new training programme, for specialist sexual assault and child abuse investigators, we concentrated on three themes:

- knowledge of the dynamics of sexually abusive relationships
- positive attitudes towards victims
- skills development (particularly investigative interviewing)

We identified these themes as both critical to investigators' effectiveness and most lacking in previous policing practice. None of them would be enough on their own, so a unifying concept was needed to make that happen. We have been working on the Whole Story methodology for over ten years now, and it's had quite an impact, particularly on investigators' attitudes towards victims and their stories. This need not apply only to the police, though, as we are all community influencers, fact-finders, and potential jurors.

Whole Story is based on an understanding of the dynamics of sexually abusive relationships. There is usually abundant relationship evidence to explain what the offender was doing, and why the victim reacted in the way that they did, if investigators know where to look. Importantly, you cannot gather the whole story without good interviewing and communication skills. Some interview training was already available and effective, but it needed to be complemented by a more comprehensive understanding of sexual offending. It may be a while before the impact of Whole Story is routinely seen in court outcomes, although evidence suggests it can be used effectively,[5] but it has already helped change both attitudes and practice. After the low point of public confidence that led to Mark and I being employed, the only way was up. Ten years later, in 2015, the Victim Support Agency in our area published its annual report.[6] It stated that victims of sexual crime were more positive about their experience of police than any other victim group. This change came about for a variety of reasons, of which Whole Story was an important factor.

Understanding offender behaviour and abusive relationships, listening thoroughly to complainants' stories, knowing what questions to ask, and eliciting all available evidence. These are the starting points of effective sex crimes investigators.

13

Police

'Police employees do not live in a vacuum,' said a 2015 report into the working culture of the police force where I have been working. 'They are individuals and community members as well as employees, whose attitudes reflect and inform broader community and societal attitudes about the identity, roles, assumptions and expectations about how men and women should be, what they should do, and how they should interact.'[1]

In short, they are us. Full of the same myths and misconceptions as we are. They represent a microcosm of the attitudes and beliefs that make investigation and prosecution so hard, and victims so reluctant to come forward. So, if you want to change the way we all see sexual crime, policing is a good place to start. The police are also, crucially, gatekeepers to the entire criminal justice system. There has always been a lot of focus on courts and conviction rates, but most case decisions are made by police.

I had not always had good experiences with the police, although most of my encounters were relatively minor. If we were not aware before, we certainly should be now, that for many people fear of police is a tangible and ever-present experience. When it comes to relationship violence and sexual offending, where women are disproportionately affected, the cultures and practices of police have strongly inhibited reporting. With these issues all in mind, therefore, I was full of trepidation when I started working for the police myself. I also knew that I might be unwelcome, that I would never be an 'insider', and that it would take a long time to make any of the changes required.

Then, when I started, there were the tests, like the investigator who wanted to show me porn on his computer, to check if I was 'one of the guys', and questionable jokes I was expected to laugh at. As I got to know the detectives in our field, half of whom were women, other stories began to emerge. One woman told me of her first experience on a detective squad, a decade or so before. In those days she would have been a relatively rare female presence. Everyone had a nickname, and the senior officer decided that hers would be LOBIT. It stood for 'Little one, big tits', which she put up with because she felt she had to. Another officer told me of her first day 'on the van', fresh out of the training academy, accompanied by an experienced senior constable. When their van had a flat tyre, and they had to wait for the support vehicle to fix it, her senior colleague suggested a way they could pass the time. 'How about a blow job?' he said. A few years ago, the Chief Commissioner of Victoria Police, where I have been working, called for an independent report into sexual harassment and abuse within the force. The Human Rights and Equal Opportunity Commission survey [2] was the most responded-to of any survey in the history of the force. It said exactly what you would expect: that policing was a male-dominated culture, and that sexual harassment and discrimination were commonplace. In fact, it found harassment rates higher than in the general population. Shocking as the findings were, the report also signalled a willingness to acknowledge the flaws in policing culture, and to set about making change.

There were also surprises in the job, as the longer I worked in the investigative units, the more they started talking about themselves, particularly when other colleagues were not around. There were numerous occasions where someone who may have been quiet in a group, or even blokey, would open up in private. Women detectives, in particular, would seem freer to express their views and not hide their personality. I realised how much group culture shaped their public personas, as it does in most workplaces. They would tell me they were Buddhist, had a passion for Second World War history, or went salsa dancing at the weekend. They would talk about the parts of the job they found hard, the work they took home with them, and the cases they could not get out of their heads. I will never forget one veteran detective, who had worked in homicide and other crime squads, well up with tears as he recalled how much of his children's lives he had missed because of his job.

I have met lots of the other kinds of policemen and women too: rigid and rule-bound, boorish, entitled, aggressive, puffed up by the badge. But those are not who I got to work with. The police I know are mostly compassionate and thoughtful people, who have joined to do good and have an old-fashioned notion of public service. We find, from our research, that most detectives work in the sexual offending and child abuse area because they want to help victims. Some do come for other reasons, like career advancement or intellectual interest, but most are there because they are passionate, or have become passionate, about this work. I asked one of them why he had come to work in a sexual offending and child abuse unit. 'Because I became a copper to look out for people who can't look out for themselves,' he said. Another once told me that, when he imagined what kind of service victims needed, he thought of his own children, and how he would want them treated.

It is not easy working with the police and, when it comes to dealing with outsiders like me, who have come to make change, they can be difficult. Once they believe in what you are saying, however, and the way you are saying it, they can quickly get on board. A senior officer from one of our units told me that, when Mark and I first started the new training programme, there were quite a few detectives who did not want to go. I asked him how long it was before we persuaded them of the training's value.

'About a year.'

Early in the reform process, two management decisions helped to protect the officers who joined our area of work. After the shock of being told how bad they were at sexual crime investigation, and how little victims thought of them, the police leadership decided to pilot two new specialist units, to see if the response could be improved. It could, and it was, and there are now twenty-eight units, with over 450 specialists in them. Reporting has risen significantly.[3]

They also decided to make all specialist sexual crime investigators into detectives, which was vital, because detectives have high status in police culture. The management of sexual crime victims had traditionally been the realm of non-detective officers, who were often women, and the work was accorded low status. The change was intended both to elevate the status of these kinds of investigations and to make people want to investigate these kinds of crimes. It was not a popular move with some of the old-school brigade, or with many senior officers, who wanted to use their detectives as they saw fit and didn't want them tied up doing only one kind of case.

One researcher describes traditional police cultures as 'hyper-masculine, results-oriented, emotionally detached, loyal, insular, hierarchical, authoritarian and hostile to the scrutiny of outsiders.'[4] There is some truth in these descriptions but, as usual, it's more complicated than that. If you are going to walk into dangerous environments, deal with drugs and alcohol, knives, and guns, you would want the next officer to have your back, wouldn't you? Problems might only arise if loyalty to a colleague superseded loyalty to the community, or to the truth, perhaps. Hierarchies are not inherently bad either, but they can limit initiative and creative thinking. And we have all met Mr Hyper-masculine, who is never going to be able to do victim-centred work.

In developing the specialism of investigating sexual assault and child sexual abuse there are three elements, from the researcher's list, that we spent most time trying to deal with: results-oriented, emotionally detached, and insular. Traditional police focus is often on what is called volume crime, such as property offences and car thefts, so called because there are a lot of them. Senior police members are held accountable to a computer analysis of crime statistics, which will show how effectively they are responding to crime in their area, so there's pressure to keep crime low on their patch. Resources follow the crime pattern, so money and staff will be put where senior officers perceive the greatest need. The problem with relationship-based crime is that it is relatively low volume by comparison to something like a spate of burglaries. It is also constant, and investigations are time-consuming. There is an ongoing struggle, therefore, to justify the resources and the specialism. So, one of the other good leadership decisions was to have an *increase* in reported crime as a goal of the reform process. It is highly counter-cultural for increases to be considered a good thing but, when you know how few victims report, it was a huge step in the right direction. It is good to be results-focused, but you need to know what results are needed.

The key criticism that led to the reform process was that victims disliked the way they were treated by police, particularly male detectives. They found them dismissive and disbelieving.[5] Emotional detachment can be useful in policing, particularly when dealing with traumatic events and situations. It is also essential to keep an open mind, which can be hard to do if you are emotionally attached to people involved in investigations. On the other hand, if you want victims to be open in interviews, so you can gather the best possible evidence, you need to be empathic and patient. You need to understand trauma and be responsive to victims' needs. Most importantly, you need to listen and have impeccable communication skills. It is not easy to make all these elements of policing come together.

Although police are often criticised for their negative attitudes towards victims and for not believing them, the solution is not to replace this with a culture of belief, but rather a culture of *listening*. Detectives cannot believe everything they hear before they have completed an investigation. Most police forces have a mantra in their detective ranks that runs something like, ABC. Assume nothing. Believe nothing. Check everything. Good sexual crime investigators know how to balance the detective ABC with the communication skills required in relationship-based crime investigations.

A young woman came into one of our units, alleging sexual abuse by her father. After she had completed her statement, she wrote a letter to the investigator. She thanked them for 'representing' her when they investigated her case and interviewed her father. She also said she realised that, during the investigation phase, they would 'walk the line between empathy and distance'. What the investigator and I both took her to mean was that, having compassionately taken her statement, they were then required to act dispassionately, as they undertook an investigation. She was spot-on, as that is exactly what detectives are required to do.

Investigative culture and practice can be slow to change. Detectives are typically trained by other detectives, who were usually trained at the same school, by detectives from their own force, and so on. The process can produce a thoroughly stagnant culture. Experience of the job, which means following long-laid-down protocols and processes, is often prioritised over training. Every organisation needs the latest information and someone to come in and ask: Why do you do this and why do you do that? We have found that the more experience one of our course participants had, the longer it generally took for them to absorb new ideas and practice. They were also less likely to be able to develop new skills that could be sustained over time. It is easier to train someone from scratch than to de-train and re-train them. However, ideas and practices that were new or even radical when we began are now embedded in the culture, so the issue has become less of a problem.

There is a point in all investigations when the detective will let victims know what may happen should their case progress through the criminal justice system, and all police forces have a version of this conversation.[6] This options talk requires a high level of communication skill, tact, and compassion. At a time when people are at their most vulnerable, they need to know what to expect and what choices they have. Investigators need to be frank and realistic, but also sensitive and reassuring. As you can imagine, in the past, this talk was a way for investigators to get rid of cases they did not think they could win, even if they believed the victim. The process was ripe for abuse and, if the victim did not fit their expected profile, evidence seemed sparse, and the prospects of winning in court slim, they would simply show scepticism and negativity, which was usually enough for the complaint to be withdrawn.

An expert in victim behaviour regularly came to our training, to describe what victims go through when they report. She told the tale of a young woman who, after years of abuse at the hands of her father, finally reported to police. She described how the woman sat on the edge of her chair, knees facing the door, eyes focused on the expression of the investigator. What was she looking for? Doubt. If she had seen any at all, she would have run away immediately. Such had been the burden of the secret, the pain of coming forward, and the fear of not being believed, that she would not have been able to bear it. She would then tell the audience, at the end of the story, that the woman in question was her.[7]

Sometimes the problems in policing sexual crime come not just from individual officers, or police culture, but also from connections in the wider community, as in the following case.

A woman lived in a rural town, small enough that it felt like everyone knew everyone else's business. Her husband was abusive, and eventually she left him. He did not take it well, and she was forced to take out an intervention order, which was not effective. He constantly left his calling card: taking vegetables from 'his' garden, dropping by unannounced to stand outside the kitchen window and clap her, sarcastically. And then there was the texting – at every hour of the day and night. He always seemed to get her number, however many times she changed it. She complained repeatedly to the local police, who told her there wasn't much they could do until he 'did something'. The rules on such behaviour are changing now, and breaches should be taken more seriously, but only a few years ago this would have been a typical response. (In the UK, for example, Domestic Violence Protection Notices (DVPNs) and Domestic Violence Protection Orders (DVPOs) only came into effect in March 2014.)[8]

The woman asked what her ex-husband had to do before she could get some action. The police didn't know what to say, so they became irritated with her. They also knew her husband and played football with him in the local team. He had always said she was 'painful', and with her persistent complaints she began to feel that way to them too. One night she came home to find him in her bedroom and, knowing what would happen if she resisted, submitted without a fight. That night she went in to report the rape to the local police, telling them that something had now happened, and she demanded action. She also insisted on a forensic medical, to which demand they reluctantly agreed. The next day one of the investigators saw the ex-husband doing his shopping and told him he needed to come in 'for a chat'. He let him finish his shopping first. The ex-husband said the sex was consensual and they left it there. Desperate, but undeterred, she complained to head office, and a crew of specialist detectives was sent to take over. They had no local ties and were trained in sexual offence and family violence investigations. They looked at the evidence and the likelihood that she would, after so many violent and abusive incidents, and multiple reports of breaches, consent to sex under the circumstances he had described. The cumulative weight of evidence, including the medical, supported her story. A jury believed her too, and the man went to prison. Specialism and knowledge helped to overcome the boys' club of a country town and local policing, and let this case through the gate, eventually.

Sometimes, to be fair to good general detectives, it doesn't need a specialist to provide open-mindedness and investigative rigour. Maintaining the ABC of investigations can yield unexpected results, and change minds that have closed too early, as in the next case.

A man in his early thirties walked into his local police station to report a sexual assault. There were no specialists there, so he got two general detectives, who were surprised to learn that the man was reporting that he himself had been the victim of a rape. He reported that he had stopped off to relieve himself at a roadside toilet block, on his way home from getting take-away for himself and his fiancée. As he was leaving, a man in full Second World War army uniform, including a helmet with insignia, stood in his path. Holding up a large, strangely curved knife, he motioned for him to move behind a row of bushes, where he made him kneel and perform oral sex. When the offender was finished, he was told to close his eyes and count to a hundred before moving. A short while later he heard an engine start and decided it was safe to move. As the offender's vehicle moved under a streetlight, he saw the car and part of the number plate.

As he told the detectives the story, he could tell they did not believe him. He felt stupid and humiliated. They said they would check it out, but he didn't think they would. The two detectives, unfamiliar with this kind of crime, had come up with a theory. A 'closet' gay man, caught out cruising, had come in to get himself a cover story. Their sergeant, a wiser head, told them to check it out anyway, so they looked up the vehicle and number plate. To their surprise, it matched the car of a local tradesman, married with kids, who lived in town. The complainant must have mistaken the number, they thought, because that could not be right. Check it out anyway, said the Sergeant ... again. So, they went to the address and, looking in the window of a vehicle like the one reported, they got another surprise. On the back seat was a Second World War army tunic and helmet. A search of the garage also revealed a Gurkha combat knife, with a distinctively curved blade.

To their credit, they followed up thoroughly, including an apology for their obvious scepticism, and the offender was prosecuted. A bit of specialist training would also have told them that it is common for men who define themselves as straight to rape other men.[9] We now tell this story in training, as a warning to understand the crimes you are investigating and not to make assumptions, however hard the story is to believe. It is a reminder we all need, from time to time.

Detectives who investigate sexual assault, rape, and child sexual abuse need a combination of qualities and skills. I conducted some research,[10] asking 100 investigators to explain which skills and qualities were most needed in their work. They completed questionnaires at the beginning of training, at the end of training, and after they had been in their specialist roles for approximately twelve months. After time in the field, they said the five most important qualities were, in order: empathy, good communication skills, patience, open-mindedness, and good investigative skills. It is not a combination that everybody has, nor are some elements easy to teach. We try, however, and participants spend a lot of time practising the application of these five skills and qualities. They spend many hours interviewing real people, in mock scenarios, including children (although the children are not interviewed about the subject of abuse). The children, who come from a local school, get a magic show performed by one of our people. It is not particularly good, but the kids are only six and they seem to enjoy it. The next week they come to the Academy and our trainees are given the task of finding out what happened. They are not told about the magic show, so they must find that out. There are also red herrings and false leads, all of which they need to navigate. It is a great day, but I always get a sad feeling when I see the children there, realising for the umpteenth time why we need to teach these skills.

Our students also get to interview volunteers with a variety of cognitive impairments and disabilities. It is a day my police colleague, Tony, is passionate about, and he loves running it. Taking statements from vulnerable groups is a critical area. Disadvantaged groups of all kinds are more likely to be targeted by offenders, and less likely to report, so getting better at listening to all these groups is a priority. When the people with cognitive impairments come in, I can see our trainees getting nervous. It is important to understand that past failings in this area weren't only because of a lack of care, or a belief that the cases wouldn't go anywhere. It was also because of the much more human problem of anxiety, about coping with difference, and a fear of making a fool of oneself.

Anxiety is not the only mental health issue that specialist sexual crime investigators face. Secondary trauma, compassion fatigue, noble cause corruption, depression, and paranoia are also common among those who spend their days hearing stories of sexual crimes.[11] There is added pressure in modern policing from the massive volume of online child abuse imagery that police are required to view, catalogue, and assess. I always tell our investigators that these stories are *supposed* to make us sad and angry, as both these states can be motivational, as well as reminding us that we are human. There is a curious double bind here, though, in that one of the qualities that makes some of our officers so good at this work is also a potential weakness: empathy. If officers are to last long in sexual crime investigation, they must learn to understand and develop their empathic side, but also know how to protect it. Like so many other things in sexual crime investigation, it is not an easy task.

An investigator friend and I once spoke about how the work had affected us. She has worked in sexual offending and family violence for many years. She told me about a time she had been at a music festival, with family and friends. It was a hot day, with music rocking and wine flowing, so her guard was down. Her sister went to find the toilets and was gone for a long time. Too long, she felt, and her mind raced to the inevitable, irrational conclusion, that something bad had happened. When her sister finally returned, she tore into her, about how irresponsible she had been, and that she needed to be more aware of the dangers. The group calmed her, but questions were later raised about her reaction, and whether she needed some help. The next morning, reflecting on her partner's description of her being 'out of control', she also wondered about the effect of this work. As is typical of police officers I have spoken to about the effects of the work, she wasn't sure much could be done about it, and accepts it as a part of the job.

Incidentally, I have regularly sought assistance for similar troubles. I have also noticed, in writing this book, that my mood has been affected, particularly when deciding which stories I would *not* write about. They are the ones I find hard to bear and do not want to put in your hearts and heads. They come into my mind intermittently, often prompted by an innocent association in my own life. I know, intellectually, that this is because sex offenders manipulate the patterns and fabric of daily life, making occasional associations inevitable, but that doesn't lessen the impact. I noticed that it was usually something in the grooming process, rather than the offending itself, which was most upsetting – typically an act of emotional cruelty or betrayal. I also realised, as I went through them, that the cumulative effect of those stories, and moments, sometimes undermines my belief that people are fundamentally good, and erodes my sense of safety in the world. I used to be afraid of the stories but, thanks to regular therapeutic support, the fear has lessened, and I can refocus the upset to provide motivation to keep working. I will never, ever, forget them.

14

Memory

In no other area of crime investigation is memory as important as with sexual offences. As we say in training: *memories are our crime scene*.

One might expect that people who experience a traumatic event would be able to remember it clearly and precisely, because it would have been so dramatic. There is an enormous amount of evidence to say that memories of trauma do not work like that,[1] but the belief has persisted, nonetheless. The central problem is that the expectations of the justice system do not match how people remember, how memory recalls trauma, or how victims tell their stories. My colleague Mark used to say that the system was being 'biologically disrespectful', which neatly sums up the disparity between scientific knowledge and legal expectation.

There has also been debate about the recovering of childhood sexual abuse memories, which has been a protracted and bitter dispute.[2] Some have argued passionately that any memory recovered should be taken seriously, while others have pointed to flaws in processes that produced the memories, particularly memory recovery associated with therapeutic techniques such as hypnosis, or guided imagery.[3] There is also some criticism that sexual abuse researchers have focused too much on the traumatic nature of the experience. Some researchers suggest that sexual abuse is not traumatic for all children, particularly where the perpetrator is a known and trusted adult.[4] They may experience the abuse more as 'weird, confusing, or uncomfortable'. Importantly, despite such criticisms of the trauma model, victims who said the experiences had not been traumatic when they were children, became highly distressed when their adult selves revisited the experiences. More than a quarter then showed signs of PTSD, and every single one of them said the abuse had negatively affected their lives in many ways.

In all the cases I have worked on over the years, the two most common historical memory issues have been these: people who can't stop thinking about it, with the memory of the trauma repeating endlessly in their head, and people who suppressed the memories, while knowing, on some level of consciousness, that they were there all along. Victims often remember at significant moments in their lives. The two most common times, in my experience, have been when they had children, or when their children reached the age at which their own abuse took place. It does not take a psychiatrist to work out why that might be. The memories can often resurface when either the perpetrator, or one of their parents (usually their mother) dies. I have known cases where memories were prompted by such things as a car accident, a smell, a song on the radio, or a report of abuse in the paper. These have never seemed like recovered memories to me, but rather those that were tucked away, for all the same reasons that victims often stay silent, and then released by some irresistible force.

In the field of sexual crime investigation, perhaps more than any other crime theme, we are particularly concerned with the memories of children. Until as recently as 2013, in our court jurisdiction, there was a warning given to juries about the unreliability of children's evidence.[5] These types of warnings, which still exist in other systems, are based on two ideas: that children's memories are substantially worse than the memories of adults,[6] and that children's memories are often influenced by the coaching of adults.[7] The first premise is just wrong, even though research shows that approximately a third of people believe it.[8] While their capacity will sharpen as they age, research is clear that children as young as four can remember events clearly and accurately.[9] There is some truth to the second premise, in that children's memories are more fragile than adults and can be corrupted, particularly under aggressive questioning.[10] They are more resilient, however, than one might think. Problems related to children's memories are usually caused by interviewers, rather than the children themselves,[11] although the field of child interviewing has advanced significantly in the last two decades.

The criminal justice system prefers that people remember events in a linear way, from start to finish, in a continuous and coherent form. It also requires that individual sexual offence events be recalled precisely, as each recollection will form the basis of charges laid against the accused person. The process is called particularisation,[12] and investigators are trained to place great emphasis on it. The law now recognises that, in cases of abuse over extended periods of time, particularisation may be difficult, and has made some allowances.[13] In some jurisdictions it is possible to lay charges such as *persistent sexual abuse*, or specify acts that took place between certain times, or in a particular year. In the days before these changes, inability to particularise would have ended an investigation. Even now, it will reduce the number of charges laid.

Our memories are extraordinarily complex, comprising numerous mechanisms and pathways to help us encode, consolidate, store, and retrieve them. It may seem that memory is a neutral process, and a factual record of what took place but, when you think about it, it cannot ever be that. There is no such thing as memory that is objective and neutral, as memory is meaning-based.[14] That is, a memory of what we experience is automatically connected to a person's understanding of it, *at the time it is encoded*. This has implications for what is remembered and how the memory is retrieved. It may seem that memory is only an experience of the mind, but all our memories are connected to the way we feel. Many victims will be trying to understand the meaning of what has happened to them, as they recall events, and may latch on to anything suggested by the interviewer. It is critical, therefore, that anyone trying to understand the story, particularly forensic interviewers, avoid any suggestions, implicit or explicit, that may alter the story.

The memory-is-meaning-based factor also helps us understand why victims' narratives often have gaps in them. Victims remember most clearly the elements of the event that impacted on them, which may be different to what others might expect. It would not be unusual, for example, for a victim to remember smelling smoke on an offender's breath during an assault, but not remember all the sexual things he did to her. In those moments, the smell may have been most significant, because she was trying not to gag when he kissed her, so other details of the assault receded in significance.

For anyone trying to understand a narrative, you need to know that memory is also reconstructive.[15] This means that each time the memory is retrieved, it is reconstructed from its components, so gaps are common here too. Memory tends to fill in those gaps, so that when the memory is communicated to another person it is coherent. The gaps are usually there because the elements were not meaningful enough, either to be encoded in the first place, or retained over the intervening period between encoding and retrieval. The more you ask someone to remember something, the more details they may fill in, which are likely to be progressively less consistent. Pointing out inconsistencies of memory[16] is one of the most common tactics in the defence counsel playbook, challenging the reliability and credibility of the victim's story. Care must therefore be taken by interviewers to make sure complainants, as far as possible, do not guess, or fill in gaps.

We reconstruct our memories not only in response to the questions we are asked, but also because of who we are talking to. For example, a victim may recall and report the details of events differently in response to questions posed by their partner, their counsellor, their best friend, or the police. If you had a bad sexual experience with a partner, would you tell your mother the same details as you would your best friend? Each version may be accurate in its own way but appear quite different. This feature of memory and story-telling has been widely abused within the criminal justice system, in creating doubt, even though changes in the way any story is told are a normal function of the human memory system. Where these differences occur, we instruct investigators to ask why they are different, because most changes are explainable.

Police investigators would prefer that complainants only gave them a complete, linear version of events, accurately stored, and retrieved from their long-term memories, but this is simply not possible. Problems arise in the context of sexual assault investigations, not only because simple recollection is complicated, but also because the brain and its memory processes have been interrupted by trauma. Experts agree that, as one put it, 'It is enormously difficult to organise one's traumatic experiences into a coherent account – a narrative with a beginning, a middle, and an end.'[17] There is also the relentless sameness of long-term abuse, where victims find little to distinguish one abuse from the next. When reporting, victims of such abuse will often say things like, 'He used to ...', or, 'He would often ...', because repeat offending blurs the lines of accurate coding and storage, turning episodes into general meanings and understandings.

After traumatic events victims report a fog of confusion and inaction, and an inability to think clearly or make decisions. The effects will be different depending on the type of assault and the length of time over which it occurred, but each abuse will make some impact. For example, in one case, a woman was assaulted outside her home by a man who was holding a knife. When questioned by investigators she could not recall much about the man, what he was wearing, what he said, or even the abusive acts. She did, however, remember in which hand he was holding the knife, and that it had a long silver blade. This is a typical example of what is known as the 'weapons effect', for obvious reasons.[18] When under threat, we focus on the most dangerous element of that threat. When investigators question why parts of a victim's experience are not remembered, I ask them to imagine that they are shut in a room with a snake and consider if, under such circumstances, they would notice the pattern of the wallpaper.

In other cases, it is not that there has been *too much* focus on one aspect of the offence, but no focus at all. Victims regularly report a process of dissociation during abuse, particularly when it is a regular occurrence.[19] The dissociation is a protective mechanism, where the brain can diminish the physical and psychological pain of the experience by creating an alternate state, sometimes with vivid visual and narrative elements. The problem for investigators is, obviously, that it diminishes the memory of the offence itself, leaving a complainant's story fragmented and lacking cohesion and coherence. As another trauma expert put it, 'In sharp contrast to gratifying or even troublesome memories, which can generally be formed and revisited as coherent narratives, "traumatic memories" tend to arise as fragmented splinters of inchoate and indigestible sensations, emotions, images, smells, tastes, thoughts, and so on.'[20]

For example, as in this short narrative, which I have constructed, a typical initial description might go like this:

It could have been over summer the last time because the room was really hot and stuffy. The light came into the room in a funny way and it made a pattern on the carpet. I just stared at it while he was doing it and, in my head, I went to the clifftop where we had our picnics when we were on holiday. You could hear the sound of the waves and one time we saw a seal. He smelt of beer. It really hurt when he was back there, but I kept thinking about the picnics, except when he made this grunting sound and called me names. Mum even took me to the doctor's once. When he stopped, I used to get a raspberry ripple ice cream. I think he was a friend of dad's brother ... Bill, we called him I think, or Billy.

This kind of fragmentation is common, with elements of different memory all jumbled together and recalled in a scattergun effect. If this is the initial recall of the abuse, an investigator will need to take great care to extract all the other elements of her memories from the fragments described here. Inexperienced interviewers may become disheartened by the brevity and disorganised nature of her story. More experienced ones will see the cues for further questioning, some of which can be corroborated: that there were multiple occasions when the abuse occurred, the visit to the doctor, the clifftop picnics, what names the suspect called her, the reference to beer, the timing of the abuse, the ice cream etc.

On further questioning some elements may be recalled in extraordinary detail, with other parts left blank. This can be very frustrating for investigators, who know that every detail is important and will build the story. Tempting as it might be to keep asking questions, in the hope that they can eke out more, it is vital that they get only the memories that are there and do not prompt an unreliable recall. The temptation to keep asking questions derives from a fundamental flaw in the process of investigations prior to Whole Story, of focusing entirely on the events and not the relationships. With so little to go on, investigators would ask relentlessly about any detail they felt might help prove what took place. What colour was his shirt? What car did he drive? What type of underwear was he wearing? Sometimes it led interviewers to ask the most ridiculous questions, like, how many times did he hit you, or what did his penis look like? Frequently, investigators would get frustrated at complainants' inability to answer these questions, partly because they did not understand why those memories weren't there, and partly because they felt a jury would not convict without them.

Best practice sexual crime investigation requires an understanding of how people remember and how memory is affected by trauma. Investigators need great skill to elicit those memories without altering them as, in this crime theme, the story is everything.

15

Interviewing victims

Most problems with complainants' evidence are created by interviewers. A prosecutor complained to me once about a case they had lost. They felt that doubt had been created in their client's story unfairly, because of her answers to interviewers from two different parts of the system. When interviewed by police, with our open question format, she had said, 'He put his fingers in me.' When questioned by a forensic medical practitioner, she had said it was 'a finger'. The defence counsel had made great play of the fact that she appeared not to know the difference between one finger or more, suggesting any truthful woman would know exactly how many fingers were put inside her. The prosecutor felt this was a factor in undermining her credibility and creating doubt. The most likely explanation for the discrepancy, however, is that the medical practitioner and the investigator asked different kinds of questions. If the investigator said simply, 'Tell me what happened,' then the victim would have been free to answer in any way she chose. If the forensic physician, following the more succinct formats of the medical profession, asked a forced choice question such as, 'What did he put in you? Was it an X … a Y … or a finger?' then the answer would be 'A finger', thereby creating an inconsistency.

Sometimes police interviewers create problems all on their own. In one case, a twelve-year-old girl was being interviewed about abuse by her stepfather, that had taken place while her mother had been out. The interviewer felt it was important to determine a timeline of events, so he asked the girl how long her mother was out for. The girl said, 'I don't know,' which should have been the end of the matter. The investigator either did not listen clearly, or felt the issue was so important that he needed to ask again. When he returned to the subject a short time later, she said, 'I'm not sure.' He still did not take the hint, so asked a third time. Most complainants, particularly children, will assume that repeated questioning about a subject requires them to come up with an answer, or that any previous answer must have been wrong, which is what happened in this case. To the third question she came up with an answer, which turned out to be provably wrong. By his repeated questioning, the interviewer had given the defence barrister an opportunity to call her a liar.

Complainant interviews involve gathering a story the investigator will not have heard before, so it is hard to plan for, and good technique is critical. Interviewers must carefully extract as much detail as possible, while allowing the storyteller to describe events in their own way. There may also be elements of the abuse that victims will not wish to disclose, which require tact and skill to elicit. Crucially, as they listen to the story, interviewers will need to anticipate what may later be asked in court, to elicit answers to potential future questions. There is often a time lag for reporting, so the interviewer will need to guide the complainant through the process of retrieving long-stored memories, without interrupting or altering the essential nature of those memories. I hope this brief description shows what a high-level skill set interviewing is, and why police spend so much time teaching it.

Interviewing witnesses is more straightforward, though they may have complex motivations in talking to police, or divided loyalties between complainant and suspect. They may also not be aware of which of their memories could be important in court, so interviewers need to guide them carefully.

Interviews are made up of three distinct skills and tasks, those of rapport-building, listening, and asking questions. As with any professional interview, such as a medical appointment or job interview, if the professional treats the interviewee with respect, and carefully explains the process to be followed, they will deal better with whatever stress and anxiety they are feeling. The goal of rapport-building is to establish the template for a productive conversation, whatever the difficulties, and talking to someone about sexual abuse is about as difficult as it gets.

Interviews in this work can also be tough to navigate simply because of the subject matter. When was the last time you talked to someone about your sexual experiences in graphic detail? Sometimes, in training, we asked participants to break into pairs and talk to each other about their last sexual experience. You can imagine the looks on their faces, and these are only consensual experiences we are asking them to discuss. We don't make them go through with it, of course, but it makes the point about how victims might be feeling when they tell us their stories. It also begins the conversation about why victims may choose to omit or change aspects of their story. They may struggle to discuss anal penetration, for example, or the fact that they experienced an erection during the offending. It is one of the key skills of our specialism, to be able to discuss sexual behaviour without anxiety or embarrassment. My colleagues and I do a lot of role playing during training, where all the role-play interviews are about sexual abuse of one kind or another. Some student interviewers get so embarrassed about the sexual elements of offending that they can barely get the words out. It usually goes something like, 'Well, she alleges at this point that you ... a-hem ... what she's saying is that you put your ... a-hem ... penis ... in her a-hem ...' It is hard to watch them wrestle with an uncomfortable subject, but they need to learn, because any embarrassment on their part will inhibit disclosure.

Believe it or not, simple listening is the hardest interviewing skill to master. It is a skill we could all improve, and one I often found wanting in my early training with police. They are so used to taking charge and pressing people to tell them what they need to know, that they often leave little room for interviewees to talk, particularly suspects. The best interviewers know the value of silence.

It may also seem obvious that good interviewers need to be able to ask good questions, but not everybody will be able to.[1] Choosing the right question can make all the difference. Closed questions are the most used in everyday life, but the least effective at information-gathering in forensic interviews. *Yes/No* questions are the most common and can be effective in interviews, if used sparingly. A *forced choice* question like, 'Did he drive you there in the white car or the blue one?' (asked because the suspect's vehicles are white and blue), gives an interviewee limited possibility for answers. But what if they had taken the train, or borrowed a friend's car? Then the interviewer just caused a potential problem for any future prosecution. The most problematic of all are *leading questions*, which suggest to the interviewee what answer is required of them, such as, 'And he threatened you with violence if you didn't go through with it, did he?'

During a training of detectives in a rural region, we were trying to convey the importance of correct question technique, using stories of cases they had investigated. One of them told of a case he had investigated, a few years earlier, which had taken place during the holiday season. A young woman had been drinking with a couple of men, one of whom she invited back to her room for sex. She reported to the police that she had started to feel unwell and attempted to change her mind, but the man had insisted. She was then taken back to her room, by both men, where she was raped multiple times over several hours. The police were sceptical of her story. The next day, when they knocked on the door of the adjacent room, they were met by an irate mother, who had been sharing the room with her husband and two children. When the detective opened with, 'We're investigating a rape that is alleged to have taken place in Room X last night,' the woman erupted. 'Rape? Bullshit!' she began. 'You should have heard the racket coming from them last night. We couldn't sleep a wink with all the yelling, especially her. I even sent my husband over to tell them to be quiet, and the guy said they'd keep it down.' As the woman continued, their scepticism grew. After tactfully suggesting that a Whole Story investigation would have considered a lot of elements they hadn't bothered about (like why and how she felt unwell, what they were drinking and who had paid for drinks, interviewing the barman about what he saw and heard, what he served and who he served it to, finding CCTV of their movements etc.), we turned to the topic of interviewing questions.

After discussing the questions that they had asked, we canvassed possible alternatives. What if you had begun by saying something more neutral, like, 'We're investigating an alleged offence that took place last night … can you tell me everything you saw and heard between X o'clock and Y o'clock?' Finally, we had their attention. We asked what they thought the answer would be and they agreed that the possibilities were much broader. She may have described what kind of noise they had heard and, rather than focusing on her own annoyance, may have given details relevant to the victim's story. Could she discern any words or phrases? What did the man tell her husband when he came to the door? Were there any connections with statements made by other witnesses? I don't know if we persuaded them that she was probably telling the truth, but we left them confused, and that's a good start.

Open questions[2] are much more important and useful than closed questions, but they are harder to master. They comprise a group of questions that allow interviewees a free recall, without specifying what they should be addressing with their answer. Open questions elicit much more information and relationship detail. An *open invitational* question might be used at the start of an interview, such as, 'Tell me what you're here to talk about today.' It isn't even a question really, just a statement with a pause, and an invitation to fill that pause. Next would come an *open breadth* question, such as, 'Tell me what happened on the day of the party ... Then what happened? ... Then what happened?,' used to gather the full scope of the story. In a lot of our work this might necessitate covering several years' worth of material. *Open depth* questions are then used once the scope of the story has been elicited, to gain further detail on key times and events, like, 'So you said earlier that you went on a camping holiday with Uncle Bob. Tell me more about that holiday.' If possible, with both complainants and suspects, it is preferable to use open questions for almost all the interview, asking as few questions as possible. Inexperienced interviewers often feel they need to stay in control of the interview and must therefore ask a lot of questions. Control of an interview can be more easily achieved from active listening and less frequent, more judicious questioning.

For example, in training we set up a role play of a child who has come in with an allegation about their babysitter. Incidentally, such an interview would be similar with adults, but I am going to start with a child example, as the process is more obvious. The pattern for an inexperienced interviewer might go like this.

Q: Tell me what you're here to talk about today.
A: When the babysitter touched my rude part.
Q: What's the babysitter's name?
A: Muriel.
Q: How old is Muriel?
A: I don't know.
Q: How many times has she babysat?
A: A few times maybe.
Q: How old is she?
A: I don't know. Older than me though.
Q: What part did she touch?
A: My rude part.
Q: What do you mean by rude part?

As you can see, it is a very inefficient way of getting information. From a more experienced interviewer it may go more like this:

Q: Tell me what you're here to talk about today.
A: When the babysitter touched my rude part.
Q: Did this happen once, or more than once?
A: More than once.

Q: OK, please think back to the last time this happened and tell me everything you can remember, starting at the beginning and trying not to leave anything out?

A: Well, Mum came back from her dance class last night and took Muriel home. I had to go with them in the car, but I didn't say anything. I told Mum I didn't want to go to school this morning and she said why – and that's when I started to cry and told her that I didn't want Muriel to come around anymore. (She pauses and looks upset.)

An inexperienced interviewer will probably butt in at this point and ask a question, while a better interviewer will wait, either saying nothing, or only something like, 'Uh-huh', 'I see', or, 'What happened then?'

A: Then Mum asked me why and I told her it was coz she touched my Minnie and Mum cried and got really angry and phoned Muriel. Muriel told her it was an accident, but it wasn't … (She pauses and looks at the wall for several seconds.)

So, the instruction was to go back to the beginning, but the complainant started where she wanted. Again, inexperienced interviewers can get rattled by this, and rather than letting the story come out naturally they might be tempted to say, 'OK, well, let's go back to the beginning,' etc., instead of waiting to see how much the complainant already covers in the way she wants to tell the story. The child has also mentioned the offence itself, so there is also a temptation to say, 'What do you mean by Minnie?', or 'Tell me about her touching your Minnie?' Good interviewers will just make a note and come back to it.

Q: What happened then?

A: Mum told her that we were going to come here to see you, and I heard Muriel crying and saying she was really sorry, and she didn't mean it. Then Mum told me that it wasn't my

fault and that I needed to tell you all about it. I told Mum that
Muriel said it was our secret and I wasn't supposed to tell and
then we came here.

*Q: OK, well, what you've told me is important, but I want
to make sure you tell me as much as you can, so if you could go
back to the start now and tell me everything that happened from
when your Mum first went out.*

*The child would then go back to the beginning, with details
being filled in along the way. Only after this free narrative had
been fully developed might an interviewer ask a range of specific
questions. For example, they would need to make sure there was
clarity about what 'Minnie' meant, what 'touched' meant, and
so on.*

When you watch a good interviewer at work it seems so
easy, as they appear to do so little, but it is the 'doing little'
that's the hard part. Once our investigators start using open
questions and pauses, we ask them to practise them as much
as possible, particularly with any children in their lives. If you
have kids, or spend any time with them, you already know that
talking to them can sometimes be a frustrating experience.

Q: How was your day at school?

A: Fine.

Q: What did you do?

A: Nothing.

Q: What do you want to do now?

A: Dunno.

Aaaaagh!

But if you use open questions, and leave long pauses after
them, you can see remarkable changes. It works particularly
well with primary school children, but can also be effective
with teenagers, if you really stick to the process. For example:

Q: Tell me what happened in your day!

If you know they had something on that they liked, you could always try, 'Tell me all about drama club, or football,' etc.

Pause.

No joy yet? Try ...

Q: Tell me all the good things that happened today.

Pause.

If you get silence, or 'It was all boring,' try ...

Q: Tell me about the worst parts, then ...

Pause ... Pause ...

Don't be tempted to ask again, or go to a closed question, because what you're trying to do is set a template for future conversations. If it doesn't work the first time, or even the fifth time, keep going. The template you want is, 'I am interested in you and what you have to say, and I am here to listen.' Our investigators, most notably the male ones, frequently report that it has transformed not only their conversations with their children, but also the connection they feel to their children's lives. If you do not have children, it can work just as well between adults, as our investigators often say it has transformed their relationships there too, making them feel more connected to partners or friends. The key to that sense of connection: open questions and simple listening.

Interviewing adults should be easier, particularly their ability to answer open questions, but there are complexities here too. There is the fragmentation of memory we saw in the previous chapter, and the challenge of producing a linear narrative from tangled elements of memory, sense, and feeling. Complainants also do not know what memories may constitute evidence so, without altering the memory, the interviewer must ask questions to help complainants remember what might prove crucial in helping fact-finders understand.

Let's take the story I described earlier in the book, of the woman who was offended against when she went for a massage. The interviewer would have built rapport, asked her what she'd come to talk about, and given the instruction to start at the beginning, and not to leave anything out, even if it seemed unimportant. This is what the woman said, as her first recall:

> Well, I went there because I couldn't get into my usual place. The clinic had just opened, so they had a special on too. He seemed very professional, so when he said to take all my underwear off, I didn't think much of it. He didn't leave the room when I changed, either, but he did turn away. When he turned around, I was a bit shocked, but he didn't stare at my boobs or anything. I didn't want to make a fuss. The massage was good, so I relaxed. Even when he brushed one of my nipples, I didn't get too alarmed. It was when he was massaging my thigh muscles that I got nervous, coz he didn't put the towel back properly after the first one. Then, when his fingers went in, I just froze. I couldn't believe it. He said something to me afterwards, but I just couldn't wait to get out of there. I even paid. Then I called my sister and told her all about it. She said to call you guys, but that freaked me out. I only called after I couldn't go to work this morning. It's messing up my life.

When the complainant has finished their first recall, as in interviews with children, the real interviewing challenge begins.

Without altering the complainant's memory, or suggesting answers, interviewers must help bring the fragments of her story together into a coherent narrative. They must also, remember, cover as many answers to possible juror misconceptions as possible. The benefits of good work here will come later, when a court decides what parts of the story will and will not be heard by a jury, and what is considered relevant information for fact-finders to hear. As you can see, from the description she has given, all the core elements are there, but the details are scant, and there are several elements a juror might find hard to understand. Most of the details can be covered with questions of depth, like, 'Take me back to the part where he ... tell me more about that.' Good interviewers will elicit exactly what he said and did, at each stage, as well as the interaction with the reception staff and the conversation she had with her sister.

Questions about misconceptions can be trickier, as they need to be done without breaking rapport or prompting feelings of shame and self-blame. Most interviewers will start with a preamble, to establish that their motivation is information-gathering only and that questions are being asked without judgment. Then they will cover all the questions they believe a fact-finder will have, which I suspect you have already noted – Why did she take her underwear off? Why didn't she ask him to leave when she undressed? Why didn't she cry out? Why did she pay? Why didn't she report to police straight away? – and so on. Sometimes complainants cannot answer such questions, but often they can articulate exactly why they didn't do what may have been expected. So, in order, her answers may have been: He told me the oil might damage my underwear. I didn't want to make a fuss, and I was already half-naked. I was shouting in my head, but I was so scared that the words wouldn't come out. I just wanted to get out of there. I didn't know if anyone would believe me and I thought he'd just deny it anyway, so what's the point?

Interviewing complainants in sexual crime matters is one of the hardest jobs in policing. It requires tact and patience, polished rapport-building skills, and flawless questioning technique, all wrapped up in a completely non-judgmental approach. As it happens, all the same skills and qualities are needed when it comes to interviewing suspects.

16

Interviewing sexual offence suspects

Interviewing suspects is surprisingly like interviewing complainants, as free narrative, open questions, and an overall information-gathering style are critical to both. The main object of all forensic interviews is engaging the interviewee in conversation, to elicit a complete narrative of events from their perspective. There are a few crucial differences between the two interviews, however. In talking to suspects, interviewers have the advantage of having heard the story before, at least the complainant's version, so they can plan what to ask and how to ask it. Although this is an advantage, suspects still hold the strongest hand. For a start, they are not required to speak at all, if they don't want to, so interviews may be peppered with 'No comment', or silence. Next, suspects will have thought long and hard about what to say should the offending ever be reported. They will have prepared to minimise culpability, shift focus, and lay blame. Offenders' grooming processes will also have drawn responsibility away from themselves, so sometimes their version of events can be surprisingly persuasive. They will usually feel significant fear and anxiety, which interviewers must understand, if they are to get them to talk.

In suspect interviewing, there are two schools of thought about the most effective method: dominance and humanity.[1]

You have probably seen a lot of the former on television, particularly in US shows, where suspects are intimidated into co-operating. The second approach, thankfully, is more common in UK policing, as well as in Europe, Canada, Australia, and New Zealand. The dominance method assumes that all suspects are reluctant to talk, will lie and be deceptive when questioned, and need to be pressured into conversation or dialogue. It is also focused on confession as a goal of the interview. Humanity methodology is based on an information-gathering style, in which suspects are assumed to have a variety of motivations, and rapport-building is the central task. The goal is to encourage conversation and dialogue through respectful interaction, where the process of conversation is prioritised over confession. We use a humanity style in our training for two key reasons. First, there is evidence that sexual offence suspects are particularly sensitive to any perceived hostility from their interviewer, and therefore the quickest to shut down dialogue.[2] Given the shame and guilt associated with their offending, this is hardly surprising, but it should rule out any use of pressure tactics. The second reason is that there is clear evidence, despite the allure of more aggressive tactics, that respectful rapport-building and an information-gathering style lead to the disclosure of more correct information, and fuller accounts, from suspects.[3] Ironically, they also lead to more confessions.[4]

When I started working for the police, one of my core responsibilities was to improve their interviewing of sexual offence suspects, and Mark was tasked with improving their interviewing of children and other vulnerable victims. After seeking out information from a wide variety of sources, we concluded that the two tasks were almost identical, which surprised us. We both had extensive backgrounds in forensic interviews for therapeutic purposes, having worked with offenders in treatment, so interview styles that were motivational, rapport-building, and centred on information-gathering, were not new to us. What we did not know, before we started, was that all these concepts were used in policing. Thanks to the pioneering work of forensic psychologists like Eric Shepherd, Ray Bull and Becky Milne, the UK led the field in the development of new suspect-interviewing practice. Shepherd called his approach Conversation Management,[5] which sums up the move from the more traditional style of 'I'll ask the questions and you give me the answers!' to a more shared process, where interviewers build rapport with their interviewee. The techniques of the humanity style are relatively easy to teach but, at the time when we began the training programme, the idea of rapport-building with sexual offence suspects was anathema to most police. Investigators know that suspect interviews can be a vital element of any case presented in court, however, so we found the most effective argument, for those that were sceptical, was that building rapport with sexual offence suspects was essential to help victims. It took a while, but the rapport-building style is now well entrenched, particularly in sexual offence investigation. If police forces are not using it, their sexual offence and family violence investigations will not be effective.

There are elements of rapport-building that are uniquely challenging when interviewing sexual offence suspects. One young detective told me of an interview she had conducted where, because she had built good rapport, the child molester she was interviewing appeared thoroughly engaged in the interview process. At one point, he tried to explain why he abused children. He pointed to her wedding ring and said, 'You know the way you're sexually attracted to your husband? Well, that's the way I look at children.' She was outraged at his connection of their sexualities, and her fury would have been plain to see. Whether he was naïvely trying to explain himself, or deliberately trying to get under her skin, her reaction was a judgment of him, and would have been unproductive. Whatever they do or say, you cannot take things personally.

A lot of policing practice is inherently anti-rapport. For a start, there is a huge power imbalance in the relationship between investigator and suspect, and arresting people is about the least rapport-building thing you can do. Fear and anxiety pervade every aspect of the process. With complainants, typical fears are of judgment, and not being believed. With suspects, fears will be of judgment, punishment, and the consequences of admission. So, rapport-building is essential, followed by developing a conversation about the relationship between them and the complainant. Interviewers already know the story, so focus is on laying that narrative in front of the suspect and inviting him to give his version of events. The more effectively this is done, and the more the suspect perceives a weight of evidence against him, the more likely he is to talk.

The effective disclosure of available evidence is a traditional investigative skill that we have tried to enhance for sexual offence investigation. Since all we have is the story, this needs to be done with great care. It requires investigators to be thorough and to utilize as much of the story as possible, particularly any unique elements. For example, it is common for offenders to give gifts as part of any grooming process. If it can be confirmed in a suspect interview that gifts were given, then it is more likely to be admitted in evidence and count against him. Whether he admits it will be dependent on two factors: the detail about the gift elicited from the complainant and the quality of the questions asked in the suspect interview. Think about the difference between these three questions ...

Q: Did you give him a toy?

The answer will probably be 'No'.

Q: Tell me about any toys you gave him.

This might get something, but there could be a variety of responses, like, 'Only stuff on his birthday', or 'I don't really remember.'

Q: Tell me about the blue and gold remote-controlled car ... pause ... the one you gave him for his thirteenth birthday ... pause.

If the question is accurate, he will remember that car and, while you are pausing, he will be thinking about it and remembering the time he gave it to the boy. He still might avoid answering the question, but you will have established both a template for the conversation, and a memory prompt he could not avoid. These types of questions also create an impetus for him to start talking, as they will show him the level of detail in the evidence against him. The template here is, 'I've been thorough in my investigation and I know a lot about you, but I really want to hear your side of it.' The impetus is, 'I've got a complete picture here, which shows a strong case against you, so you'd better give me your version or you're in trouble.'

The blue and gold remote-controlled car is a unique signifier,[6] one of the elements crucial to the effectiveness of the Whole Story training. Investigators are taught to capture complainants' memories in fine-grain detail, gathering as many of the unique elements of each abusive relationship as possible. Unique signifiers take people's memories back to time and place and can have a powerful effect on suspects' motivation to talk. Often, but not exclusively, they are elements of the offending relationship known only to the offender and victim. One famous example, which we use in training, occurred when Bill Clinton was questioned about his relationship with Monica Lewinsky.[7] Because Lewinsky had been taped without her knowledge, she had given extraordinary detail of their sexual behaviour, including the use of the President's cigar as a sexual aid. Clinton was obviously unaware that the interviewer had this unique signifier, and you can see the effect it has on him in the interview. He appears shocked that the interviewer knows about it; his breathing changes, and he shifts awkwardly in his seat. He becomes less coherent and seems distracted, possibly running the memory through his mind. In the space of a few moments, he goes from being charming and relaxed to tongue-tied and tense. It is not a good forensic interview, incidentally, and could have been much more effectively handled, but it makes the point about the need for relationship detail and unique signifiers. I get emails from investigators saying, 'I had a Clinton moment,' and they can have a big impact on the success of an investigation.

The next hardest challenge we experienced was persuading investigators that most suspects *want to talk to them*. We never had any trouble getting men to talk in treatment, even adolescents, but police were sceptical that the same motivations would apply in the higher-pressure environment of a police interview. Certainly, the odds are diminished, but our view was that the same drivers, of feeling the need to be understood and wanting to explain themselves, would be present in both environments. We encouraged investigators to see the interview as an opportunity to tap into the suspect's desire to explain himself. We suggested they see the beginning of complainant and suspect interviews the same way, both offering an invitation to tell their story. So, either interview might begin, for example, with an invitation like, 'Tell me what you're here to talk about today.' Although some suspects might counter with, 'You're the fucking detective. You tell me!', a surprising number will give a comprehensive answer to the question. One suspect, who had been accused of raping a woman with an object, answered the question with, 'I'm here about sticking the bottle in,' so it can be highly effective. Even when suspects begin an interview with 'No comment', it is surprising how many will then start talking, if the process is right. In training, we always ask how many participants have had a suspect move from 'No comment' to full or partial admissions, and almost all the hands go up. They go up because, deep down, we all want to explain ourselves, particularly if we fear judgment from our listener. In one case I worked on, a man accused of rape and false imprisonment asked to speak to a lawyer during the interview, as it became clear to him that police had a strong case. The interviewer fully expected that, after the call, he would make no further comment in the interview. On recommencing, we decided to stick with an invitational question, then continue where they had left off. After a significant pause, he said, 'Oh, boy ... my lawyer's going to kill me,' before giving a lengthy answer to the question.

When a suspect began an interview with, 'No comment', one investigator colleague would artfully say, 'Well, would you like to know what's been said about you?' The requirements of a suspect interview insist that my colleague go over the allegations anyway, but he preferred this method because it is so hard to resist. Everyone wants to know what others are saying about them. He claimed that it never failed to provoke a response.

Sometimes, you don't even need skill, or an artful question, as suspects make it all too easy. One man, after being cautioned about his rights, said his lawyer had explained to him that, if he were innocent, he should tell the police everything. On the other hand, he claimed to have been told, if he were guilty, he should make no comment. The man then went on to answer every question with 'no comment'. He went to prison for eleven years.

Perhaps the biggest advantage in suspect interviews is the opportunity to plan. Interviewers can not only prepare for the personality they are going to meet, having learnt all about him during the complainant interview, but also how best to lay the story out in front of him. The goal is not, as many novice interviewers believe, to get a confession, but to engage the suspect in a guided conversation and elicit their version of what happened. Any admission, whether partial or complete, will come about as a side effect of this approach. There are several levers interviewers can use to encourage conversation, all of which are dependent on a thorough understanding of the complainant's story and time spent planning. The story must be used to create pressure on the suspect, without coercion, to give their version of the relationship with the complainant. Most police forces are required to follow strict rules about using coercion. Rules usually state they must not overbear the will of the suspect, or words to that effect, so many of the interviews you see on television would be thrown out, and rightly so. The phenomenon they are most trying to achieve, and a legitimate technique, is called cognitive load.[8] The process is intended to create pressure on the suspect to give his version of events, and to make it harder for him to maintain a coherent false narrative, without making a mistake. It can be created by good questions, the perception of the weight of evidence, and the judicious use of silence and pauses, which I will talk more about shortly. If you want to understand cognitive load, try telling a story in these different ways. First, tell a true story, in linear fashion, from beginning to end, allowing the listener to ask questions. So far, so easy. Next, tell the same story backwards, and you will find your brain beginning to work harder. The questions may also seem more difficult to answer, even if they are the same ones you were asked in the first run. Thirdly, construct a story that is not true, again allowing the listener to ask questions. Not only will your brain now have to remember the lie, but it will also need to imagine all the potential consequences of each element of the lie, or the story will lose cohesion. This is not easy, particularly in the stressful context of a police interview.

Good interviewers also understand the importance of, and the difference between, shame and guilt. In short, shame can shut people down, as it is experienced as a direct criticism of their self. Guilt, on the other hand, can open people up, coming as it does with the potential for remorse, just desserts, and the possibility of moving on. Even when the stakes are high, these phenomena hold true.

Just as with interviewing victims, the two most powerful tools in an interviewer's repertoire are the ability to listen and the ability to sit in silence. Silence is a skill we ask them to practise, as it is counter-cultural. Think of the last time you were at any kind of social gathering. The chances are any silence was quickly filled by the assembled company, to avoid a sense of embarrassment. It is only with those closest to us, typically, that we allow silence to be a connection, rather than a severing, of relationship. This feeling of intimacy, created by silence, is highly effective in suspect interviews.

The pause is the most underused tactic in policing, where the culture usually says to take charge and drive the interview forward. Any cognitive load, created by effective exposition of the complainant's story, is most effective when suspects are given plenty of time to think about it. The longest pause I have experienced, in a suspect interview, was fourteen and a half minutes. The suspect had suggested, almost an hour into the interview, that the people around him had been concerned about his behaviour. This comment had been prompted by gentle, probing questions about his relationships with the complainant and other family members. 'What were they worried about?' the interviewer asked, after he had let slip their concern. As she watched on, the suspect gradually retreated into his mind, obviously remembering those concerns and associated events. As he reflected, he put his head in his hands and slowly slumped onto the table in front of him. At the twelve-minute mark of the pause she said, reassuringly, 'Take your time,' before allowing silence to fall again. When she repeated the question a couple of minutes later, he began a full disclosure of all the offences he was being interviewed about, along with a couple that the victim had not even mentioned.

Sometimes, suspects are unable to disclose without a little additional prompting, so we use a range of simple techniques to help that happen. The most common would be the judicious use of unique signifiers, as we have discussed before, where interviewers ask about unique elements of the narrative, often known only to the offender and victim (like the use of cigars!). Where possible, visual aids can also be helpful. One investigator asked me to help plan an interview for a man who was accused of committing two rapes (that we knew about), over a decade apart. The most recent offence was committed against a young woman, who had been dragged into a car in a railway car park. Elements of her statement identified links to a similar crime, on deserted ground next to a nearby station, some thirteen years earlier. In the earlier case the victim was much older and was also suffering from dementia. In that case, he had apologised for raping her, before running away. Missing clothing, and very distressed, she stumbled into a local car repair business after the attack. A young apprentice, despite his shock, found her some clothes to put on, and cared for her until the police arrived. When it came to the interview, and after some time, the offender made admissions to offending against the younger woman. The interviewers then took a break, leaving a map of the city on the table, where it had been placed before the interview began, open at the page where the first attack had taken place. The waste ground was circled in red, and the suburb name underlined. When they returned, and the interview formalities were completed, the offender was asked, 'Is there anything else you'd like to talk about?', followed by a long pause. He looked at the map, then down at the table. 'Yes,' he eventually said, 'I've always felt bad about that one.' It was just as well he admitted it, as the older woman's dementia had become much worse and would have prohibited her giving evidence. After the interview and admission, investigators went to see the young apprentice, now a man in his early thirties. When he opened the door and saw the detectives, the first words out of his mouth were, 'Did you finally get him?' When they nodded, he burst into tears, telling them that he thought of the woman often and had never forgotten that night.

Sometimes the prompts need to be more elaborate. In one of the most important historical child sexual abuse cases I worked on, the initial victim's statement pointed us to eight other victims of the same offender. Interviewing suspects in historical child sexual abuse matters presents significant challenges, especially with multiple complainants and when the offending has taken place over several decades. It is common for suspects to feign memory loss, and easy for interviewers to lose track and get confused. To aid the interviewer, and to ensure the suspect was aware of the extent of the evidence, I suggested we spend the first part of the interview laying out all the children and offences we were going to interview him about, before asking any questions. We found photos of the boys at the age they were offended and placed them on the wall in chronological order. Each photo was accompanied by key details of each relationship. The man had employed them in his business, and in a volunteering capacity for a local sports club, so there were pictures of the boys in both uniforms. It was explained to him that we would talk about each boy, one by one, and for the next twenty minutes their stories were outlined to him. He was told he could say or ask anything he wished, but he just stared at the pictures on the wall, or the interviewer, throughout. Utterly overwhelmed by the breadth of the investigation, and the detail of the presentation, he eventually admitted all the offending, as well as a further six victims. The process worked so well that I started teaching it on the course.

Another crucial technique is the pretext call.[9] The idea is that the complainant, or someone related to the case, such as their mother or brother, will come up with a pretext for calling the suspect, and attempt to engage him in conversation about the abuse. Police are not allowed to coach the caller in any way, nor tell them what to say, so results can vary. We can suggest they ask questions, rather than do the talking, or jot down what they want to know from him, as a way of suggesting a structure for the interaction. It is important to prepare people to make the call, as far as the rules allow, because hearing the offender's voice can have a profound effect on them. Sometimes, when he first speaks, they may lose their temper and start abusing him, which usually means no useful discussion takes place. Preparation helps them not only to adjust to the prospect of hearing his voice, but also to focus on what they are ringing about and the questions they want to ask. When we ask course participants what they think those questions usually are, the answers are always the same: Why did you do it? Why me? Did you do it to my sister/anyone else? Do you have anything to say to me? and so on.

Suggesting they ask questions can also help with the typical pattern that occurs in these calls, where offenders slip back into their grooming method as soon as they hear the victim's voice, attempting to control them as they did during the abuse. This part of the process is hard to listen to, as you sometimes hear victims go back into the relationship that trapped them in the first place. It is crucial, therefore, that victims only put themselves through this process if they feel up to it. Many do and cannot wait to get him on the phone. At other times, it will need to be another family member, or maybe a case of not doing it at all, as the investigative process is supposed to help people recover, not re-traumatise them. Incidentally, this process can also be done in person, where victims wear, or carry, a listening device. This is riskier, for the reasons already mentioned, and because of the potential for an aggressive reaction, so it doesn't happen very often.

I have heard many of these calls over the years, with a wide variety of results. Some suspects put the phone down, others are suspicious and guarded even, on occasion, mentioning the prospect of being recorded. Most use grooming, to shut the caller down, or guide the conversation away from discussion of the abuse. There is also a common strategy, where the offender will apologise for what happened, while claiming to have no memory of it, which can be very frustrating for the caller. However, when the calls work, they can have devastating consequences for the offender. First, and the reason I have included this technique in the interviewing chapter, is because interviewers can later ask, 'When was the last time you spoke to ...?' If he acknowledges contact, then the conversation can be explored by the interviewer. If he lies, which is common, and says something like, 'I haven't heard from her in ages,' then the interviewer can choose to either expose the lie, leave the lie to be exposed by a prosecutor in court, or play him some of the conversation and get his reaction. Any of these three outcomes will probably show him in a poor light. Secondly, and even more important, pretext calls can be cathartic for victims. Whether he admits the offending or not, and offenders regularly do, victims frequently report feeling empowered afterwards, and having gained a sense of control back in their lives.

In a recent case, the victim had taken her father's car without permission and driven it around, deliberately damaging it before returning it to him. She had done so after years of trying to draw attention to the abuse had failed. Unfortunately, this tactic did not work either, but resulted in so much conflict that she left home to live with relatives. Several years of estrangement later, after finally reporting to police, she called him up. He asked her to call back in an hour. When she did, his voice was changed from the initial call, now calmer and more measured, just as it had been during the abuse. Instantly, she recognised his grooming voice. He proceeded to lecture her about the breach of trust she had perpetrated in taking his car, during which she remained silent. Finally, recovering her voice, she steered him repeatedly back towards the abuse. All he could say was that they had a lot to talk about, offering neither denial nor apology. The objective listener would have been in little doubt that the abuse had taken place as she described. She told investigators that the call had been an important step for her. She went on to call him again, several times, which is not unusual. While he never made admissions, he corroborated many aspects of her story, unwittingly participating in some important steps in her recovery, and his own prosecution.

I have heard offenders say they are glad the victim called, as they have long wanted to apologise. Some offer money, or bribes, in attempts to ensure continued silence. Typically, they say things like, 'Well, I'm not sure who's going to believe all that,' or, 'I really don't know what you hope to gain from all this,' perhaps not realising how guilty it makes them sound. They rarely make convincing denials.

Interviewing, of both complainants and suspects, has come a long way in the last twenty years. New techniques, designed to prioritise information-gathering over confrontation, have created a more even playing field. Rapport-building, treating suspects with respect and without judgment, gathering a thorough narrative from complainants, good interview planning, thoughtful questions, time and space for suspects to think, and feel: these are the ingredients of a good suspect interview, none of which is easy, and all of which take time and practice to perfect.

17

Getting the Whole Story

I remember one detective, in the early days, explaining to me why so few police liked working on sexual crime cases. He said that, when it came down to it, most did not understand them, or think they would lead to a prosecution. The traditional questions asked by detectives used to be, 'What went where, how far did it go in, and can anyone back up what you're saying?' They were looking to catalogue the act, to determine what the charge might be, and to decide if it could be verified by a third party. As one researcher put it, 'Ideally, cases need to contain independent proof of non-consent, such as physical injuries, independent witnesses or other physical or forensic evidence.'[1] As we have seen, in sexual crime cases, none of these elements is usually present. These are the hardest investigations of all. They test every investigative skill, challenging investigators personally and emotionally. We would always say, in training, that if you can investigate these stories successfully, you can investigate anything.

When you understand sexual offending as a crime of relationship, rather than an act or series of acts, it changes everything. From the moment an offender first contemplates what he would like to do, the offending relationship begins, and in forensic terms, evidence is being generated. In the past, victim narratives were often taken by uniformed police members, usually women, who frequently included relationship details in the final statement. The statements were then passed to a detective, who was usually a man. It was clear from the detectives' notes that they rarely considered the relationship would provide any relevant evidence.

All investigations have a series of points of proof that must be confirmed before a case can be authorised for prosecution. For the most part, these are straightforward issues, such as whether a law has been broken, or the suspect has been correctly identified. Traditional investigative techniques mirrored those used for general offences, rather than being relevant to the unique elements of relationship-based crime, so the avenues of inquiry followed the usual format: statements, finding potential witnesses to the acts, and a search for CCTV. CCTV of the offence itself is rare and, even when present, is generally not that helpful. Remember my colleague on the train, who froze when sexually assaulted by a fellow passenger? Despite CCTV showing him behind her on two separate occasions, having followed her across the carriage, the CCTV evidence was deemed 'inconclusive'.

Then there are the checks of computers and mobile phones, including exhaustive reviews of social media posts and images. Sometimes these yield important results, but mostly they do not, or at least are not as helpful as one might wish. Social media posts and photos can outline a pattern of abusive behaviour and grooming, but often they show a more complicated relationship, so juries may be confused about what is alleged to have taken place. One rape victim, exasperated by cross-examination from a defence barrister, about how much she and the suspect appeared to be in a positive relationship, snapped, 'Haven't you ever seen a rape in a marriage before, but they still love each other?' He was following that line of attack because the array of communications appeared to show their relationship in a positive light, which he hoped would damage the credibility of her complaint. Appearances can be deceptive, however, and what people post is often only a fraction of the story. From a police perspective, gathering a complainant's phone and social media material is a necessary, but very time-consuming, task. From victims' perspective, it is an unnecessary intrusion into their privacy, for no good reason. For defence barristers, it provides an opportunity to create doubt.

Focus on the sexual act, as the primary area where evidence may be elicited, also led to a belief that science would hold the answers to improving case outcomes. Contrary to popular opinion, forensic medical examinations can seldom determine what kind of act took place, let alone whether the act was consensual. A suspect may argue that the child had come into the bed where he and his partner had just had sex, or he had masturbated, or that their clothing had all been in the wash together. One of my forensic colleagues explained to me, in gruesome detail, how long semen can last outside the body after ejaculation, and that it may even still be present after clothing or sheets have been washed. Only semen on or inside a child's body, without possible explanation, is hard for suspects to argue against. In adult cases, it may prove that sex took place, but will seldom reveal whether the act was consensual.

In both adult and child cases, there can be injuries that are unmistakably connected to a sexual act or acts, but nowhere near as often as one might think. When I started working regularly on cases involving medical examination, I knew injuries were unlikely to be present due to the offending relationship, and because of victims' common freeze reaction. What I had not realised, as my forensic colleague also explained to me, was that injuries are also rare because, despite the traumatic and abusive circumstances, the body is usually being asked to do something it already does. Not only that, but victims will usually position themselves to minimise the pain or discomfort of the offending action, making visible injury much less likely.

The reliance of sexual crime investigations on stories, rather than forensics, brings us to the biggest problem: corroboration, or rather the lack of it. Corroboration is an important element in expectations of how to judge whether something is true or not. How can you find someone guilty if it's only one person's word against another's? In fact, there is no legal impediment to a finding of guilt based on the evidence of one person and, in many legal jurisdictions, judges no longer give a warning about the dangers of conviction on uncorroborated evidence.[2] If you think about the way you make up your mind about stories, you can see the process in action. I don't mean quick value judgments without thought, but listening to stories and deciding, based on the elements of each narrative, which version has credibility. In the research literature it has been said that juries respond to the qualitative elements of a story.[3] What this means is that people connect with the parts of a story they can relate to, which explain what is going on and why people are behaving a certain way. Even if people hold misconceptions about offending, these connections with a story can get them to change their view. Rather than follow their own beliefs, they can understand someone else's actions, even if they believe they themselves would have done something different. In training, I sometimes set our students a task to help explain how people come to understand stories. I ask them to seek out, over the course of an evening, several television dramas, and suggest that they watch each one for ten minutes or so. They are asked to find characters who, under the circumstances depicted, behave in a way they would not have done themselves. Did they come to understand that character's behaviour and, if so, how did that understanding come about? Odds on it was the qualitative elements of the story.

There is a lot of research literature on the effective use of story, as well as a body of literature on legal storytelling. As one legal scholar put it, '[The] law always begins in story ... it ends in story, too, with a decision by a court or jury, or an agreement between the parties, about what happened and what it means.'[4] Many academics and practitioners have commented on the inability of court processes adequately to describe offending relationships, and how often narratives are distorted, or incomplete.[5] Others have suggested that the better juries are assisted to understand the story, and the more complete those stories are, the more likely it is that court outcomes will be just.[6] There are researchers who see the greatest need for a focus on stories when trying to understand the narratives of children.[7]

Traditional investigative methods see evidence in narrow ways, trying to find evidence *in* the story, like witnesses or photographs. But what we were teaching was that the story *was* the evidence, particularly in descriptions of the relationship. So, what is relationship evidence and where is it found?

In the story of the woman who was sexually assaulted on the massage table, despite the whole process taking under an hour, there is a huge amount of evidence that a prosecutor should argue is relevant to the case. There are all the manipulations of the masseur, of course: suggesting she take off all her clothes, not leaving the room when she undresses, the ambiguous testing of her reaction to touch, asking her if she enjoyed the experience, and so on. Other employees can also testify to her behaviour before she left the premises, such as paying but not making another appointment. This last element might seem counter-productive, because paying may also suggest she was satisfied with the service. The issue will get raised by the defence anyway, so jurors will need an explanation, which will be much better in her own words. The two weeks after the assault can also raise a problem, because she waited so long to report. However, that period also provides a wealth of explanatory detail, from the moment straight after, when she rang her sister, through the sleepless nights and absences from work. And finally, any investigator worth their salt would see this man's behaviour as practised and would be canvassing potential victims from other places he had worked. The more complainants the better.

In the story of the girl who has been groomed to initiate sex with her father, there is at least ten years of evidence to be gathered. This can take multiple interviews. The girl in the story can chart a range of grooming behaviours, as far back as she can remember. Again, it is important that potential problems, like seeming to initiate sex and wearing lingerie (which I have heard defence use to say young victims are 'worldly'), be explained in her statement. Jurors will need to see the behaviour as a part of his grooming, rather than her action, so prosecutors need to be upfront about such issues. Now, with a more appropriate investigative process, we see these elements as an essential part of persuading the jury, rather than issues that need to be avoided or hidden. It is also important to remember how much the mother and brother know about the offender's grooming tactics, despite both being unaware of the offending itself. This may include details of the unfair punishments given, to keep the boy out of the way, and the campaign waged by the offender to encourage his wife to do evening volunteer work, as well as basic corroboration of the nights of the week she was out of the house, which matched the nights her daughter said she was abused.

A young detective once challenged me to demonstrate how the Whole Story method might work if the victim and perpetrator did not know each other or had no verbal interaction. He worked in transport policing, where most of his cases were stranger assaults. After admitting that it was harder with such cases, I asked him to detail the last one he had worked on.

A woman had reported an assault on the train. She was seated in the last carriage and a man had sat opposite her. After several minutes, he began masturbating as he stared at her. I asked the detective to tell me everything he knew about the man and his movements. The man was a plumber, he said, who had recently begun travelling on this line to work on an apartment block project. CCTV confirmed the suspect had sat opposite the woman, but his lower body was obscured behind a screen, next to the doorway. He told me that these seats were commonly used by offenders, because the cameras could not view them if they sat there. In his unit, he said, they were known as 'the wank seats'. I asked him what else the CCTV picked up, and he said the suspect had got on the train in one of the middle carriages. At each stop he had moved down a carriage. He had been in the last carriage for several stops before he sat opposite the woman, only doing so when there were no other people left in that section. So, in effect, the suspect had been in a 'relationship' with her for quite a while, I suggested, waiting for the power and control to be in his favour before offending. His movements, should a fact-finder see them all, are corroboration of the victim's story, even without witnesses to the act itself. The investigation was ongoing, so the detective decided to take another statement. He called me after the course and said the investigation had discovered the man had only used that railway line on four previous occasions, as the building site was new. They were attempting to review the footage of those trips.

Over the last ten years, I have seen many investigations changed by a better understanding of abusive relationships and a thorough gathering of victims' stories, like these next three cases.

Case 1

Twenty years ago, a teenage boy reported being sexually abused by a man he had met while skateboarding, with his older brother, at his local skate park. The man lived nearby and skated himself. He also told the boys that he was a photographer and could take pictures of them if they wished. The boys agreed, and they made plans to meet up for a photo session. These sessions became a regular occurrence, after which the boys began to spend time at the man's house, watching skateboard videos and playing video games, as well as drinking beer. On some occasions the boy went without his older brother, who now had a girlfriend, and it was during these visits that the man introduced him to pornography and smoking marijuana. Then the abuse began, which continued for several months, during which time the boy became insular and surly, his schoolwork was affected, and he started to smoke marijuana more regularly. His mother was concerned, and eventually persuaded him to tell her what had been going on, although he only disclosed a fraction of what had happened. She insisted he told the police, although he did not want to. The boy left out a lot of detail when being questioned, but the core of the complaint was there. Problems arose when the investigating officer, who had not taken the statement, met the complainant. The boy was withdrawn and hard to communicate with, leading the detective (non-specialist) to be sceptical of the story. He also felt the boy would not be considered credible by a court. His view was confirmed when the boy changed elements of his story under questioning and the investigator suggested that the chances of success were poor. Against the mother's wishes, the case was dropped.

Two years ago, a specialist detective took a report of sexual abuse from a young man. The allegation was historical, but relatively recent. The offender had approached him several years before, he said, when he was out on his mountain bike. The man had said he was part of a bike club, as well as being a photographer, who could take pictures of him and his mates if they liked. He named the man and, after taking the statement in Whole Story detail, the detective looked him up on the system. When he read the statement of the boy from the skate park, he immediately saw the patterns, particularly in the grooming 1. He was disappointed, but not surprised, to see that the original case had not been authorised for prosecution, and he decided to reopen it. Not only might it assist in his own case, he believed, but he saw no reason why the first boy's evidence couldn't be revisited in a current, and more complete statement, nor that his credibility issues couldn't be explained to a jury. He also realised that the offender had effectively created a photographic record of his abusing, which might identify other possible victims. At the time of writing, both investigations are ongoing.

Case 2

The investigator in a historical child sexual abuse case went to interview the suspect. He had moved to a country town some distance away, so the interview took place at the local police station, where he made a 'no comment' interview. During the interview, she noticed that he struggled to make eye contact whenever she asked about the abuse, particularly when talking about his relationship with the victim. Some days later, she returned to visit the man at his home where, during a relatively brief conversation, she told him what she had seen. She asked whether his reaction might have meant that he felt bad about what had occurred, to which he made no reply. She then suggested that he might, at some later stage, like to talk about what had happened. She told him that, if he ever wanted to talk, she would like to hear what he had to say, and she left her card. She delivered her message with respect and without judgment. A week later, her phone rang.

Case 3

A young woman reported that she had been raped by a stranger but, as the investigator listened to the story, she felt that it did not seem quite right. The complainant couldn't pinpoint where it had taken place, and the description of her movements and his actions didn't add up. The investigator felt that something had taken place, just not what the woman described. She decided to broaden her inquiry, in the hope that the woman would gain the confidence to tell her the real story. As she asked about the woman's family the atmosphere shifted. She went quiet and stared at the floor. Undeterred, the investigator waited, politely suggesting that the woman take her time and go back to the beginning of the story. Slowly, over several hours, the woman detailed abuse at the hands of her brother. She told the investigator that he was the family favourite, and that she thought her family would not have believed her, had she told them what was going on. She explained her fears of rejection, but said the weight of the secret, and the fear of more rapes, had become intolerable. She completed a statement about her brother's abuse, including a section explaining why she had originally told police it was a stranger, and her fear of family backlash and ostracism.

Without specialism, all these cases may have been consigned to an archive nominated as (in order) complaint withdrawn, case not authorised, and probable false report. Policing has come a long way in understanding and responding to sexual crime. Harder tests are to come, however, when these stories reach the courts.

Part IV

Justice and the courts

Courts play an important role in our culture, as arbiters of community standards, where the decisions of guilt and innocence influence our attitudes and beliefs. As Helena Kennedy QC wrote in *Eve was Shamed*,[1] a comprehensive critique of the law's treatment of women and their stories, 'The law is symbolic, playing an important role in the internalising of ideas about what is right and natural.' This is never more important than when these ideas are about sex and relationships.

Victims, it may seem obvious to say, do not get to decide whether their case is heard in court. Once a complainant's story has made it through the investigation phase, the decision to proceed will be made on two criteria: is prosecution in the public interest and is there a reasonable prospect of conviction?[2] If police or prosecutors feel the answer to either of these questions is no, the case won't proceed. One might imagine, given the seriousness of the decision and the impact on people's lives, there would be extensive processes for working through any decision, but that is not so. There are only guidelines, and much of it is based on guesswork, leaving us with three words that frame the whole system: reasonable, relevant, and credible. *Reasonable* is connected to the notion that there is a common standard of understanding in our community, where we can come to a collective agreement about what a reasonable person would do, or should believe.

Relevance[3] is a term for what can be included as evidence in court. In law, this is open to argument. *Credibility*[4] is a measure of what a reasonable person would consider believable, which, inevitably, is dependent on subjective judgments and attitudes.

When the criminal justice system tries to deal with sexual crime it works in a problematic and circular way, known as downstream-orientation.[5] Everyone involved is, in effect, required to guess the likely thought processes of the next decision-maker down the line, attempting to anticipate their views. Victims imagine what the community and police will think of their story. Detectives imagine whether their bosses are likely to authorise the case for prosecution, and prosecutors imagine what any magistrate or juror will think. Throughout this process decision-makers are basing their assumptions on beliefs derived from a community information base that is, to say the least, ill-informed.

Courts also differ on any given day much more than one might imagine, mainly because all the individuals involved are different. It might be comforting to believe that the system would deal with two similar stories in the same way, but it probably won't.

In the period of developing our training, and listening to police, I was frequently struck by how often they mentioned court and their experiences in the witness box. Most comments were negative, as each investigator seemed to have a memory of being made to feel stupid, or having their credibility undermined by a defence barrister. It did not seem to matter how many times they had been successful, the cases lost loomed larger in their minds. In some jurisdictions, police are also liable for court costs, should they lose the case.[6] In discussions with senior officers in our field, there is a variety of opinion about how much difference this makes. Some insist it has no effect on their judgment whatsoever, while others say it does. Police at senior level are both investigators and managers who, if they wish to be considered for promotion, will need to manage budgets efficiently. Losing a case is an expensive proposition, which must surely weigh on the minds of those who seek advancement. A 2017 Australian Royal Commission[7] called for an end to the practice.

Authorising cases for court is a litmus test for the effectiveness of the entire adversarial process. The call from key stakeholders, like sexual assault centres and law reform commissions, has been that the process of investigation, authorisation for court, and prosecution, should be *'consistent, transparent, and accountable'*.[8] In the adversarial justice system, of all the elements that need changing, abiding by those three words will prove the biggest hurdle.

The Director of Public Prosecutions in the UK has been criticised for suggesting, in recent training guidelines, that more 'weak' cases should be dropped.[9] This amounts to a policy shift by stealth. While the stated goals are to improve conviction rates and provide better outcomes for victims, the move is the antithesis of victim-centric justice. It also demonstrates that our adversarial system struggles to deal effectively with relationship-based crime. The system can transform itself as much as possible but, hanging over any change, will be the information base of any decision-making and the powerful effect of downstream-orientation. Until we all understand how this works, change will never come.

18

Reasonable

Our justice system is not about a search for the truth; it's about finding a winner.[1] The term adversarial justice tells you what's coming: a fight. Not only is the adversarial process about winning, but any decision will require a uniformity of thought from fact-finders. This process is made more difficult, obviously, by the depth and breadth of misconceptions held by those tasked with any decision.

Some say that we are moving to an era of trial by social media, that movements like #MeToo have gone too far, and that all allegations should proceed through 'due process' rather than the court of public opinion. It is hard to disagree with the notion that processes of justice must be fair, but challenges to current systems are occurring because the due process we have created is *not* fair. One researcher described what victims face as 'attrition, re-traumatisation, and disparate treatment across gender, class, and ethnic lines'.[2] Sexual crime victims describe a decidedly untherapeutic process that is weighted against them. They find its processes gruelling and unsatisfying, leaving them worse rather than better, an impact known as critogenic harm.[3] As a leading trauma expert put it, 'If one set out intentionally to design a system for provoking symptoms of traumatic stress, it might look very much like a court of law.'[4]

A Royal Commissioner, who had just spent five years listening to victim narratives and analysing the justice system's response to child sexual abuse, said that the law was too heavily weighted towards the benefit of the accused. Despite changes in the system, he said, 'The pendulum has barely moved.'[5]

If you want to win a sexual assault, rape, or child sexual abuse case, the bar of truth in adversarial justice is set beyond *any* reasonable doubt. The suspect had a *reasonable* belief that she consented ... the jury should consider what a *reasonable* person would believe ... etc. It is based on the presumption that any decision-maker will be able to reason, and use sound judgment, to come to a just decision. But what if the decision-maker thinks 'going back for coffee' is tantamount to consent, or that children's memories are flawed, and they are easily coached to lie? People who hold these views still think their beliefs are reasonable. Adversarial justice is not that good for accused people, either. Does 'not guilty' mean he didn't do it, or just that it couldn't be proved beyond reasonable doubt? With so few cases getting through the system, it is the one time that the flaws in the system work against accused people, leaving a question mark hanging over their heads.

When a victim enters the adversarial system, they will tell their story to an investigator: by any measure, a huge leap of faith. If the investigator is not a specialist in this field, it's an even bigger leap. From that moment, they do not own their story, as it becomes the property of the law and its representatives. First, the property of the police and then, if it does progress, of the prosecution service. Should it reach court, both the victim and investigator then become merely 'witnesses for the prosecution'. Once the story arrives at court there will also be legal argument about what the jury can hear, so the story is whittled down further. By the time every participant in the investigative and prosecutorial process has finished with it, the original story can be substantially changed.

In court, a jury will have explained to them how the story should be listened to, with rules of law explained to them endlessly, until their brains hurt.[6] There will be warnings about not assuming this and not thinking that, finding him not guilty if x, y, or z. They will be told that, just because they don't believe *his* story, it doesn't mean that they must believe *hers*,[7] as well as more positive recent innovations, like not assuming delays in complaint mean falsehood.[8] There is debate as to whether jurors can understand the complexity of law in directions put before them and what effect, if any, they have on decision-making.[9]

Then there's cross-examination, during which the job of the defence barrister is to create doubt. The tactics they use can be cruel and clinical, although not usually aggressive, as this can be counter-productive with juries. A barrister colleague, with many years of experience defending sex cases, explained to me what they are required to do. 'You have to pick apart the witness,' she said. She emphasised that it was one witness, because these cases usually rely on the testimony of the victim, as the only witness. I said, 'So you try to get them to make a mistake?' 'Yes,' she said. 'And you only need one. You need to go over the case to see where you can find that mistake and work out how you would then sum it up to the jury, so you can prompt that doubt.' Even though I like her, it was hard to listen to, as I know she would have been particularly good at it. Occasionally she helped genuinely innocent men get off the charges, she thought, but more often she helped guilty men get away with it, just by doing her adversarial job.

In 2016, researchers examined whether the tactics used
by defence barristers in rape trials had changed between
the 1950s and the 2000s.[10] The short answer was no, which
is disappointing, if not surprising. Some of the fine print
was fascinating, however, as the 1950s cohort referred more
frequently to the defendant's good character, suggested victims
should have resisted, or that lack of injuries raised doubt.
The group from the 2000s focused more on inconsistencies
of memory and delays in reporting, and suggested victims
maintaining a relationship with the accused after the alleged
offence should raise doubt. Some of the change in tactics has
come about because of new judicial directions and prohibitions
on certain tactics, leaving defence barristers to focus on
whichever myths and misconceptions are left. With so many
still floating around in common use, they haven't had to work
that hard, or change that much, leading these researchers to
conclude that both groups were 'merely pursuing the same
goals in slightly different ways'.

With children, as we have seen, the job of defence can be
even easier. Our prosecutors ran a case where a young girl said
her elderly neighbour had sexually abused her. The matter
came to light when her mother noticed redness in her groin
area during bath time. The child said it happened in the game
she played when she went to his house. The neighbour had
befriended the mother and child over a long period, so the
girl regularly played in his garden, or with his guinea pigs
(her mum and she didn't have any pets). One of the planks in
the fence between the properties was missing, creating a gap
for her to walk through. He kept tubs of lollies in his kitchen
cupboard, which she said he gave her after each offence. 'What
kind of lollies?' demanded the defence barrister, quietly. It

seems logical doesn't it, that anyone, however young, would remember what kind of sweets they were given at such important times? He repeated the demand, but she could not remember and became confused, which point the barrister gently drove home, leaving the jury little option but to acquit. I suspect everyone in that courtroom thought the little girl was telling the truth.

So, when all is said and done, guilty or not guilty, a magistrate or jury will hand victims their story back, in whatever shape it is finally left in, and with the new ending filled in by the court. We have ended up with a system of justice that is utterly disempowering, so that even when victims win, they can feel like they have lost. The system takes over their story at every juncture, turning people into observers of their own lives. There are other systems, however, which we should consider.

First and foremost, any system needs to understand the experiences of victims, as the cornerstone of any forensic practice. This is particularly important for police and, in our training, we carry out many presentations and exercises designed to help them understand victims' experience of abuse, as well as disclosing, reporting, and coping with the investigative process. In one simple exercise, they are asked to write down what they think victims might need from any justice system, and what victims might consider to be 'success'. Their lists include all sorts of elements that have nothing to do with the courts, and our investigators begin to realise how many elements of the system could benefit victims, like: being listened to, being represented, having their story thought worthy of investigation, having the offender spoken to, having their experience 'on the record', having people know about his behaviour, trying to stop others being abused, trying to help others come forward, to begin to move on and leave the abuse behind, to have him held to account, to have him punished, to have him imprisoned, and so on.

Many years ago, I was working in a support group for parents of child sexual abuse victims, which was organised by a therapeutic agency working with such children and their families.[11] The parents, who were all mothers, spoke of their guilt, shame, and confusion about the abuse, emotions which were evident on their faces. Many felt they had let it happen, even though they were unaware of the abuse at the time. I was there to talk about offenders and how they operate, explaining the processes of grooming, including the strategies offenders use to manipulate potentially protective adults. As I was speaking one woman let out a terrible groan, a howl of anguish which shocked and silenced us. After a long pause, she said she now understood something, and was struggling to deal with what it meant. She had long suffered from a bad back, she explained, which flared up painfully on occasions. When these episodes had started, her husband occasionally slept on the sofa, giving her space in bed to help her recover. In recent years these offers, she had just realised, had become more and more frequent, even when her back had not been too bad. It had obviously been a ruse, she now believed, to provide opportunity for the abuse of their daughter. She said she was both devastated and relieved, as it finally showed him for who he was, and gave her some respite from the guilt and self-blame. She hoped that understanding the abuser's behaviour could also release her daughter from any feelings of responsibility, and that it might help to heal a rift that had grown between them, created by the offender and his grooming.

This story reminds us that there are many people affected by abuse, not just victims themselves. In our adversarial system of justice, the state is the injured party. Messages to the community, from the judicial system, are mostly about punishment and deterrence, paying only passing attention to the ripple effects of abuse out into the wider community. Other cultures see the harm done in a broader way. New Zealand, for example, with its strong Maori culture, frames responses to abuse and violence around the notion of Whanau: language which denotes the interconnectedness of individuals, family, and community. Justice processes are set around repairing damage to those connections, acknowledging victims' stories, and having the community participate in holding perpetrators to account.[12] The concepts of restoration and prevention, inherent in their system, come from an understanding that acts of abuse and violence traumatise both the community and the individual.

The phrase 'trauma-informed'[13] is now ubiquitous in the therapeutic professions. It is designed to draw us to the notion that harm comes from trauma and is intended to produce therapeutic interventions that are both effective, and respectful of traumatic experiences. Obviously, this is most pertinent for those harmed by abuse. However, it is argued that work with offenders should also be trauma-informed, in order both to acknowledge the harms done to them, as they are disproportionately likely to have suffered many forms of abuse and neglect,[14] and to maximise the effectiveness of offender treatment processes.

So, if we are to be trauma-informed, and provide a process that moves beyond a fight, focusing on the needs of the affected person *and* the community, what are the choices? The most obvious replacement for an adversarial justice system is probably an inquisitorial one, although there are arguments that the processes are not as separate as one might think.[15] While some suggest inquisitorial systems might overcome problems with jury trials, others argue that judge-only trials, in an adversarial system, might offer better conviction rates.[16]

Civil courts are also touted as a clear alternative to the criminal courts. The bar for a finding in civil court is 'on the balance of probability', so the prospects for acknowledgement of wrong are greater. However, civil justice also includes the concept of comparative fault,[17] where determinations are made about the percentage of fault, for any action, that may be attributed to either party. This is, potentially, a recipe for victim-blaming, and therefore anathema to anyone who has been the subject to abuse. The process may offer some comfort for victims, though, albeit in a largely monetary form. When judgments are about money it may be seen to undermine victims' cases, as critics may say their claim is solely made for financial gain. Others argue that the money is symbolic, and rarely more than a minor part of victims' motivation. In a recent high-profile case, one victim felt compelled to clarify his motivation after such criticism. 'Some commentators have suggested that I reported to the police somehow for my own personal gain,' he stated. 'Nothing could be further from the truth. I have risked my privacy, my health, my well-being, my family. I have not instructed any solicitor in relation to a claim for compensation. This is not about money and never has been.'[18] I have heard victim/survivors say many things about their motivation to come forward. Money has rarely been mentioned.

Restorative justice[19] is, as the name suggests, based on the notion that the fabric of victims' lives, and community safety and cohesion, have been harmed and need to be restored. Unsurprisingly, given how New Zealand understands harm, the model has been widely used there. It is also used in some parts of the US and Australia, mostly around offences committed by young offenders.[20] Restorative justice is available in the UK for many offences, including sexual ones. There are a variety of processes, the most common being 'group conferencing',[21] where all those harmed may confront the offender, in a moderated and prepared environment. Listening and addressing needs are prioritised, with the victim at the centre, and collective discussion allowed about possible justice outcomes and reparation measures.

The biggest complaint from survivor advocates, should sexual crime matters be handled under a restorative model, is that it de-criminalises offending behaviour. However, restorative justice models do allow offenders to face consequences. The most persuasive arguments I have heard about restorative justice models have come from survivors, who talk about a sense of empowerment they get from the process.[22] Research also shows that victims experience a reduction of fear and anger towards offenders. All parties involved in restorative processes, whether offender or victim, report that they find the process fair.[23]

A new model, kaleidoscopic justice,[24] also deserves attention. Its authors, the UK academics Clare McGlynn and Nicole Westmarland, developed the model from talking to survivors about what justice meant to them, and what kinds of justice they most needed. They want to move away from conventional notions that the only positive outcomes are the conviction and punishment of offenders, recognising that survivors are typically more focused on prevention and connectedness. The kaleidoscopic element refers to the way each person will have a unique experience of abuse, and justice needs that will change over time, which require a more nuanced and multi-faceted response from the community and justice system than is currently available. Their work, to date, has focused on identifying key themes, each requiring elements of the models discussed above: consequences, recognition, dignity, voice, prevention, and connectedness. I hope their vision becomes a template for change.

No system of justice is perfect, despite claims some might make, so a combination of processes will offer more promise. If we listen to victims, look through the kaleidoscope, and understand how these crimes tear at the fabric of the relationships that connect us all, maybe we can put together a system we can all have faith in.

19

Relevant

When telling a story, in law, relevance is everything.[1] Prosecutors will generally want to include as much explanatory and contextual information as possible, whereas the defence will want the opposite. Each side is trying to control the story and define the parameters of the narrative. All evidence, or potential evidence, must go through hurdles to be heard in a court. If the right arguments can be made, what is considered relevant can change. The side that wins the relevance debate will probably win the case. As far as victims are concerned, if a court says it is not relevant, *then it is no longer a part of their story.*

We ran a conference a few years ago, focusing on how narratives were presented in court during sexual offence trials.[2] The key discussion was about the breadth of evidence decision-makers should be allowed to hear, when victim narratives were heard in court. I was discussing aspects of the upcoming conference, with a senior judge, when the topic turned to relevance. Having often been disappointed with what was allowed in trials I said to her, 'Do you think it would be OK for me to say that victims' narratives are sliced and diced by the adversarial process until they are almost unrecognisable?' She laughed. 'No,' she said, 'you can't say that.' But she didn't disagree. She just knew that if I said it so crudely judges and lawyers might stop listening.

There are, of course, variations in different jurisdictions, but most have similar hurdles any story will be forced to clear.

It has been common practice for defence and prosecution to meet pre-trial, to determine what elements of the case they will, and will not, contest. Prosecutors' beliefs about jury behaviour, as well as myths and misconceptions, have tended to make them err on the conservative side. This is a practice that has frequently exasperated investigators, who often feel that elements of their investigation are given away without a fight. I have lost count of the times an investigator asked me to talk to the prosecutor in their case, in the hope that they could be persuaded to include certain evidence. It nearly always concerns grooming behaviour by the perpetrator that has gone unrecognised, or confusing victim behaviour, provoked by the alleged abuse. What I usually discover is that the prosecutor is not sure how to argue for the inclusion, or what to say should the defence argue the point. This is not surprising, as many prosecutors do not receive specialist training in understanding sexual offence dynamics.

To show relevance, prosecutors are required to demonstrate what is called a 'chain of reasoning' between any relevant evidence and the fact in issue (usually just the alleged sexual offence). If they cannot show the connection, it will not be included. A suspect's violent behaviour, for example, will need to be linked to the grooming process, the offending itself, or any of the victim's response to it, if it is to be included. Even if something is considered generally relevant, it may still be excluded. The court will decide whether it has probative value,[3] in explaining elements of the case, outweighing the possibility that the information may prejudice the jury against the accused. For example, a sexual offence suspect may have a drug problem and commit acts of family violence. If a prosecutor cannot make a compelling argument to connect these behaviours with the sex offences, then the evidence will be considered too prejudicial, and a jury will not hear about it.

The highest bar is set for evidence that a prosecutor suggests shows the accused is of bad character,[4] or tended to behave in the way alleged in the case.[5] In the UK, there is a range of criteria for the admission of evidence of bad character, most notably the potential for the evidence to explain any elements of the offending, or victim reaction. In Australia, tendency rules used to prescribe that the defendant's behaviour be 'strikingly similar' to what was alleged in the complainant's statement. This language was so precise that such evidence was seldom admitted. Although the language has softened in some jurisdictions, it is still hard to get tendency evidence admitted. The difficulties of introducing tendency evidence are so great that even cases of multiple abuse against family members are often run as separate trials, which is highly contentious and deeply frustrating for police and prosecutors. To illustrate these hurdles, here are some examples. These stories are disturbing, but each says something about the way offending works, what evidence can be presented to juries, and why these cases can be so hard to prosecute.

A woman reporting historical abuse from her stepfather described the day, when she was about twelve years old, that she decided to challenge him about the abuse. They lived in a high-rise building, several floors up. He was on the balcony, having a cigarette and playing with his small dog. She went outside to confront him, threatening to tell her mother about what he was doing, unless he stopped. In an instant, he picked up his dog and dropped it over the railing of the apartment. She shrieked in horror, unable to comprehend what had just happened. Her mother ran out onto the balcony to see what the commotion was about. The offender immediately explained that the dog had leapt onto the table, near the rail, and had then fallen over the edge. He appeared devastated, and she looked to her daughter for confirmation, unable to believe that such a thing could happen. The girl said nothing, and so that became the story of what happened, and the abuse continued. Whether this act of terrible cruelty was conscious, or an instinctive act of desperation on the offender's part, it was effective, because it took another twenty years for her to come forward and tell the story. The investigator was thorough, taking her through the incident to find out every detail she could recall. She remembered the shock and disbelief, and the fear of him that permeated her in that moment. If he would do that to his beloved pet, what might he do to her? Most of all, she remembered thinking that her mother would not believe her, if she told the truth.

When it comes to prosecution, the inclusion of this episode presents a problem, with the first legal test of relevance. Does this evidence speak to the fact in issue?[6] I am sure most of us would agree that this was a critical moment in the story of the abuse, and so it meets that test. It ensured her silence, trapping her in a terrible lie. Her stepfather became a frightening and unpredictable figure, ensuring she stayed silent rather than risk the consequences. Perhaps you would also agree that a jury ought to hear this story, so pivotal is it to explaining the continued abuse? Remember though, its value in explaining what happened has to *outweigh* its potential to prejudice the jury, so the onus is on prosecutors. So, does this evidence contain sufficient probative value to outweigh its prejudicial effect? It is an important test, because we all do things that we shouldn't, and that would make people think less of us.

Every time we do something wrong, is every single one of our transgressions relevant to the commission of any subsequent act?

So, if someone threw a dog to its death, the prosecutor is required to show that the act of killing was relevant to the commission of the sexual offence. Common sense says it is, because it is connected to the silencing of the victim, but the law is not looking for what is common, it's looking for what's specific to each case. In general terms, is a man more likely to commit sexual abuse if he is violent towards people, or animals? Research says that it is a statistically significant link,[7] but the law insists on evidence, not statistics. Evidence must relate to particular acts, on particular days, not what *generally* happens.

In another case, a woman came into a police station and reported that her father had sexually abused her throughout her childhood. She said that no one ever knew, she did not report it at the time, and was only doing so now because her mother had recently died. She felt her mother would have suffered terribly if she had disclosed earlier. She was also afraid that she would not have been believed and would have been shunned by the rest of the family. This may have been, in part, because her father was a lay preacher at their church and, by all accounts, 'a lovely man'.

The investigator asked her to recall when the abuse started. Around the time she started school, she remembered being alone with her father, and playing with the family dog. She recalled that he had got angry with the dog but could not remember why. This was a side of him that she hadn't seen before and was only to see again during the abuse. He started to hit and kick the animal repeatedly. It died, right in front of her.

She did not know what happened next, but assumed a story had been concocted, to cover the shock death of a beloved pet. The sexual abuse, she recalled, began a short time later. She never spoke of the killing or the abuse to anyone, until she walked into the police station twenty years later.

The same questions arise. Is it relevant and is it too prejudicial to be heard by a jury? Not long after I heard this story I was meeting with a retired judge, to discuss the work we had been doing with police investigators. He was conducting an inquiry into child protection issues and was meeting with people from relevant agencies.[8] I used the story as an example of tactics used by offenders to groom and silence children, and I brought up how hard it was for many of the relationship details to make it to court. I asked him if the story would have been heard in his courtroom. 'No,' came the firm reply: too prejudicial. What if, during her statement, we had asked what she remembered of the experience, and she had said something like, 'I was just so scared of him after that, I did whatever he said'? Would it get in then? 'Probably not'. Still too prejudicial, despite being more clearly seen as an act of grooming. What if, I asked, the offender later whispered to her, 'Remember what happened to Scruffy,' when she threatened to expose the abuse. Would it get in then? 'Maybe'. A clear threat, designed to ensure compliance, and yet still only a maybe.

This shows how hard it is for evidence to be included, even when it seems crucial to understanding the story. It also shows that the law has a certain flexibility, which we can use to include relevant information, if we are smart enough about it. The crucial factor here is that laws can change, or rather the rules of law can change. Decisions made by different courts will change the interpretations made by courts that subsequently look at similar issues. The higher the court, the more binding such interpretations are on lower courts. It is one of the ways law can keep up with the times, without resorting to governments enacting legislation that forces change. Case law is not permanent and may be altered by future judgments, so every case has the potential to be a part of a bigger change.

I had the opportunity to meet with the same judge a second time, some months later. He is a kind and cordial man so, despite my previous challenges, he was happy to discuss our work further. As luck would have it, there had been a significant court judgment in the meantime, when a case had been sent to the Court of Appeal for review. Appeals courts are significant, because they rank more highly than Magistrate and County courts, so are important in creating case law. The matter at issue involved a man who was found guilty of sexually abusing his children. He was also charged with physical violence towards his family. One of these acts of violence was the killing of a family pet, in front of the family. He was found guilty on both sets of charges. Evidence of violence, including towards the pet, was introduced in the sexual offence trial, as well as evidence of sexual abuse being introduced in the trial regarding his violent behaviour. The convictions were appealed, partly on grounds that the evidence of killing the pet was too prejudicial, and irrelevant to the commission of the sexual offences. To our surprise and delight, the appeal was denied. The appeal judges decided that the evidence spoke to 'the states of mind of the complainants', making specific reference as to why they submitted to the abuse and why they delayed their complaint.[9] I reminded the judge of our previous discussion and showed him the court's decision. He read it carefully and then said, 'I agree with that.'

Prosecuting sexual crime presents some unique challenges, demanding counsel be excellent storytellers. The process they use to gather their story together, and persuade fact-finders of their narrative, is done through the development of a case concept. Jurors arrive at court with a set of expectations about sex and relationships, including sexual offending, which come from a set of stored personal and community beliefs, sometimes called narrative scripts.[10] As we have already discussed, these scripts often include a range of misconceptions which can have a significant effect on their judgments.[11] Research suggests, however, that if prosecutors can present a clear narrative as to why people acted in the way they did, then these expectations may be overcome. They must contain explanations for the behaviour of complainants and accused persons, giving reasons why jurors should understand a changed social reality.[12] In other words, a well-constructed narrative can give jurors clear reasons for the circumstances they are examining, rather than those in their personal scripts. For such an understanding to take place, the well-constructed narratives must be *coherent, consistent, and complete.* Research also suggests that both lay people and police investigators are most likely to change their opinions, or re-evaluate their judgments, when advice is offered that contributes novel information, particularly when offered in a way that is unorthodox or incongruent.[13] The Whole Story process, with its focus on relationship, and explanations for behaviour that runs counter to community myths and misconceptions of sexual offending, offers an opportunity for effective presentation of such novel information.

As I am writing this section, the example that comes to mind is a case in which a woman accused her ex-boyfriend of sexual assault and attempted rape. He had come over to her house to win her back. When she declined the offer, he became verbally abusive, pushed her up against a wall and grabbed her between the legs. As he took down his trousers and forced her to her knees, she wriggled free and ran to a neighbour's house to call the police. The neighbour reported that she appeared distressed. He also said that, despite it being a cold and rainy winter's evening, she did not have any shoes on. Defence argued that the absence of shoes was not relevant. The court disagreed, the evidence was considered relevant, and the ex-boyfriend was found guilty. Asked to decide between two competing narratives – the shoes, or rather the lack of them – may have proved the difference. The prosecutor who argued that case also trains the police prosecutors who work in our jurisdiction, in Victoria. He calls our method 'the Why' and teaches its use in developing case concepts. Without 'the Why', he argues, fact-finders will be left with doubt. As you know, in the adversarial justice system, doubt means acquittal.

20

Credible

Next to reasonable and relevant, the most important word in the adversarial system of justice is credible, even though its meaning is subjective and there are no instructions or guidelines as to how it should be determined. When senior investigators come to decide whether a case should go to court, the $64,000 question is, 'Will she be a credible witness?'

What they are asking is actually *two* questions, the first of which is, 'Will she be able to cope with telling her story in court?' It is a necessary question, as the process will be rough. Remember the fourteen-year-old girl in the park, right at the beginning of the book? The prosecutor in her case, detailing to the girl and her mother what cross-examination by barristers for all three defendants would be like (they would all have been part of the same trial, so she would have been cross-examined by all three), explained that the process would be 'brutal'.[1] The prosecutor also anticipated that she would be in the witness box for two to three days. Even the most robust individual will find the rigours of adversarial justice nerve-wracking, so we should not put people through it unless the process and the outcome may be of some benefit to them. The official line on why this process is necessary will be because her evidence must be tested. The upshot is that, in an adversarial system, the central job of a defence barrister is to undermine the credibility of the complainant.

The second question they are asking is, 'What will a jury make of her?' This is even more problematic from an ethical standpoint, and a pernicious aspect of the downstream-orientation process. If you were hoping that the law would guide each step of this decision, you are going to be disappointed. Many elements of criminal justice decision-making are known as 'extra-judicial factors',[2] which simply means 'nothing to do with the law'. In the theatrical world of adversarial court, where advocates attempt to draw decision-makers towards their version of events, appearances are all-important. Jurors will be persuaded to make judgments about the victim herself rather than the credibility of her story. As one defence barrister told a researcher, when questioned about her tactics in rape cases, 'You'll put your chap's facts and obviously controvert her facts. They're less important than undermining her personality. It sounds sinister but that's what you're trying to do, make her sound and appear less credible.'[3]

Knowing defence tactics, prosecutors also place great emphasis on credibility issues – in particular, focusing on how she might appear to the judge or jurors as much, if not more, than analysing the breadth of relevant evidence.[4] One study, analysing forty-seven intimate partner sexual assault cases, showed that all the cases filed by the prosecutor 'involved incidents where the victim was not engaging in any behaviour that could be interpreted as damaging her credibility'.[5]

It is hard to resist judgments as to who does, and does not, have credibility. The lessons we learn growing up become our collective social knowledge,[6] there to help us organise the world into a coherent form, so we don't feel overwhelmed.

The trouble is, attitudes and beliefs can be hard to change, particularly if they are about sensitive subjects like sexuality and relationships. It used to be a free-for-all, with all sorts of tactics allowed, including disclosure of her previous sexual history, irrespective of its relevance to the fact in issue. Although this practice has been somewhat curbed, it is still admissible in some cases.[7] Even though the worst abuses have been eradicated, the process is heavily weighted in favour of the accused. For example, in many jurisdictions, any previous criminal history on behalf of the complainant is required to be disclosed in court.[8] No such disclosure can be made about the accused however, without going through argument about its potential to prejudice the jury.

In one case, lawyers for Cardinal Pell, who was subsequently convicted of child sexual abuse, before being cleared by the High Court, tried to subpoena the medical records of the complainants.[9] This is common practice, but it's more likely to be the subject of a contest now, as the system is slowly improving. They were looking for two things: inconsistencies in any other statement complainants may have made, and anything that might suggest the complainant has, or has had, mental health problems, or behavioural issues. Any issue would then be used to damage their credibility, irrespective of its relevance to their allegation.

We once ran an investigation into the organised abuse of teenage girls in the Melbourne care system, where a loose collective of abusive men was conducting a co-ordinated grooming process on targeted girls. This phenomenon is common throughout the world, unfortunately, as numerous UK cases can attest. After a period of getting them used to absconding from their residence and 'having a good time', the girls were invited to parties. When they got to the parties, they were expected to have sex with the men there, in return for money and gifts. Even though investigators gathered a considerable amount of evidence of the abuse, there were only two prosecutions. In one case the offender pleaded guilty and the other case only went ahead after heavy lobbying by police, because prosecutors had initially wanted to drop it. The offender was subsequently found guilty. The girls were not seen to be credible witnesses. You can guess why, because they were a bit rough around the edges, had tattoos and told people to 'fuck off' when they got angry. Our system of justice appears available only to those who fit a certain profile of worthiness. Even if she does fit the mould, other prejudices will be pandered to. In 2018, when a young woman in Northern Ireland alleged gang rape, the defence barrister suggested her story didn't ring true because there were other 'middle-class' young women at the party, where the alleged rape took place, who would have heard her cries.[10] The men were acquitted.

The 'perfect victim', if they are a child, will be between five and ten years old and have no family problems or behavioural issues of any kind. Any younger and their memory will be called into question. Any older and their complicity will be implied, particularly once they are over fourteen.[11] Any troubling behavioural issues and that will be game over.

Research suggests that the three variables most associated with guilty findings in child sexual abuse cases are similar fact (tendency) evidence, evidence from a witness to the offending act/s, and positive medical or DNA evidence.[12] We have already seen how hard they are to achieve. There are other factors, however, that show a positive association with convictions, such as good recent complaint evidence and partial acknowledgement of inappropriate behaviour by the accused (that did not include admission of guilt). The more positive factors show the value of good interviewing, of both complainants and suspects.

If the victim is an adult then total absence of criminal history, drugs, alcohol, or other problem behaviours is a must. And their behaviour before, during, and after the assault will need to be unimpeachable, otherwise it's no-go. There are anomalies, however, such as research showing drunk victims might still get a guilty verdict, particularly if the prosecution can show that *he* bought the drinks. If she got herself drunk, judgments of her will be damning.[13] Some victims who stand outside the mould of so-called 'real rape' scenarios[14] can also get a guilty verdict, occasionally. There is research that suggests complainants who resist the punishment of cross-examination effectively can be perceived as likely to have also resisted the offender, thus bolstering their credibility.[15] If it all just feels like a roll of the dice to you, and a process lacking in credibility, then I'm inclined to agree.

In this discussion of defence attacks on complainants' credibility there is also the cruellest of ironies: that the trauma created by sexual abuse, leaving victims with a range of possible mental health and behavioural issues,[16] is then used, extra-judicially, to undermine their credibility in court. In late 2017, the Royal Commission into Institutional Responses to Child Sexual Abuse in Australia[17] handed down its final findings, based on the testimony of thousands of survivors, and hundreds of forums with criminal justice professionals and advocacy groups. One of its central conclusions for improvements to the criminal justice process, relevant to every kind of sexual crime, was that investigations and prosecutions should be based on the credibility of the complaint, rather than the credibility of the complainant. If we were to commit to such a change, then we just might end up with a system that provides justice.

21

Consent

I was discussing consent with a colleague once when she started talking about her kindergarten days. When she was three or four the teachers had a ritual that, when children arrived, they had to say, 'Good morning'. They could choose how they did it, however. They could wave, give a handshake, or a hug. As they got to the door, the children knew to point to their preferred greeting, displayed by large signs, and that is what would happen. I asked her what the process was when she went on to primary and secondary school. She told me that there was no similar process around choice and consent, for any practice, and that sex education had focused on biology, pregnancy, and avoiding STDs. How strange, that consent should drop out of the curriculum just at the time when young people most need clarity. In no area is this lack of education about consent more apparent than when it concerns sexual assault and rape.

The crime of rape, as we now understand it, is a relatively recent phenomenon. In patriarchal cultures, where women and children were property, rape was considered a crime against the man who was her husband, rather than an abuse of the woman herself. Men's sexual rights have been enshrined in law well into modern times.[1] You can find the hand of the seventeenth-century lawyer Matthew Hale here too, as he argued that a husband could not be guilty of rape, as the marriage contract gave him permanent consent.[2] His view lasted for over two centuries, until debates and dissent about the law, begun in comprehensive form by feminists in the 1970s, led to repeal.³ In the UK, rape in marriage was only recognised in law in 1991.⁴

The Sexual Offences Act (UK, 2003)⁵ states that 'a person consents if he agrees by choice and has the freedom and capacity to make that choice' (note, in passing, the use of 'he'). How well does it work?

In a 2018 newspaper interview the Director of Public Prosecutions in the UK, Alison Saunders, informed women that they should, when being sexually assaulted, give a clear 'no' to their assailant. If they did not, she warned, the offender would be likely to assume consent.⁶ What does that say about the way we see sex and consent? The dynamic offered is still that of seeking permission, where *she* will say yes or no to *his* request. If he persists, she is to give an unequivocal verbal signal that she does not wish to proceed. Acquiescence, even clear non-verbal signals, will not be sufficient.

Low conviction rates for rape show that juries have a hard time coming to unanimous decisions as to what constitutes a rape. Some jurisdictions have tried to solve these issues by substituting other charges, but this has not only failed to improve conviction rates, but also made some victims feel diminished by the reclassification of their experience. The changes were made with good intentions, though, as fact-finders have trouble with the use of such a loaded word to describe a wide variety of experience. All rapes contain three elements: they are acts of power, control, and aggression; they involve penetration (with differing definitions); and they are perpetrated against someone's will. After that, there are many potential differences. Is the act of a man who takes a condom off, during what had hitherto been a consensual experience, the same as the act of a man who bullies his wife into sexual submission? Is the act of a man who penetrates a sexual partner anally, when that had not been discussed as a part of what was desired, the same as rape by a stranger at knifepoint? If these cases make it to court defined as rape, which every one of them is, a jury might see all except the last one as not meeting the common-sense definition. Even if they agree all acts were non-consensual, their views about responsibility and guilt will be framed by their beliefs about male and female sexual behaviour, by different interpretations of language, and probably by some myths and misconceptions. They may also believe the punishment, of being branded a rapist, imprisoned, losing their job and status, and suffering social stigma, does not fit each crime equally. What might a jury make of this next case, for example?

A woman in senior management attended her company's annual conference, which was held some distance from her home and office. One of the directors of the company, who had propositioned her at a previous conference, came up to her at the first 'icebreaker' gathering. In front of colleagues, he complimented her on her looks, her dress, and her hair. He told her she was 'the best piece here' and loudly suggested he should hire more like her. Startled by the crudeness of his approach she said, 'I'll take that as a compliment,' and tried to laugh it off. Some of the assembled company were later called as witnesses to the cordial relationship between them. He came up to her as she was getting a drink at the bar, put his arm around her and pulled her in close. He whispered that they had 'unfinished business', told her his room number, and that he would give her 'the ride of her life'. She froze, unsure of what to say, and how to rebuff him without causing a scene. He removed his arm, but stayed in her personal space, as he kept up his charm offensive. After a short while she recovered her composure, said she had just seen someone she needed to catch up with 'about a business thing', and escaped his attentions. Worried about how to deal with the next two days of the conference, she found a woman she knew from the HR department and asked, off the record, for advice. Her HR colleague said he was notorious for 'womanising' and that she would 'have a word with him'. Retreating to her room, she ordered dinner and called her boyfriend. Later, as the party was winding up below, she got a phone call. So sorry to have caused offence. It was just a bit of harmless fun. 'Can I please apologise in person? I just feel so awful about it.' She said he could. Once inside her hotel room he pulled her to him again, kissed her forcefully, picked her up and laid her on the bed. She was silent and rigid as he removed her underwear and penetrated her. Later, he admitted they had sex, but claimed it was consensual. The jury could not arrive at a unanimous decision, beyond reasonable doubt, so he was acquitted.

Iceland changed its laws (23 March 2018)[7] to make consent an explicit, rather than implicit, process. Consent in Icelandic law is now constructed as a dialogue, rather than a statement or an unspoken understanding. *All parties* are expected to assure themselves of the willingness of the other/s to participate throughout the experience. Accused people will now be required to demonstrate what steps they took to ascertain consent at each step along the way. As the main advocate of the change expressed it, 'It has to be clear when you engage in a sexual act that you have approval, and that it is not enough to expect or assume you have approval. There must be no question that you have consent.'[8]

The new legal model has also become law in Sweden (1 July 2018).[9] These changes represent a fundamental shift in expectations of sexual relationships, particularly as few European countries even have consent-based rape laws at all. Countries that don't use consent as the basis of sexual offence laws generally use the presence of violence, and the overcoming of resistance, as the benchmark for rape charges.[10] Even countries with enlightened policies on other social justice issues can remain archaic in their laws around rape and consent. Finland, for example, generally seen as progressive around issues of gender equality, was widely criticised recently for its outdated rape laws. At the time of writing, in Finland, rape can only be proven if violence is used or threatened, or the victim is rendered helpless by fear and unable to defend herself. Matters came to a head with a court ruling, that a man could not be charged with the rape of a ten-year-old girl, because he did not use violence and she wasn't seen to be in fear of him.[11] With so many countries still not even using consent laws at all, never mind moving to progressive models such as Iceland and Sweden, it's no wonder so few rapists are held to account.

The Swedes have introduced two new offences, of Negligent Rape and Negligent Sexual Assault, with maximum sentences of four years.[12] It is clear, in their decision to pass such laws, that they are trying not only to change the construction of consent in Sweden, but also to develop a process that holds more transgressors to account, with sentences that juries are more likely to find appropriate. They are also in the process of developing guides for educators, to help citizens, particularly young people, adjust to the new rules for negotiating sexual relationships.

In rape trials outside Iceland or Sweden there are two key hurdles that prosecutors must overcome to gain a conviction (three, really, if you include all the myths and misconceptions about sexual offending). The first is that the burden of proof is on the prosecution to show that consent was *not* given.[13] So the UK's Director of Public Prosecutions was right, in law, that without clear signals, particularly verbal, accused men will probably be given the benefit of reasonable doubt. Rape defendants will also then be given a second chance, because the law allows his defence team to argue that, despite whatever signals given, he still had formed a reasonable belief that consent was given.[14] This next case highlights how problematic this can be.

A group of twenty-somethings went out clubbing and, in the early hours of the morning, they all went to crash at one of the group's place. A young woman and man, who were acquaintances, were left to share a mattress on the floor. He approached her for sex, but she said she was not interested. A short while later he tried again, and she rebuffed him again, saying she'd be forced to sleep in her car if he continued. He told her that he could go to the car, but she said he didn't have to, as long as they just went to sleep. They continued to share the mattress. Sometime later she was woken up, being anally penetrated by him.

At his trial he was found guilty of rape, so case closed, you might think. His defence team appealed against his conviction, claiming that he had formed a reasonable belief that she was consenting. Despite two clear refusals, and her being asleep, the court of appeal accepted his version, and the conviction was overturned.[15] As it happens, this case went to a further appeal. On the day the High Court was bringing down its judgment, the atmosphere in our office was tense and pessimistic. People were commenting that if the second appeal was lost, we should all pack up and go home. In fact, the High Court denied the appeal, thank goodness, bringing down a damning judgment, saying legal statutes were out of step and that the Appeals Court judges were flawed in their decision-making.[16] The relief we all felt was palpable, before everyone felt flat and depressed, with the old-fashioned absurdity of it all. It is an inescapable conclusion from this process that the law, despite recent reforms and attempts at change, still prioritises the state of mind of the accused over that of the complainant. Nearly always, in court, this means the experience of men over women. As one researcher put it, when describing the law's construction of *mens rea*, the concept that knowledge of wrongdoing constitutes part of the crime,

> the manner in which *mens rea* is constructed in sexual assault trials poses particular difficulties. This is because a woman's experience of sexual assault may be denied based on the mental state and knowledge of the defendant. That is, a defendant's honest but inaccurate belief in consent is privileged above a woman's actual knowledge of her non-consent.[17]

Drugs and alcohol are also a significant factor in sexual assaults, particularly those against young people.[18] It really blurs the way we see consent and it turns up a lot in these cases, particularly those sometimes deemed 'regrettable sex'.

Is it possible to determine whether consent was present when both parties were drunk? Yes, is the short answer. Although alcohol has a negative impact on memory recall, particularly on recollection of peripheral detail, memory is surprisingly robust under the influence of alcohol, particularly for significant actions or events.[19] Sometimes we do things we wouldn't usually do, under the influence of alcohol, but we still know when something is against our will. For example, an undercover operative (u/c) once told me of a case where they used a lip reader to 'listen' to a suspect in conversation, because it was easier than using electronic devices in a public setting. On one occasion the suspect was in a bar with a woman, whom he asked back to his place. She replied that he would need to buy her a few more drinks, as she only fancied him when she was drunk. When the lip reader repeated this the u/c laughed out loud, which was understandable, if unprofessional. The point is, she knew what she wanted, drunk and sober. Victims of rape know the difference, and sometimes suspects can express it clearly too, albeit unwittingly. One man, interviewed over a rape allegation, described how much the woman had drunk, including slurred speech and unstable walking. He also told interviewers how he had helped to take her clothes off, as she couldn't really do it herself. He was trying to show how drunk they both were, but he ended up talking himself into a whole lot of trouble.

When it comes to issues of children and consent, countries draw the line in different places. Even when ages of consent are clearly defined, as in the UK, there can be a lack of clarity about what that means. In 2017, the UK Criminal Injuries Compensation Authority considered whether compensation, in sexual offence matters, should be given to those over twelve.[20] Its thinking, which was later overturned after an outcry from children's advocacy groups, seemed to be based on the notion that children over twelve are somehow more culpable, and therefore unworthy of compensation. As I am sure you are aware, the age of consent in the UK is not thirteen.

In a case in France, in 2018, there was debate about whether an eleven-year-old girl should be considered a woman. As there is no official age of consent in France, the argument was made by her lawyers that their twenty-nine-year-old client did not commit rape,[21] but rather had consensual sex with a willing participant, who should be considered a woman. The lawyers could do so, in part, because French law only permits a possible charge of sexual abuse for those fifteen and under, but not rape. They were also able to do so because the only ruling on age and consent in France, at that time, said that children of five years and younger cannot consent under any circumstances.[22] Children above that age, it could be argued, may have consented, and could therefore be thought of as adults. There was debate among lawmakers about introducing an age of consent, but they were unable to agree. The man on trial was acquitted.[23]

Remember the case of the girl who goes to her father's bedroom? When she got to his room, following the non-verbal cues he had taught her to decipher for so many years, he would feign surprise. 'What are you doing here?' he would say, in yet another tactic to make her feel responsible. He was not the only one to make her feel that way, however. When the girl's father was convicted in court, in the late 1980s, the judge admonished the daughter for having taken part in sexual acts with her father. She was fourteen at the time, and it had been going on since she was six. In case you're thinking that was the 1980s, and those words would not be spoken today, I refer you to the thinking of the Criminal Injuries Compensation Authority, from 2017, still confused about the complicity of thirteen-year-olds.

The law has slowly been dragging itself into the twenty-first century on children's issues, as it used to be a lot worse. In child cases, there were general warnings given about the unreliability of children's evidence.[24] Children also used to give evidence in the court itself, whereas there are now a range of provisions for giving evidence in a separate space, psychologically protected from the presence of the accused. In some UK jurisdictions, thanks to pioneering work by organisations like Triangle,[25] intermediaries can help children cope with the process of giving evidence.[26] This practice is gaining widespread recognition but is not available in all courts.

In adult cases there used to be a range of judges' warnings given to juries. The most common, in cases that hinged on consent, was that it would be dangerous to convict when allegations were of a historical nature,[27] or solely on the testimony of the complainant, without corroborative evidence.[28] Given that such evidence, in the traditional sense, was rarely available, you can imagine what effect it had on juries. Lots of courts no longer give these warnings.

Whether it is the age at which we believe children can consent to sexual acts, or the way we negotiate sex in adult relationships, notions of consent are still old-fashioned. We have become so confused about the rules that charging and conviction rates for rape have plummeted in recent times, prompting the UK Victims Commissioner to suggest that rapists can now act almost with impunity.

If the systems most countries operate to find justice in cases of sexual crime were businesses, they would have closed down long ago. Few people use them, attrition is high, convictions are low, and 'customer' satisfaction is poor. And yet most systems have existed, largely unchanged, for many years. As the Australian academic Rachael Burgin puts it,

> In one sense, the system isn't 'broken' at all – it is working exactly as it was intended to. And that's the problem: the law is out of touch with reality. It's out of touch with community expectations. It's out of touch with women's lived experience of sexual violence. It lags behind academic evidence and research into what we know about sexual offending and those who perpetrate sexual violence.[29]

It is not just the law, but the core construct of consent underpinning it, that needs to be changed. Similar problems exist at every stage of the justice system. Surely it is time to make some bold decisions and move to more effective models and practices? We should start by following the lead of Sweden and Iceland, setting new standards for consent in sexual relationships. Once that principle is set, so many others might follow: Education in sex, relationships, and consent throughout childhood and adolescence; prioritising consent communication; changes to the penalties for offences; encouraging reporting of abuses; prioritising prevention and early intervention; specialist courts; specialist training for all investigators and adjudicators; non-case-specific education for jurors, or turning jurors into professional roles;

a kaleidoscope of justice choices for victims, including restorative practices ... the list of potential improvements goes on and on. Perhaps then, if we made these changes, those who work in the system would have more confidence in it, and more victims would feel free to tell their stories.

Part V

Where to from here?

22

Difficult conversations – close to home

We may be talking more about sexual offending now, and reporting rate rises are testament to that, but the conversations are just beginning. Over the years I have developed a personal marker for how that change is happening, from the number of people who get in contact to talk about what happened to them. It would probably be no surprise to you that many people, in work connected to sexual offending, have experienced abuse first-hand. What may surprise you is how few have ever told anyone or reported the crimes. When they do come to talk, reporting is rarely the first thing on their mind, although it usually becomes part of the conversation. Typically, they are more concerned about whether doing this type of work is right for them. They usually feel passionate about it, for obvious reasons, but are beginning to feel the strain. These are complex issues, often requiring several conversations, about the effect of the abuse, finding the right therapeutic help, and where the supports are in their personal and professional lives. Remarkably, after working through their issues, most of those I have talked to have stayed in the work.

The other conversation I have had more frequently, in recent times, is with people working in this field who have not experienced abuse first-hand, but want to know how best to respond, should family or friends disclose to them. When they are confronted with the reality of offender behaviour, what many who come to work in this field find most unsettling are the myriad elements of grooming, that we are most at risk from those we know, and how common sexual offending is in our communities. Among the many questions these realisations provoke is, 'What do I do if my friend/partner tells me that they were sexually assaulted or abused as a child?'

There is no set script for this kind of conversation, but there are helpful responses. 'I'm sorry that happened to you' can be a good start, or, 'I'm really glad you told me, as that can't have been easy for you.' It needs to be about them and not you. If you do not know what to say, then say so. Remember, they have often been living with this for a long time, but letting the secret out, or saying it out loud, is a big deal. Some people feel relief, while others are consumed by fear and anxiety at the consequences of disclosure. Particularly in romantic or other intimate relationships, there will be a fear of rejection or judgment, or that this new knowledge might change the way you see them. Reassurance is vital.

After initial disclosure and reaction, it is important that they maintain a sense of control over the consequences of disclosure, so sentences like, 'Do you want to do something with this? If so, what? Is it useful to try and work out the next part together?', might be helpful. This response will need to change, of course, if their disclosure identifies someone at immediate risk. If they do not want to seek further advice or help, but you are worried about them, you could ask if *you* can talk to someone. There are lots of good specialist services who can give advice without them having to identify themselves. And finally, you may want to ask them if they have considered reporting the abuse to the police.

The next common question I am asked is, 'I'm having issues at work and I don't know what to do about it.' They are usually talking about sexual harassment. Again, there is no set template, simply better starting points, like, 'What is happening to you is wrong,' or, 'They should not be doing that.' I have worked on so many cases where the first response was more like, 'Are you sure? – he's such a nice guy?' or, 'Maybe he's just a bit ...' Often, what they are telling you is only the tip of the iceberg, to test how you will react. People have usually been putting up with the behaviour for a while, so may be confused and wracked with self-blame, even though they have done nothing wrong. Fears for their job, their career, and their reputation may be uppermost in their minds. As before, ask them what they would like to do about it, and how you can help. Whether they intend to report it or not, suggest they keep a record of every incident and comment. Even if they never report it, it can help them gain a sense of perspective about where the real responsibility lies, and how significant the abusive behaviour is. Finally, you may ask them if they need help finding out what their options are, whether it's therapeutic help they want, or to make a formal complaint. It is hard for people to navigate these kinds of decisions, as harassment can make people lose touch with their usual self. Sleeplessness, anxiety, and depressed feelings are all common, so they may need your help for a while, until equilibrium is restored, and they reconnect with their old selves. Here are the key themes again: listen, ask questions, and make it about them. Acknowledge the behaviour as wrong and that they bear no responsibility. Ask if they know what help they want. Ask if they would like help working out their options. If it is a current situation, suggest they keep a record. Leave all choices up to them, unless you believe there is someone else at immediate risk, or that they are a serious risk to themselves. And don't forget that they have chosen to tell *you*. It is an important acknowledgement of the connection they feel.

Then there is the question, only ever asked by women, of how to spot the signs of risk in relationships. The question usually concerns issues with adult relationships, but women with children also ask about risks, particularly if they are starting new relationships. There is no definitive answer to these questions, but there are some obvious red flags, which are best seen as cumulative. Remember the woman in the massage story? If she had seen his behaviour as connected, rather than dismissing each of her concerns individually, would she have broken the conventions of polite behaviour and challenged him, or simply changed her mind and left? Maybe. Once, when I discussed the same case in training, a detective told us about going to a masseur a few times, without any issues, when he made suggestions about 'future areas to work on'. It was not what he said, but the way he said it, that bothered her. She never went back.

In relationships, if they have a reputation for abusive behaviour, it is worth noting that people *can* change, but not without a mighty big shove in the right direction. They might have a list of things they want to be different about you, don't get on with your friends and family, want exclusivity and encourage you to spend less time with others that you love. There may be unpredictable changes of emotion that they always imply, or tell you directly, are your fault. They may use belittling language and make 'jokes' at your expense. If you see these signs, look out, and remember that risk is cumulative, so each issue should be seen collectively, not in isolation. It is way more difficult than this in real life, of course, because things may start off fine, and problems often arrive slowly. When they do accumulate, if it feels too difficult or dangerous to bring up concerns, or they are dismissed when you do, then the writing is on the wall. Leaving relationships is the most dangerous time, particularly if there has been physical violence and abuse. Seek advice from agencies that know how to help.

For those who are parents, or planning to be, the problem with recognising the risk of sexual abuse for children is that it can be hard to differentiate problem men from those who are a positive influence. Sometimes 'He's so good with kids' means just that, or that offering to take your child on a fishing trip is a simple kindness. There are potential signs, however, and, as with adult relationships, these should be accumulated rather than seen as separate, including: encouraging secrecy and exclusivity, playing favourites and treating children differently (particularly if one is treated as 'special'), disrespecting children's boundaries or insisting on being treated by them in a certain way, changing family rules about touch, or encouraging sexualised language and behaviour: these are all red flags. It may be advisable to leave children out of any online dating profiles, too, as some offenders use profiles to target. It is a difficult juggle, of course, because the subject is sure to come up in early encounters. Deciding when a new relationship has reached a stage for introductions to children is hard, but the key rule is that it needs to be on your terms, with your timing. 'I'd love to meet your family' is one thing, but pressure to do so should count as a warning sign.

This brings up the next point: instincts. If it does not feel right, explore that feeling. This rings true whether we are talking about adult relationships or concerns about our children. I have known a lot of cases, particularly with children, where matters came to light because someone 'felt something wasn't right'. If you get that feeling, or something concerns you, then act on your feeling, or at least talk it over with someone. It is not always easy to find that someone, of course, but there are agencies and helplines who will listen to your concerns.

Not trusting anyone is about as helpful as trusting everybody, so where is the middle ground? What about not making up your mind until you have enough information to feel able to do so? Obviously, this will differ depending on your life experience, as those of you with histories of rape, sexual assault, or child abuse know all too well.

Detectives in this field often say they cannot unknow things, and that their adult relationships and parenting styles have been altered by their work. Vigilance is not necessarily a problem, as it can help us make better decisions. Hyper-vigilance, however, may affect relationships. It can also affect a child's overall sense of safety because they will pick up on our anxiety. It is a hard balance to strike. For those concerned about their children, check out what organisations like the NSPCC or Save the Children suggest, or local services if you have them. There is plenty of good child-safe information out there, and suggestions for how to talk about these topics with your children. It can also be helpful to talk with family/ friends who care for your child, about the approach you are taking, and ask for their support. Openness about these topics and listening to children's experiences are the best measures of prevention, as well as the best protection for them should anything go wrong.

Here are the key messages again, for both adult relationships and child safety:

- trust should be earned
- don't dismiss your concerns
- see red flags as cumulative
- pay attention to your instincts
- seek advice

Listening to someone tell you about abuse can be upsetting and unnerving, whatever your relationship with them. Even second-hand, the realities of the conversation can upset our world view, leaving us anxious or unsettled. It can be just as disconcerting to think through the risks to oneself or one's children, as it undermines our sense of safety. Participants on our courses often work through a range of emotions, both during the training and in the formative stages of their specialist work. It is hard to find out just how cruel and destructive people can be, but still maintain a positive outlook on the world. Someone usually asks if there are any useful strategies for coping with the effects, to which my standard reply is, 'When you left here on Friday afternoon, what were you looking forward to?' You can imagine their replies, as the answers are the same the world over. Connections to people, place, hobbies and enthusiasms, and a sense of purpose when we return to work on Monday morning. What we now know can make us and our children safer, and it doesn't have to overwhelm our sense of safety and goodness in the world.

23

Difficult conversations – prevention and change

The first step to imagining a world without sexual offending or family violence is to understand the breadth and depth of abuse in our communities, which means honest conversations about what is happening. The desire to deny and minimise is understandable – 'Can't we talk more about the men who *don't* do this?', 'You can't put us all in the same basket', etc. When I was at university, way back in the 1980s, the phrase used on placards and in chants at rallies such as 'Reclaim the Night' ran, 'Every man is a potential rapist,' and I hated it. When I challenged it once a female friend explained why they were shouting the phrase. I still didn't understand, so she called me 'a typical product of the sexist, male-dominated, elitist environment you've grown up in', words that still ring in my ears to this day. She was right, unfortunately, as I had grown up with all the values of that world, even though I'd hated the school, and most of what it stood for. It took me ages to begin to understand that she was expressing the way the world felt to *her*, and what it was like to negotiate love, sex, and relationships with men. It isn't just the night that needs to be reclaimed, dismantled, and rebuilt, but also our relationships and culture. The stories are right in front of us. Will another backlash prevail, or will change finally come?

All countries and cultures have significant problems with sexual offending to varying degrees. Most have the same range of myths and misconceptions about offending, too, particularly about victim behaviour. Even the most progressive of countries will struggle with certain issues. A senior police colleague, in a highly enlightened northern European country, wants to start using our training techniques. He recognises, within the fabric of his community, what he describes as 'traditional thinking'. By this he means victim blaming and a culture of disbelief, wrapped up in phrases like 'family values' and 'common sense'.

Across cultures, we are all on a continuum of knowledge, understanding, and change about the sexual harms in our communities, so judge not lest we be judged. There is always room for optimism, however, because people and cultures change. A researcher in Canada looked at sexual attitudes, and adherence to rape myths, in students who had grown up exclusively in Canada, and students who had migrated from other countries. Some student groups had more conservative attitudes to sex than the Canadian-born students, and stronger adherence to rape myths. However, when researchers factored in their length of residency in Canada, they found that the longer they had been exposed to the values of the new culture, the less they adhered to those myths.[1]

There is a phrase I have always liked, although I don't know where it comes from, as I heard it at a conference, many years ago. It goes, 'For every complex problem, there is a simple solution ... and it's wrong.'

In Michael Moore's documentary *Bowling for Columbine*, made after one of the many US school shootings, he asks people their theories about why there are so many gun deaths in America, and why other countries don't have a similar problem. The answers are all simple: it's about poverty, or unemployment, or too many guns, or violent video game culture, and so on. Moore demonstrates that each of these phenomena is present in other countries, who do not have substantial issues with gun violence, suggesting that the prospect of change lies only in a more complex analysis. Moore also confronts some of the vested interests behind the gun lobby, provoking us to see how many people and institutions stand against any prospect of change, even though one might think that trying to prevent the violent deaths of schoolchildren would require little motivation. The same applies here, in responding to the breadth of sexual offending in our communities, with obvious interests standing against changes to the justice system or creating communities of genuine equality. The task is just as pressing but, unlike the gun issue, exists in every country around the world.

I once met with a survivor of child sexual abuse who was going to help us educate our investigators. Two things struck me most about our conversation, the first being that she felt she had now fully recovered from the abuse and was a better person for it, as she had learned so much about herself. The second was her ironclad conviction that the system she had experienced needed to be changed. She had been abused for eleven years and spent five years navigating the criminal justice system, only for him to be given a four-year sentence. 'You do the maths,' she said. She is now on a government committee looking at improvements, focusing on secondary prevention strategies for high-risk groups.

Whatever the risk to our communities, somebody some-where is doing something creative to address it. Here are just a few examples. There is an advertising campaign in Germany, promoting a therapeutic programme that targets people who are thinking of sexually abusing children, called the Dunkenfeld Project.[2] The programme estimates that there are approximately 250,000 men with paedophilic interests in Germany, and argues that the best community protection measure is to work with these men before they abuse. The UK and Ireland have a similar project, originating in the US, called Stop It Now, which offers counselling and support to people concerned about their online behaviour, or their thoughts towards children. Interestingly, almost a third of referrals to UK Stop It Now come from police.[3]

Nightclubs in my hometown of Melbourne, spurred on by reports of abuse in their venues, have introduced zero-tolerance policies for sexually harassing behaviour, illustrating their approach on the walls of the venue, training staff in how to deal with such behaviour, and encouraging reporting.[4] University campuses in many countries, having finally recognised the level of abuse occurring within their walls, are beginning to take concerted action. The risks are most acute in the first term of the year, when new students attend alcohol-fuelled events, but have relatively few friends to look out for them.[5] In 2013, the US enacted Federal legislation to mandate policies and training for universities to follow. Some of these policies, unfortunately, were overturned by the subsequent administration.[6]

The most important strategies, which also represent the biggest challenge, are those of primary prevention, stopping problems from developing in the first place. As far back as anyone can remember, prevention strategies have been about teaching women and girls to protect themselves – be careful what you're wearing and where you go, don't talk to strangers etc. Not only has this failed, but it has contributed to a culture of victim blame. Offending starts with offenders, so most measures need to start with strategies for educating boys and men.

I have asked a lot of people what they think would stop offending happening in the first place. The most popular answer, by far, was a community defined by equality. Inclusivity and respectful relationships came up a lot, too, without which we continue to allow vulnerabilities that offenders can exploit. In terms of sexual relationships, lots of people pointed to our construct of consent as a critical problem. It is not only a legal word, used to define what is not wanted, it's also supposed to express what we do want. What would happen if we moved, like Iceland and Sweden, to an understanding of consent where taking steps to understand what the other person wanted was normal, and everybody was taught how to ask, 'What are you up for?' A friend once told me that the sexiest sentence she ever heard, during the early stages of a passionate encounter, was, 'What do you like?' God, I wish I had known that earlier in life. I may not have had more sex, but I bet it would have been better sex. Some people suggest that it would be too difficult for young men to adjust to such changes. If that is true, and I do not believe it is, what does it say about the distinctions we draw between the ways young men and young women see sex? And what an indictment of the way we educate young people about sex, relationships, and sexuality.

In some countries, the traditional sex education models of biological instruction and warnings about STDs have been replaced by models prioritising relationships and communication, or 'instruction on living together', as Sweden calls it.[7] The idea is for young people to see sex as a natural part of relationships and to reduce fear, shame, and silence. Research is clear that young people who receive sex education, in this model, have sex later than those who don't, and have fewer STIs and early pregnancies.[8] Abstinence-only-based models are not nearly as effective in achieving those aims,[9] showing yet again that young people need to be given the right information.

When I speak to people about this book, women have shown much more enthusiasm for it than men. One male colleague, required to read the book for legal vetting, told me that some of it was interesting, but he finished by saying, 'I didn't know you were … (long pause) … like that.' I was not entirely sure what he meant, but I'm certain it was not a compliment. Several of the women who've read it have said, 'I don't think it's the kind of book my husband/partner/any man would want to read, although I'd love him/them to read the part about X, or Y.' Their reasons have been varied: that there is too much about this topic in the news already, that men are sick of hearing about it, men are feeling under siege/criticised etc. I read a newspaper column yesterday, provocatively proposing that the reason women still experience so much abuse and hurt, and that men still advance at their expense, is because men don't even have the curiosity to care about women's lives. The very next article I read was about a man who is going to be confirmed in a position of considerable power, mostly by other men, despite the testimony of several women that he has a history of sexually abusive behaviour.

I have spent my career listening to men and boys tell me about their behaviour. It was easy to see them as separate entities, or men who had 'crossed a line'. It took me ages to understand that it is not a line. The most uncomfortable aspect of understanding sexual crime, at least for us men, is that sexual abuses are overwhelmingly perpetrated by our fellow men. I don't know if I would have absorbed this fully if I hadn't seen and heard it in my work so relentlessly, because it is profoundly uncomfortable to see your likeness in a pool of abuse and violence. We exist in a space where this behaviour is a part of our road map of life. It takes a long time to realise the map is there and to decide to be a part of redrawing it.

In Laura Bates's definitive guide to misogynistic misery, *Everyday Sexism*, her arguments wrap around the testimony of women and girls who have written in to her Everyday Sexism Project, numbering more than 100,000 and counting. She memorably describes women's abuse and harassment experiences as 'moments that slip like beads onto an endless string to form a necklace that only you can feel the weight of. It can drag you down without another person ever witnessing a single thing.'

All too often, men are responsible for the beads. I know women sexually offend too, and that they can be violent and abusive in relationships, but the scale is different. If you piled up all the beads, one would be a hillock and the other a mountain. As men, we may be caught in abusive and disheartening relationships, but we are rarely afraid for our lives. Neither do we prepare ourselves, each day, for the potential hostilities of the world around us. I was discussing harassment with a female colleague at work, recently, when she began telling me about her morning routine, as she decides how to deal with the world she will inevitably confront: on public transport, walking through the streets, at work, and for whatever she might choose to do after work. She explained how she moderated her dress, hair, make-up, and accessories, to minimise the inevitable unwanted attention she receives. She also described a form of psychological routine she would follow, to prepare her for what would lie ahead. Most men do not do this. The strongest evidence I have found of a culture where sexual aggression is tolerated, and even promoted, is in the morning routines of my colleague. If anyone still wants to say that the harassments of daily life are not that serious, suggest they go to YouTube and search '10 hours walking in New York City as a woman'. Ten hours of pestering, being followed, hassled, commanded to smile, intimidated ... it's awful, and exhausting, and it's not even happening to you. If that does not get them, suggest they ask the women in their life.

It could be different. As it happens, I know lots of men who care deeply about these issues. I suspect if you are a man reading this chapter you care about them too. You probably also recognise, like me, when you have contributed to the problem. Growing up in the era that I did, the messages I was taught seem positively archaic. Add to that, an all-boys private school system, surely the epicentre of English patriarchal, privileged, and misogynistic thought, and you can imagine the language and values I inherited. I'm sure every man can also remember the times, like me, when we either said something regrettable, laughed at something because we felt we had to, or stepped back rather than forward when there was an opportunity to intervene. We simply cannot do that anymore. Abusive men often do things away from the eyes and ears of others. If that is the case, all we can do is listen when victims come forward and tell us about it. But when they do it in public, we need to

witness it, challenge it, and do something about it. I apologise
for the cliché, but it really is as simple as: if you are not part
of the solution, then you are part of the problem. It does not
need to be a heroic act. It can be as simple as not laughing at
the joke. I asked my friend Maree what change would look like
and immediately she said, 'Well, not calling anyone "a girl", as
an insult, would be a start.'

In case you're wondering how not laughing at a misogynistic
joke can make a difference, particularly to tackling the sexual
abuse of children, which might seem a distinctly different, and
distant, problem, then Maree's answer holds the key. Using
'girl' as an insult, with its inherent disrespect of gender, creates
an inequality, which creates a vulnerability. And offenders
target vulnerability. While the vulnerability may be greater
for girls, boys also suffer from a culture's lack of respect for
the voices of children. The vulnerability created by disrespect
and inequality also helps us understand why so many groups,
outside the dominant norms, are disproportionately affected.

If challenging inequality and disrespect is the start, what's
next? In the early days of acknowledging and tackling child
sexual abuse, there was a lot of focus on creating 'aware
cultures', which could better prevent and respond to abuse,
in organisations that worked with children. Step one was
acknowledging the extent of the problem, followed by
information and training. Then came the creation of rules for
conduct, attempting to make offenders visible should they try
to break them. Finally, developing pathways for disclosure and
reporting that children could have confidence in, knowing
they would be listened to, understood, and protected. The
work is still developing, of course, but it's a model that could
be used to counter sexual harassment and assault in our

workplaces: understand the extent of the problem, create prevention strategies, put boundaries in place, and establish cultures of listening and safety. Whatever organisations, institutions, or workplaces you are involved in, do they have these practices?

I started the book by suggesting that both child and adult victims of sexual crime, when they come to decide whether to report what has happened to them, are afraid of us. At the heart of this fear is the belief that we won't understand, may not believe, and will even blame them. The huge change in police attitudes, once knowledge and victim-centric practice arrived, suggests the same approach might work with all of us. Without a move from victim-blaming, listening to science and eradicating misconceptions, we are destined to repeat this miserable, terrifying part of our history and culture. Judith Herman suggests that, while our current community standards remain, any justice system is destined to fail, because 'the so-called community cannot be counted on to do justice to victims because public attitudes toward these crimes are ambivalent at best ... The community support that victims so ardently desire does not presently exist.'[10] She wrote those words in 2005. Was she right and, if so, do these words still hold true, or are we finally turning awareness into action? If we are, then the change will be us.

History will see the way we treat each other, in the early twenty-first century, as primitive. In a hundred years, I hope they look back on us with a mixture of disgust and admiration. Disgust that we let so many suffer for so long, and admiration that, in this time, change came sweeping in. Real, wholesale, permanent change.

We are at a crossroads, with an opportunity to change the dynamic of our relationships and find better ways to justice.

It is a time to be brave, and to ignore the inevitable backlash from the status quo and the vested interests. A time for us men to get off the sidelines and be on the right side of history. A time to be allies and brothers, give up the privileges we enjoy at others' expense, and discover something better. We will all need to choose a side, because it's going to take a while, and it is not going to be pretty.

There is a song I like, written by friends of mine. They live their values more clearly than anyone else I know, advocating for the planet and for social justice. Their songs often challenge the listener to wake from complacency and think about an issue. In my favourite, there is a clear provocation to consider what values and beliefs we might have at our core. The chorus line demands we think about who we stand with and what we stand for.

So, 'Who do you stand with, and what do you stand for?'

Notes

Introduction

1. Kate B. Wolitzky-Taylor, Heidi S. Resnick, Jenna L. McCauley, Ananda B. Amstadter, Dean G. Kilpatrick and Kenneth J. Ruggiero, 'Is Reporting of Rape on the Rise? A Comparison of Women with Reported Versus Unreported Rape Experiences in the National Women's Study-Replication', *Journal of Interpersonal Violence*, vol. 26, no. 4 (2010), pp. 807–32. Australian Bureau of Statistics, *Personal Safety Survey*, 2013.

2. This is an extrapolation from three different sets of statistics. If approximately one in eight adults report (Stern report/NSB UK), and one in ten children (see note 3), but only one-third of reporters do so within seventy-two hours of the offence (Victoria Police stats) – seventy-two hours is a common timeframe for designating an 'immediate' report – then the figure for overall 'immediate' reporting is about 5 per cent.

3. Kamala London, Maggie Bruck, Daniel B. Wright and Stephen J. Ceci, 'Review of the contemporary literature on how children report sexual abuse to others: Findings, methodological issues and implications for forensic interviewers', *Memory*, vol. 16, no. 1, *New Insights in Trauma and Memory* (2008): https://doi.org/10.1080/09658210701725732; Lorraine Radford, Susana Corral, Christine Bradley, Helen Fisher, Claire Bassett, Nick Howat and Stephan Collishaw, *Child Abuse and Neglect in the UK Today* (NSPCC, London, 2011).

4. Harriet Harman, *A Woman's Work* (Allen Lane, London, 2017).

5. Christine Eastwood, 'The Experiences of Child Complainants of Sexual Abuse in the Criminal Justice System', *Australian Institute of Criminology Trends and Issues*, no. 250 (May 2003).

6. K. Daly and B. Bouhours, 'Rape and attrition in the legal process: A comparative analysis of five countries', *Crime and Justice*, no. 39 (2010), pp. 565–650; doi: 10.1086/65310

7. **'90-95 per cent of sexual offenders are male.'** Office of National Statistics (UK): 'Sexual offences in England and Wales', year ending March 2017: 'The vast majority of respondents who had experienced rape or assault by penetration since they were sixteen reported that the offender(s) were male (99 per cent), with 65 per cent of victims reporting that the offender was a male aged between twenty and thirty (Appendix Table 13).' Some research suggests offending by females (who predominantly offend other females,

usually children) is under-reported, and that the real figure may be as high as 11 per cent – e.g., Franca Cortoni, Kelly M. Babchishin, Clémence Rat, 'The Proportion of Sexual Offenders Who Are Female Is Higher Than Thought: A Meta-Analysis', *Criminal Justice and Behavior*, vol. 44, no. 2 (2016), pp. 145–62.

'At least 30 per cent of female sexual offenders co-offend with a male.' Katria S. Williams, David M. Bierie, 'An Incident-Based Comparison of Female and Male Sexual Offenders', *Sexual Abuse* (ATSA), vol. 27, no. 3 (2017), pp. 235–57; Franca Cortoni, *Women Who Sexually Abuse: Assessment, Treatment and Management* (Safer Society Press, Brandon, VT, 2018).

'Eighty per cent of rape, sexual assault and child sexual abuse victims are female.' Office of National Statistics (UK): 'Sexual offences in England and Wales', year ending March 2017.

'One in five girls will be sexually abused in childhood (and one in twelve boys).' K. M. Gorey and D. R. Leslie, 'The prevalence of child sexual abuse: Integrative review adjustment for potential response and measurement biases', *Child Abuse and Neglect*, no. 21 (1997), pp. 391–8; doi:10.1016/S0145-2134(96)00180-9. N. Pereda, G. Guilera, M. Forns and J. Gómez-Benito, 'The prevalence of child sexual abuse in community and student samples: A meta-analysis', *Clinical Psychology Review*, no. 29 (2008), pp. 328–38; doi: 10.1016/j.cpr.2009.02.007. M. Stoltenborgh, M. H. van Ijzendoorn, E. M. Euser and M. J. Bakermans-Kranenburg, 'A global perspective on child sexual abuse: meta-analysis of prevalence around the world', *Child Maltreatment*, no. 16 (2011), pp. 79–101; doi: 10.1177/1077559511403920

'One in six women will be sexually assaulted or raped as adults.' UK Office for National Statistics (ONS) (2013); Australian Bureau of Statistics – *Personal Safety Survey* (1996); Australian Bureau of Statistics – *Personal Safety Survey* (2012).

'Women are far more likely to be victims of sexual harassment than men.' Stop Violence Against Women, a project of the Advocates for Human Rights, *Report on the prevalence of sexual harassment* (2010); Australian Bureau of Statistics (ABS), *Personal Safety Survey* (2005); Australian Bureau of Statistics (ABS), *Personal Safety Survey* (2016); http://www.haut-conseil-egalite. gouv.fr/IMG/pdf/hcefh_avis_harcelement_transports-20150410.pdf; 'Reports of sexual assaults on London Underground soar', PA Media, 23 September 2019; Victorian Human Rights and Equal Opportunity Commission, *Independent review into sex discrimination and sexual harassment, including predatory behaviour in Victoria Police*, Phase One Report (2015).

'Violence and sexual violence are the number one "burden of disease" issue for women.' Lori L. Heise, Jacqueline Pitanguy and Adrienne Germain, 'Violence against women: the hidden health burden' (English), *World Bank Discussion Papers*, no. WDP 255 (World Bank, Washington DC, 1994); http:// documents.worldbank.org/curated/en/489381468740165817/Violence-against-women-the-hidden-health-burden-Burden-of-disease; ANROWS,

Examination of the burden of disease of intimate partner violence against women in 2011, final report (30 October 2016); Prof. Jacquelyn C. Campbell, 'Health consequences of intimate partner violence', *Lancet*, vol. 359, issue 9314 (13 April 2002), pp. 1331–6.

'**Only one in eight women will report rape or sexual assault, mostly due to a fear of community judgment and our culture of victim-blaming. Few will do so at the time of the offence.**' Ministry of Justice, Home Office, Office of National Statistics (MoJ, HO, ONS) (2013); MoJ, HO, ONS (2017); Kate B. Wolitzky-Taylor, Heidi S. Resnick, Jenna L. McCauley, Ananda B. Amstadter, Dean G. Kilpatrick and Kenneth J. Ruggiero, 'Is Reporting of Rape on the Rise? A Comparison of Women with Reported Versus Unreported Rape Experiences in the National Women's Study-Replication', *Journal of Interpersonal Violence*, vol. 26, issue 4 (2010), pp. 807–32.

'**Up until 2015/16, fewer than two in ten sexual crimes reported to police were heard in court. In the last twelve months that number has gone down significantly.**' Ministry of Justice, Home Office, Office of National Statistics (MoJ, HO, ONS) (2013); MoJ, HO, ONS (2017); Home Office, *Crime Outcomes in England and Wales*: year ending March 2019, Statistical Bulletin HOSB 12/19 (July 2019).

'**Sexual crimes have some of the lowest conviction rates of all interpersonal crime. These rates have also declined in the last thirty years.**' K. Daly and B. Bouhours, 'Rape and attrition in the legal process: A comparative analysis of five countries', *Crime and Justice*, no. 39 (2010), pp. 565–650; doi: 10.1086/65310; J. Lovett and L. Kelly, *Different Systems, Similar Outcomes? Tracking attrition in reported rape cases across Europe* (Child and Woman Abuse Studies Unit, CWASU, 2009).

'**The chance of a rapist facing consequences for his offending is very small. Hardly any will go to prison.**' Jörg-Martin Jehle, 'Attrition and Conviction Rates of Sexual Offences in Europe: Definitions and Criminal Justice Responses', *European Journal on Criminal Policy and Research*, vol. 18, issue 1 (March 2012), pp. 145–61; Australian Law Reform Commission, *A National Legal Response* (ALRC Report 114), Section 26: Reporting, Prosecution and Pre-trial Processes/Attrition in sexual assault cases (2010; online 11 November 2010); Lovett and Kelly, *Different Systems, Similar Outcomes?*, op. cit.

Author's note

1. ONS, *Sex Offending in England and Wales*: year ending March 2017. https://www.ons.gov.uk/peoplepopulationandcommunity/crimeandjustice/articles/sexualoffencesinenglandandwales/yearendingmarch2017; 'Sexual Assault of Young Children as Reported to Law Enforcement: Victim, Incident, and Offender Characteristics', US Department of Justice, Bureau of Justice Statistics, 2000.

Part I. Victims

1. Mark Chipperfield, *Telegraph*, 28 October 2006; Mark Tran, *Guardian*, 26 October 2006. Emily Havens, 'What were you wearing exhibit?', The Spectrum, 3 April 2018.

2. Parnian Toofanian, 'Understanding post-traumatic growth among sexual assault survivors', Post-Traumatic Growth Research Group, Department of Psychology, Palo Alto University (2010; online 2014).Lovett and Kelly, *Different Systems, Similar Outcomes?*, op. cit.

3. V. Stern, *The Stern Review*: A report by Baroness Stern CBE of an independent review into how rape complainants are handled by public authorities in England and Wales (Cabinet Office, London, 2010).

1. How much is this happening?

1. *Stern Review*, op. cit; C. J. Eastwood, S. M. Kift and R. Grace, 'Attrition in child sexual assault cases: Why Lord Chief Justice Hale got it wrong', *Journal of Judicial Administration*, no. 16 (2006), pp. 81–91; Victoria Police statistics quoted in Darwinkel (2013); Australian Bureau of Statistics, *Personal Safety Survey* (2007); see introduction, note 2.

2. Ministry of Justice, Home Office, Office of National Statistics (MoJ, HO, ONS) (2013).

3. MoJ, HO, ONS (2017).

4. *Crime Outcomes in England and Wales*: year ending March 2019, Statistical Bulletin HOSB 12/19; Home Office (July 2019).

5. UK Office for National Statistics (ONS) (2013); Australian Bureau of Statistics, *Personal Safety Survey* (1996); Australian Bureau of Statistics, *Personal Safety Survey* (2012).

6. US Department of Justice figures (1997). Published online by Rape, Abuse & Incest National Network (RAINN); NSPCC (2011).

7. MoJ, HO, ONS, *An Overview of Sexual Offending in England and Wales – Aggregate data 2009–12* (2013), p. 11.

8. Cindy Tarczon and Antonia Quadara, 'The nature and extent of sexual assault and abuse in Australia', ACSSA Resource Sheet no. 5 (December 2012).

9. K. M. Gorey and D. R. Leslie, 'The prevalence of child sexual abuse: Integrative review adjustment for potential response and measurement biases', *Child Abuse & Neglect*, no. 21 (1997), pp. 391–8; doi:10.1016/ S0145-2134(96)00180-9; N. Pereda, G. Guilera, M. Forns and J. Gómez-Benito, 'The prevalence of child sexual abuse in community and student samples: A meta-analysis', *Clinical Psychology Review*, no. 29 (2008), pp. 328–38; doi: 10.1016/j.cpr.2009.02.007; Stoltenborgh et al., 'A global perspective on child sexual abuse', op. cit.; Fanslow et al., 'Prevalence of child sexual abuse reported by a cross-sectional sample of New Zealand women', op. cit.; NSPCC – figures published 2011; D. M. Fergusson, M.

T. Lynskey and L. Horwood, 'Childhood Sexual Abuse and Psychiatric Disorder in Young Adulthood: I. Prevalence of Sexual Abuse and Factors Associated with Sexual Abuse', *Journal of the American Academy of Child and Adolescent Psychiatry*, vol. 35, issue 10 (October 1996), pp. 1355–64; doi: https://doi.org/10.1097/00004583-199610000-00023

10. D. Finkelhor, R. K. Ormrod, H. A. Turner and S. L. Hamby, The victimization of children and youth: A comprehensive, national survey. *Child Maltreatment,* vol. 10, issue 1 (2005), pp. 5–25.

11. Stoltenborgh et al., 'A global perspective on child sexual abuse', op. cit.

12. John Briere and Diana M. Elliott, 'Prevalence and psychological sequelae of self-reported childhood physical and sexual abuse in a general population sample of men and women', *Child Abuse and Neglect*, vol. 27, issue 10 (October 2003), pp. 1205–22.

13. *Crime in England and Wales* (Office for National Statistics, 2018).

14. Australian Bureau of Statistics, *Personal Safety Survey* (2005).

15. ABS, *Personal Safety Survey* (2012).

16. MoJ, HO, ONS (2013).

17. M. J. Dorahy and K. Clearwater, 'Shame and guilt in men exposed to childhood sexual abuse: A qualitative investigation', *Journal of Child Sexual Abuse,* vol. 21, issue 2 (2012), pp. 155–75.

18. E. Steever, V. M. Follette and A. E. Naugle, 'The correlates of male adults' perceptions of their early childhood experiences', *Journal of Traumatic Stress*, vol. 14, issue 1 (2001), pp. 189–205.

19. D. M. Fergusson and P. E. Mullen, *Childhood Sexual Abuse: An evidence-based perspective* (Sage, London, 1999).

20. P. Parkinson, K. Oates, and A. Jayakody, 'Breaking the long silence: Reports of child sexual abuse in the Anglican Church of Australia', *Ecclesiology,* vol. 6, issue 2 (2010), pp. 183–200; William C. Holmes, 'Sexual Abuse of Boys: Definition, Prevalence, Correlates, Sequelae, and Management', *Journal of the American Medical Association*, vol. 280, no. 21 (December 1998).

21. E. Romano and R. De Luca, 'Male Sexual Abuse: A review of effects, abuse characteristics, and links with later psychological functioning', *Aggression and Violent Behaviour,* vol. 6, issue 1 (2001), pp. 55–78; N. Garnefski and E. Arends, 'Sexual abuse and adolescent maladjustment: Differences between male and female victims', *Journal of Adolescence*, vol. 21, issue 1 (1998), pp. 99–107; Australian Institute for Family Studies, 'The long-term effects of child sexual abuse' (CFCA Paper no. 11, January 2013); Myriam S. Denov, 'The Long-Term Effects of Child Sexual Abuse by Female Perpetrators: A Qualitative Study of Male and Female Victims', *Journal of Interpersonal Violence*, vol. 19, no. 10 (October 2004), pp. 1137–56.

22. Cortoni, *Women Who Sexually Abuse*, op. cit.; F. Syed and S. Williams, *Case studies of female sexual offenders in the Correctional Service of Canada* (Correctional Service of Canada, Ottawa, 1996); A. Burgess-Proctor, E. B. Comartin and S. P. Kubiak, 'Comparing female- and male-perpetrated

child sexual abuse: A mixed-methods analysis', *Journal of Child Sexual Abuse*, no. 26 (2017), pp. 657–76.

23. Lara Stemple, Andrew Flores, and Ilhan H. Meyer, 'Sexual victimization perpetrated by women: Federal data reveal surprising prevalence', *Aggression and Violent Behavior*, no. 34 (2017), pp. 302–11; Cortoni, Babchishin, and Rat, 'The Proportion of Sexual Offenders Who Are Female Is Higher Than Thought,' op. cit.

24. Jill Johansson-Love and William Fremouw, 'A critique of the female sexual perpetrator research', *Aggression and Violent Behavior*, no. 11 (2005), pp. 12–26.

25. Cortoni, *Women Who Sexually Abuse*, op. cit.; Williams and Bierie, 'An Incident-Based Comparison of Female and Male Sexual Offenders', op. cit.

26. S. Hackett, *Children and young people with harmful sexual behaviours*, Research in Practice (NSPCC, 2014).

27. Gatehouse Centre, Royal Children's Hospital, Melbourne.

28. I. Wolak, D. Finkelhor and K. J. Mitchell, 'Online predators and their victims: Myths, realities, and implications for prevention and treatment', American Psychologist, 63, 111–128.

29. Australian National Research Organisation for Women's Safety, 'Sexual Assault and domestic violence in the context of co-occurrence and re-victimisation', *Landscapes,* State of Knowledge paper (13/ 2015); P. Cox, 'Violence against women: additional analysis of the Australian Bureau of Statistics' *Personal Safety Survey, 2012'* (*ANROWS Horizons* 1, Sydney, 2015).

30. Sara-Beth Plummer and Patricia A. Findlay, 'Women with Disabilities' Experience with Physical and Sexual Abuse: A Review of the Literature and Implications for the Field', *Trauma, Violence & Abuse*, vol. 13, no. 1 (2012), pp. 15–29; Martin et al., 'Physical and Sexual Assault of Women with Disabilities', *Violence Against Women*, vol. 12, no. 9 (September 2006), pp. 823–37; World Health Organisation (WHO), *World Report on Disability* (2011); S. Murray and A. Powell, 'Sexual assaults and adults with a disability: enabling recognition, disclosure, and a just response', Australian Centre for the Study of Sexual Assault (ACSSA), Issues paper no. 9 (NCVRW, 2018). Disability statistics: US DoJ Office on Violence Against Women (2018); 'Violence against people with disabilities occurs at alarming rates', *Centre on Victimisation and Safety* (2018).

31. S. Murray and M. Heenan, 'Reported rapes in Victoria: Police responses to victims with a psychiatric disability or mental health issue', *Current Issues in Criminal Justice*, vol. 23, no. 3 (March 2012), pp. 353–68.

32. Muslim Women's Network UK (online September 2013); ONS, Statistics on race and the criminal justice system (2012); Australian Institute of Health and Welfare (AIHW), *Family, domestic and sexual violence in Australia 2018* (2018).

33. Emily F. Rothman, Deinera Exner and Allyson L. Baughman, 'The Prevalence of Sexual Assault Against People Who Identify as Gay, Lesbian, or Bisexual in the United States: A Systematic Review', *Trauma, Violence, & Abuse*, vol. 12, no. 2 (2011), pp. 55–66; M. L. Walters and M. J. Breiding, National Intimate Partner Sexual Violence Survey (published online by the Centre for Disease Control, CDC, 2010).

34. Krug et al., World report on violence and health (WHO, 2002).

35. Alexandra Neame, 'Beyond "drink spiking". Drug- and alcohol- facilitated sexual assault', Australian Centre for the Study of Sexual Assault, Briefing no. 2 (November 2003); J. A. Hall and C.B.T. Moore, 'Drug-facilitated sexual assault – A review', *Journal of Forensic and Legal Medicine* no. 15 (2008), pp. 291–7; Michael Hurley, Helen Parker, and David L. Wells, 'The epidemiology of drug-facilitated sexual assault', *Journal of Clinical and Forensic Medicine*, no. 13 (2006), pp. 181–85.

36. Victoria Police Family Violence Command statistics (2016).

37. https://www.gov.uk/government/publications/domestic-abuse-bill-2020-factsheets/domestic-abuse-bill-2020-overarching-factsheet

38. J. Campbell. et al., 'Risk Factors for Femicide in Abusive Relationships: Results from a Multisite Control Study', *American Journal of Public Health*, no. 93 (7) (2003), pp. 1089–97.

39. Heather A. Turner, David Finkelhor and Richard Ormrod, 'Poly-Victimisation in a National Sample of Children and Youth', *American Journal of Preventive Medicine*, vol. 38, issue 3 (March 2010), pp. 323–330; Australian Institute of Family Studies, *Children's exposure to domestic and family violence. Key issues and responses*, CFCA Paper no. 36 (December 2015); Sherry Hamby, David Finkelhor, Heather Turner and Richard Ormrod, 'The overlap of witnessing partner violence with child maltreatment and other victimisations in a nationally representative sample of youth', *Child Abuse and Neglect*, no. 34 (2010), pp. 734–41; Anne E. Appel and George W. Holden, 'The co-occurrence of spouse and physical abuse: A review and appraisal', *Journal of Family Psychology*, vol. 12, no. 4 (1998), pp. 578–99.

40. Zelimar S. Bidarra, Genevieve Lessard and Anni Dumont, 'Co-occurrence of intimate partner violence and sexual abuse: Prevalence, risk factors and related issues', *Child Abuse and Neglect*, no. 55 (2016), pp. 10–21; Herrenkohl et al., 'Intersection of Child Abuse and Children's Exposure to Domestic Violence', *Trauma, Violence and Abuse*, vol. 9, issue 2 (2008), pp. 84–99; https://doi.org/10.1177/1524838008314797; G. Bedi and C. Goddard, 'Intimate partner violence: What are the impacts on children?', *Australian Psychologist*, vol. 42, issue 1 (online 17 January 2007), pp. 66–77.

41. David Finkelhor and Lisa Jones, University of New Hampshire, 'Why Have Child Maltreatment and Child Victimisation Declined?', *Journal of Social Issues*, vol. 62, no. 4 (2006), pp. 685–716; S. Mishra and M. Lalumiere, 'Is the crime drop of the 1990s in Canada and the USA associated with a general

decline in risky and health-related behavior?', *Social Science & Medicine,* vol. 68, issue 1 (January 2009), pp. 39–48.

42. NSPCC, 'Child sex offence recorded on average every 8 minutes in UK' (20 February 2018).

2. The aftermath

1. RAINN. 'Effects of sexual violence' (published online 2018); Rebecca Campbell, Tracy Sefl and Courtney E. Ahrens, 'The Physical Health Consequences of Rape: Assessing Survivors' Somatic Symptoms in a Racially Diverse Population', *Women's Studies Quarterly,* vol. 31, no. ½ (2003); Fiona Mason and Zoe Lodrick, 'Psychological consequences of sexual assault', *Best Practice and Research Clinical Obstetrics and Gynaecology,* no. 27 (2013), pp. 27–37; CDC, 'Sexual Violence: Consequences' (published online 10 April 2018).

2. R. Kimerling and K. S. Calhoun, 'Somatic symptoms, social support and treatment-seeking among sexual assault victims', *Journal of Consulting and Clinical Psychology,* vol. 62, no. 2 (April 1994), pp. 333–40; P. Salmon and S. Calderbank, 'The relationship of childhood physical and sexual abuse to adult illness behaviour', *Journal of Psychosomatic Research,* vol. 40, issue 3 (March 1996), pp. 329–36.

3. Lori L. Heise et al., 'Violence against women', op. cit.; ANROWS, 'Examination of the burden of disease of intimate partner violence against women in 2011', Final report (30 October 2016); Prof. Jacquelyn C. Campbell, 'Health consequences of intimate partner violence', *Lancet,* vol. 359, issue 9314 (13 April 2002), pp. 1331–6.

4. A. Browne and S. S. Bassuk, 'Intimate violence in the lives of homeless and poor housed women: Prevalence and patterns in an ethnically diverse sample', *American Journal of Orthopsychiatry,* vol. 67, no. 2 (1997), pp. 261–78; http://dx.doi.org/10.1037/h0080230; Margot Breton and Terry Bunston, 'Physical and Sexual Violence in the Lives of Homeless Women', *Canadian Journal of Community Mental Health,* vol. 11, no. 1 (1 May 2009), pp 29–44; https://doi.org/10.7870/cjcmh-1992-0003

5. D. L. Fergusson, L. J. Horwood and M. T. Lynskey, 'Childhood Sexual Abuse and Psychiatric Disorder in Young Adulthood: II. Psychiatric Outcomes of Childhood Sexual Abuse', *Journal of the American Academy of Child and Adolescent Psychiatry,* vol. 35, issue 10 (October 1996), pp. 1365–74; M. Cheasty, A. W. Clare and C. Collins, 'Relation between sexual abuse in childhood and adult depression: case-control study', *British Medical Journal,* no. 316 (1998).

6. M. C. Cutajar, P. E. Mullen, J. R. Ogloff, S. D. Thomas, D. L. Wells and J. Spataro, 'Schizophrenia and other psychotic disorders in a cohort of sexually abused children', *Archives of General Psychiatry,* no. 67 (2010), pp. 1114–19; doi:10.1001/archgenpsychiatry.2010.147

7. J. Cashmore and R. Shackel, 'The long-term effects of child sexual abuse', CFCA paper no. 11 (January 2013); NSPCC, 'Sexual abuse: Signs, indicators and effects' (published online 2018); US National Center for Victims of Crime, 'Effects of child sexual abuse on victims' (published online 2018).

8. P. Cox, 'Violence against women: Additional analysis of the Australian Bureau of Statistics' *Personal Safety Survey* 2012', *ANROWS Horizons 1* (ANROWS, Sydney, 2015).

9. D. Allnock and P. Miller, *No one noticed, no one heard: A study of disclosures of child abuse* (NSPCC, 2013); Dr Catherine Esposito, 'Child sexual abuse and disclosure: What does research tell us?', Office of the Senior Practitioner NSW Department of Family and Community Services, December 2016.

10. M. R. Harvey, 'Towards an ecological understanding of resilience in trauma survivors: Implications for theory, research, and practice', *Journal of Aggression, Maltreatment and Trauma,* no. 14 (issues 1–2) (2007), pp. 9–32; C. Boyd, 'The impacts of sexual assault on women', Australian Centre for the Study of Sexual Assault (ACSSA) resource sheet (April 2011).

11. Judith Herman, 'Justice from the Victim's Perspective', *Violence Against Women,* vol. 11, no. 5 (May 2005), pp. 571–602.

3. Fight/Flight/Freeze/Surrender

1. Peter A. Levine PhD, *Trauma and Memory: Brain and body in a search for the living past* (North Atlantic Books, 2015).

2. Kristen L. Thompson, Susan M. Hannan and Lynsey R. Miron, 'Fight, flight and freeze: Threat sensitivity and emotion dysregulation in survivors of chronic maltreatment', *Personality and Individual Differences* no. 69 (2014), pp. 28–32; M. A. Hagenaars, J. F. Stins and K. Roelofs, 'Aversive life events enhance human freeze responses', *Journal of Experimental Psychology: General,* no. 141 (2012), pp. 98–105.

3. R. Campbell, 'The Neurobiology of Sexual Assault', National Institute of Justice (published online 3 December 2012); J. M. Heidt, B. P. Marx and J. P. Forsyth, 'Tonic immobility and child sexual abuse: A preliminary report evaluating the sequelae of rape-induced paralysis', *Behaviour Research and Therapy,* vol. 43, issue 9 (September 2005), pp. 1157–71; Kalaf et al., 'Sexual trauma is more strongly associated with tonic immobility than other types of trauma – A population-based study', *Journal of Affective Disorders,* no. 215 (2017), pp. 71–76.

4. Warwick Middleton and Jeremy Butler, 'Dissociative Identity Disorder: An Australian Series', *Australian and New Zealand Journal of Psychiatry,* vol. 32, issue 6 (1998), pp. 794–804.

5. Brunner et al., 'Dissociative symptomatology and traumatogenic factors in adolescent psychiatric patients', *Journal of Nervous and Mental Disease,* vol. 188, issue 2 (February 2000), pp. 71–77; Jeffrey A. Atlas, Kim Weissman and

Susan Liebowitz, 'Adolescent inpatients' history of abuse and dissociative identity disorder', *Psychological Reports*, vol. 80, issue 3 (1997), p. 1086.

6. Tim Barlass, 'Woman with multiple personalities to read impact statement in different "alters"', *Sydney Morning Herald* (online 31 May 2019).

4. Truth and lies

1. Penny Cooper and Michelle Mattison, 'Intermediaries, vulnerable people and the quality of evidence: An international comparison of three versions of the English intermediary model', *International Journal of Evidence and Proof*, vol. 2, no. 4 (2017), pp. 351–70.

2. Lord Justice Hale (1713), quoted in C. J. Eastwood, S. M. Kift and R. Grace, 'Attrition in child sexual assault cases: Why Lord Chief Justice Hale got it wrong', *Journal of Judicial Administration*, no. 16 (2006), pp. 81–91.

3. https://www.yorkshireeveningpost.co.uk/news/crime/its-really-hard-lady-brenda-hale-discusses-why-so-few-rape-allegations-result-prosecution-1374785

4. I. Coyle, P. Wilson, D. Field, C. Cuthbert and G. Miller, 'Out of the mouths of babes: The case for an increased use of expert evidence in the rebuttal of sexual abuse allegations by child witnesses', *Criminal Law Journal*, 33 (2009), pp. 139–164.

5. N. Trocmé and N. Bala, 'False allegations of abuse and neglect when parents separate', *Child Abuse & Neglect*, no. 29 (2005), pp. 1333–45; doi: 10.1016/j.chiabu.2004.06.016

6. H. McGee, M. O'Higgins, R. Garavan and R. Conroy, 'Rape and child sexual abuse: what beliefs persist about motives, perpetrators, and survivors?', *Journal of Interpersonal Violence*, no. 26 (2011), pp. 3580–93; doi: 0886260511403762

7. Victorian Law Reform Commission, *Sexual Offences: Final Report* (2004), p. 111.

8. Philip N. S. Rumney, 'False Allegations of Rape', *Cambridge Law Journal*, no. 65 (issue 1), March 2006, pp. 128–58; L. Kelly et al., 'A gap or a chasm? Attrition in reported rape cases', Home Office Research Study no. 293 (London 2005), pp. 46–47.

9. Gov.UK, Home Office 'No Crime' data 2012/13.

10. *The Age*, comments (18 July 2013).

11. D. Lisak, L. Gardinier, S. C. Nicksa and A. M. Cote, 'False allegations of sexual assault: an analysis of ten years of reported cases', *Violence Against Women*, no. 16 (2010), pp. 1318–34; doi: 10.1177/1077801210387747; L. Kelly, 'The (in) credible words of women: False allegations in European rape research', *Violence Against Women*, no. 16 (2010), pp. 1345–55; doi:10.1177/1077801210387748; K. A. Lonsway, 'Trying to move the elephant in the living room: Responding to the challenge of false rape reports', *Violence Against Women*, no. 16 (2010), pp. 1356–71; doi: 10.1177/107780121038775; C. Spohn, C. White and K. Tellis,

'Unfounding sexual assault: Examining the decision to unfound and identifying false reports', *Law & Society Review*, no. 48 (2014), pp. 161–92; doi: 10.1111/ lasr.12060; L. Wall and C. Tarczon, *True or False? The Contested Terrain of False Allegations* (Australian Institute of Family Studies, Melbourne, 2013).

12. M. Heenan and S. Murray, *Study of Reported Rapes: Victoria 2000–2003* (Australian Institute of Family Studies, Australian Centre for the Study of Sexual Assault, Melbourne, 2006).

13. Trocmé and Bala, 'False allegations of abuse and neglect when parents separate', op. cit.

14. Sopan Deb, 'Dylan Farrow accuses Woody Allen of sexual abuse in TV interview', *New York Times* (18 January 2018).

5. Myths and misconceptions

1. McGee et al., 'Rape and child sexual abuse: what beliefs persist about motives, perpetrators, and survivors?', op. cit.

2. Sexual Offences Act 2003, 1.2 – legislation.gov.uk

3. Australian Football League, Respect and Responsibility: pilot programme, 2005.

4. Australian Law Reform Commission, *Family Violence – A National Legal Response* (ALRC Report 114), chapter 25, 'Sexual Offences – Rape: The Penetrative Sexual Offence' (11 November 2010).

5. Thirteen-year-old was 'down with this': Quentin Tarantino defends Roman Polanski, *Age* (AAP) (7 February 2018); Stephanie Convery, *Guardian* (6 February 2018).

6. L. D. Cromer and R. E. Goldsmith, 'Child sexual abuse myths: Attitudes, beliefs, and individual differences', *Journal of Child Sexual Abuse*, no. 19 (2010), pp. 618–47; doi:10.1080/10538712.2010.522493

7. A. Cossins, J. Goodman-Delahunty and K. O'Brien, 'Uncertainty and misconceptions about child sexual abuse: Implications for the criminal justice system', *Psychiatry, Psychology and Law*, no. 16 (2009), pp. 435–52; doi:10.1080/13218710902930234

8. P. Cox, 'Violence against women: Additional analysis of the Australian Bureau of Statistics' *Personal Safety Survey 2012*, op. cit.; N. M. Heath, S. M. Lynch, A. M. Fritch, L. N. McArthur, and S. L. Smith, 'Silent survivors: Rape myth acceptance in incarcerated women's narratives of disclosure and reporting of rape', *Psychology of Women Quarterly*, no. 35 (2011), pp. 596–610.

9. M. A. Klippenstine and R. Schuller, 'Perceptions of sexual assault: Expectancies regarding the emotional response of a rape victim over time', *Psychology, Crime & Law*, 18(1),(2012),pp. 79–94; doi: 10.1080/1068316X. 2011.589389; Karl Ask, 'A Survey of Police Officers' and Prosecutors' Beliefs About Crime Victim Behaviors', *Journal of Interpersonal Violence*, no. 25 (6) (2010), pp. 1132–49.

10. Australian Bureau of Statistics, Personal Safety, Australia, 2012 (2013), 4906.0; M. L. Larsen, M. Hilden and Ø Lidegaard, 'Sexual assault: A descriptive study of 2,500 female victims over a 10-year period', *BJOG: An International Journal of Obstetrics & Gynaecology*, no. 122 (2015), pp. 577–84; Waterhouse et al. (2016).

11. Katie M. Edwards, Megan C. Kearns, Christine A. Gidycz, Karen S. Calhoun, 'Predictors of victim-perpetrator relationship stability following a sexual assault: a brief report', *Violence and Victims* (2012), vol. 27(1), pp. 25–32; doi: 10.1891/0886-6708.27.1.25

12. M. Carr, A. J. Thomas, D. Atwood, A. Muhar, K. Jarvis, K. and S. Wewerka, 'Debunking three rape myths', *Journal of Forensic Nursing*, no. 10 (4) (2014), pp. 217–25; A. Quadara, B. Fileborn and D. Parkinson, *The role of forensic medical evidence in the prosecution of adult sexual assault* (Australian Institute of Family Studies, Melbourne, 2013); G. F. Waterhouse, A. Reynolds and V. Egan, 'Myths and legends: The reality of rape offences reported to a UK police force', *European Journal of Psychology Applied to Legal Context*, no. 8 (1) (2016), pp. 1–10.

13. M. Clayton, M. D. Bullock PhD and Mace Beckson MD, 'Male Victims of Sexual Assault: Phenomenology, Psychology, Physiology', *Journal of the American Academy of Psychiatry and Law*, vol. 39 (2) (2011), pp.197–205.

14. S. Blackwell 'Child sexual abuse on trial in New Zealand', paper presented at the New Zealand Law Foundation Intensive Criminal Law Symposium, Auckland, 2007.

15. P. Tidmarsh, A. Quadara and G. Hamilton, 'Challenging misconceptions about sexual offending: Creating an evidence-based resource for police and legal practitioners', Victoria Police and Australian Institute for Family Studies (2017); https://www.aic.gov.au/sites/default/files/2020–11/ti611_misconceptions_of_sexual_crimes_against_adult_victims.pdf

16. Patrick Tidmarsh PhD, 'Training sexual crime investigators to get the "Whole Story": Investigator qualities and field adherence to training principles' thesis (2017), pp. 70–84.

17. Amy Dellinger Page, 'True Colors: Police Officers and Rape Myth Acceptance', *Feminist Criminology*, no. 5 (4) (2010), pp. 315–34; Rachel M. Venema, 'Making Judgments: How Blame Mediates the Influence of Rape Myth Acceptance in Police Responses to Sexual Assault', *Journal of Interpersonal Violence* (4 August 2016); Emma Sleath and Ray Bull, 'Comparing Rape Victim and Perpetrator Blaming in a Police Officer Sample. Differences Between Police Officers With and Without Special Training', *Criminal Justice and Behavior*, vol. 39, no. 5 (2012), pp. 646–65; Karen Rich and Patrick Seffrin, 'Police interviews of sexual assault reporters: Do attitudes matter?', *Violence and Victims*, vol. 27, no. 2 (2012); Molly Smith, Nicole Wilkes and Leana A. Bouffard, 'Rape Myth Adherence Among Campus Law Enforcement Officers', *Criminal Justice and Behavior*, vol. 43, no. 4 (April 2016), pp. 539–56; Amy Dellinger Page, 'Behind the Blue Line: Investigating

Police Officers' Attitudes Toward Rape', *Journal of Police and Criminal Psychology*, no. 22 (2007), pp. 22-32.

18. Emma Sleath and Ray Bull, 'A Brief Report on Rape Myth Acceptance: Differences Between Police Officers, Law Students and Psychology Students in the United Kingdom', *Violence and Victims*, vol. 30, no. 1 (2015).

19. Victim responsibility data:

Strong	0.72 (1.31)	0.32 (0.79)	0.61 (1.29)
Ambiguous	3.11 (2.11)	1.12 (1.34)	1.59 (1.62)
Weak	3.59 (2.31)	2.12 (1.98)	2.70 (1.96)

Part II. Offenders and offending

1. N. Smith, C. Dogaru and F. Ellis, *Hear me. Believe me. Respect me: A survey of adult survivors of child sexual abuse and their experiences of support services* (University Campus Suffolk, Ipswich, 2015).

6. Offending begins with offenders

1. The NSPCC definition is, 'Grooming is when someone builds an emotional connection with a child to gain their trust for the purposes of sexual exploitation.'

2. Evan Stark, 'Rethinking Coercive Control', *Violence against Women*, vol. 15, issue 12 (published online 22 October 2009; issue published 1 December 2009), pp. 1509–25; https://doi.org/10.1177/1077801209347452

3. R. C. Summit, 'The child abuse accommodation syndrome', *Child Abuse and Neglect,* no. 7 (1983), pp. 177–93.

4. Bullock and Beckson, 'Male Victims of Sexual Assault', op. cit.; N. Groth and A. W. Burgess, 'Male rape: offenders and victims', *American Journal of Psychiatry*, no. 137 (1980), pp. 806–10.

5. F. Cortoni and R. K. Hanson, *A review of the recidivism rates of adult female sexual offenders* (Correctional Services of Canada, Ottawa, 2005); K. Williams and D. Briere, 'An incident-based comparison of female and male sexual offenders', *Sexual Abuse: A Journal of Research and Treatment,* no. 27 (2015), pp. 235–57.

6. F. Syed and S. Williams, *Case studies of female sexual offenders in the Correctional Service of Canada* (Correctional Service of Canada, Ottawa, 1996).

7. Burgess-Proctor et al., 'Comparing female- and male- perpetrated child sexual abuse', op. cit.

8. J. C. Sandler and N. J. Freeman, 'Female sex offender recidivism: A large-scale empirical analysis', *Sexual Abuse: A Journal of Research and Treatment*, no. 21 (4) (2009), pp. 455–73; E. B. Comartin, A. Burgess-Proctor, S. Kubiak, K. A. Bender and P. Kernsmith, 'Comparing women's and men's sexual offending using a statewide incarcerated sample: A two-study design', *Journal of Interpersonal Violence* (2018), pp. 1–24.

9. Franca Cortoni, *Women who sexually abuse*, op. cit.

10. V. Poels, 'Risk assessment of recidivism of violent and sexual female offenders', *Psychiatry, Psychology, and Law,* 14 (2007), pp. 227–50; Franca Cortoni, R. Karl Hanson, Marie-Ève Coache (2010), 'The Recidivism Rates of Female Sexual Offenders Are Low: A Meta-Analysis', *Sexual Abuse,* vol. 22, issue 4, pp. 387–401; Sandler and Freeman, 'Female sex offender recidivism', op. cit.

11. ibid; see also 8.

12. R. K. Hanson and M. T. Bussiere, 'Predicting relapse: A meta-analysis of sexual offender recidivism studies', *Journal of Consulting and Clinical Psychology,* no. 66 (1998), pp. 348–62.

13. T. A. Gannon, M. R. Rose and T. Ward, 'A descriptive model of the offense process for female sexual offenders', *Sexual Abuse: A journal of research and treatment,* vol. 20 (2008), pp. 352–74.

14. M. C. Seto, L. E. Pullman, 'Risk factors for adolescent sexual offending' (chapter in G.J.N. Bruinsma and D. L. Weisbund (eds), *Encyclopedia of Criminology and Criminal Justice* (pp. 4466–4475) (Springer, 2014); doi:101007/978-1-4614-59-690-2_104; Alissar El-Murr, 'Problem sexual behaviours and sexually abusive behaviours in Australian children and young people: A review of available literature', Australian Institute of Family Studies – CFCA Paper no. 46.

15. Associations of Therapist Treating Sexual Abuse (ATSA), *ATSA Taskforce on children with sexual behaviour problems* (2006); M. C. Seto, C. Kjellgren, G. Priebe, S. Mossige, C. G. Svedin and N. Langstrom, 'Sexual coercion experience and sexually coercive behaviour: A population study of Swedish and Norwegian male youth', *Child Maltreatment,* no. 15 (2011), pp. 215–28.

16. R. A. Knight and R. A. Prentky, 'Exploring characteristics for classifying juvenile sex offenders', in H. E. Barbaree, W. L. Marshall and S. M. Hudson (eds), *The Juvenile Sex Offender* (Guilford Press, New York, 1993), pp. 45–83.

17. R. Sipe, E. L. Jensen and R. S. Everett, 'Adolescent sexual offenders grown up: Recidivism in young adulthood', *Criminal Justice and Behavior,* no. 25 (1) (1998), pp. 109–25; P. Lussier, C. Van Den Berg, C. Bijveld and J. Hendriks, 'A developmental taxonomy of juvenile sex offenders for theory, research, and prevention. The adolescent-limited and the high-rate slow desister', *Criminal Justice and Behavior,* vol. 39, no. 12 (December 2012), pp. 1559–81; M. F. Caldwell, 'Study characteristics and recidivism base rates in juvenile sex offender recidivism', *International Journal of Offender Therapy and Comparative Criminology,* no. 54 (2010), pp. 197–212; Dennis Waite, Adrienne Keller, Elizabeth L. McGarvey, Edward Wieckowski, Relana Pinkerton and Gerald L. Brown, 'Juvenile Sex Offender Re-Arrest Rates for Sexual, Violent Nonsexual and Property Crimes: A Ten-Year Follow-Up', *Sexual Abuse: A Journal of Research and Treatment,* vol. 17, issue 3 (July 2005), pp 313–31.

18. D. F. Walker, S. K. McGovern, E. L. Poey and K. E. Otis, 'Treatment Effectiveness for Male Adolescent Sexual Offenders: A Meta-Analysis and Review', *Journal of Child Sexual Abuse*, no. 13 (3–4) (February 2004), pp. 281–93; E. J. Letourneau, S. W. Henggeler, C. M. Borduin, P. A. Schewe, M. R. McCart, J. E. Chapman and L. Saldana, 'Multisystemic therapy for juvenile sexual offenders: one-year results from a randomised effectiveness trial', *Journal of Family Psychology*, no. 23 (2009), pp. 89–102; C.A. Fortune and I. Lambie, 'Sexually abusive youth: A review of recidivism studies and methodological issues for future research', *Clinical Psychology Review*, vol. 26, issue 8 (December 2006), pp. 1078–95; J. R. Worling and T. Curwen, 'Adolescent sexual offender recidivism: success of specialised treatment and implications for risk prediction', *Child Abuse and Neglect*, vol. 24, issue 7 (July 2000), pp. 965–82.

7. Why do they do it?

1. Ulf Holmberg and Sven-Åke Christianson, 'Murderers' and sexual offenders' experiences of police interviews and their inclination to admit or deny crimes', *Behavioral Sciences and the Law* (17 April 2002); https://doi.org/10.1002/bsl.470
2. Danielle Kertzelben, 'Trump accusers', NPR.org (20 October 2016); Claire Mindock, *Independent* (4 December 2017).
3. T. Ward and T. R. Keenan, 'Child Molesters' Implicit Theories', *Journal of Interpersonal Violence*, no. 14 (8) (1999), pp. 821–38; doi: 10.1177/088626099014008003
4. H. M. Wellman, *The Child's Theory of Mind* (MIT Press, 1992).
5. Devon L. L. Polaschek, Theresa. A. Gannon, 'The Implicit Theories of Rapists: What convicted offenders tell us', *Sexual Abuse: A Journal of Research and Treatment*, vol. 16, no. 4 (October 2004).
6. Elizabeth Gilchrist, 'Implicit thinking about implicit theories in intimate partner violence', *Psychology, Crime and Law*, no. 15 (2–3) (2009), pp. 131–45; Sarah Weldon and Elizabeth Gilchrist, 'Implicit Theories in Intimate Partner Violence Offenders', *Journal of Family Violence* (published online 19 August 2012); doi 10.1007/s10896-012-9465-x
7. Devon L. L. Polaschek, Susan. W. Calvert and Theresa. A. Gannon, 'Linking Violent Thinking: Implicit Theory-Based Research with Violent Offender', *Journal of Interpersonal Violence*, vol. 24, no.1 (January 2009), pp. 75–96.
8. Anthony R. Beech, Natalie Parrett, Tony Ward and Dawn Fisher, 'Assessing female sexual offenders' motivations and cognitions: an exploratory study', *Psychology, Crime and Law*, no. 15 (2–3) (2009), pp. 201–6.
9. T. A. Gannon, J. A. Hoare, M. R. Rose and N. Parrett, 'A re-examination of female child molesters' implicit theories: evidence of female specificity?', *Psychology, Crime and Law*, vol. 18, no. 2 (February 2012), pp. 209–24.

10. Asst Professor Kassia Wosick, New Mexico University, quoted in Chris Morris, 'After rough 2013, porn studios look for a better year', CNBC (14 January 2014); Gail Dines, *How Porn Has Hijacked Our Sexuality* (Beacon Press, 2010).

11. Karin Lehnardt, Senior Writer, Fact Retriever (19 August 2016).

12. TopTen Reviews.

13. D. Polaschek and T. Ward, 'The Implicit theories of potential rapists. What our questionnaires tell us', *Aggression and Violent Behavior*, vol. 7, issue 4 (July–August 2002), pp. 385–406.

14. D. Finkelhor, *Child Sexual Abuse: New Theory and Research* (Free Press, New York, 1984).

15. S. W. Smallbone and R. K. Wortley, 'Onset, Persistence, and Versatility of Offending Among Adult Males Convicted of Sexual Offences Against Children', *Sexual Abuse: A Journal of Research and Treatment*, vol. 16, issue 4 (October 2004), pp. 285–98; S. W. Smallbone and R. K. Wortley, *Child sexual abuse: Offender characteristics and modus operandi* (Australian Institute of Criminology, Canberra, 2001).

16. R. H. Aday and J. Krabil, 'Older and geriatric offenders: Critical issues for the twenty-first century', in Lior Gideon (ed.), *Special Needs Prisoners in Correctional Institutions* (Sage, 2012), pp. 203–33.

17. T. D. Miethe, J. Olson and O. Mitchell, 'Specialisation and Persistence in the Arrest Histories of Sex Offenders. A Comparative Analysis of Alternative Measures and Offence Types', *Journal of Research in Crime and Delinquency*, vol. 43, issue 3 (1 August 2006), pp. 204–29; https://doi.org/10.1177/0022427806286564; L. Sample and T. M. Bray, 'Are Sex Offenders Different? An Examination of Re-arrest Patterns', *Criminal Justice Policy Review*, vol. 17, issue 1 (1 March 2006), pp. 83–102; https://doi.org/10.1177/0887403405282916

18. Figures for the Male Adolescent Programme for Positive Sexuality (MAPPS), Children's Protection Society, AWARE programme and Berry Street.

19. T. K. Seghorn, R. A. Prentky and R. J. Boucher, 'Childhood Sexual Abuse in the Lives of Sexually Aggressive Offenders', *Journal of the American Academy of Child & Adolescent Psychiatry*, vol. 26, issue 2 (March 1987), pp. 262–7; Sonia Dhawan and W. L. Marshall, 'Sexual abuse histories of sexual offenders', *Sexual Abuse: A Journal of Research and Treatment*, vol. 8, issue 1 (January 1996), pp. 7–15; Lindsay et al., 'A comparison of physical and sexual abuse: histories of sexual and non-sexual offenders with intellectual disability', *Child Abuse and Neglect*, vol. 25, issue 7 (July 2001), pp. 989–95; Ashley F. Jespersen, Martin L. Lalumière and Michael C. Seto, 'Sexual abuse history among adult sex offenders and non-sex offenders: A meta-analysis', *Child Abuse and Neglect*, vol. 33, issue 3 (March 2009), pp. 179–192; D. A. Simons, S. K. Wurtele and R. L. Durham, 'Developmental experiences of child sexual abusers and rapists', *Child Abuse and Neglect*, vol. 32, issue 5 (May 2008), pp. 549–60; L. A. Bard et al., 'A descriptive study of rapists

and child molesters: Developmental, clinical, and criminal characteristics', *Behavioral Sciences and the Law*, vol. 5, no. 2 (1987), pp. 203–20; Jackie Craissati and Anthony Beech, 'The characteristics of a geographical sample of convicted rapists. Sexual victimisation and compliance comparison to child molesters', *Journal of Interpersonal Violence*, vol. 19, no. 4 (April 2004), pp. 371–88.

8. When young people commit sexual offences

1. R. Curnow, P. Streker, and E. Williams, *Male Adolescent Program for Positive Sexuality*, Juvenile Justice evaluation report (National Library of Australia, NLA); Bib ID2668700; D. Eger and S. Kilby, *Integrating Adventure Therapy into an Adolescent Sex Offender Program* (NLA); Bib D 5621430

2. S. Hackett, *Children and young people with harmful sexual behaviours* (NSPCC, 2014); B. L. Bonner, M. Chafin and K. Pierce, *Adolescent Sex Offenders: Common misconceptions vs. current evidence*, US National Center on the Sexual Behavior of Youth, no. 3 (July 2003); H. N. Snyder and M. Sickmund, *Juvenile offenders and victims: 1999 National Report*, Office of Juvenile Justice and Delinquency Prevention.

3. FBI, *Crime in the United States: Uniform crime report 1998* (US DoJ, 1999); National Sex Offender Public Website NSOPW – Facts and Figures 2018; J. V. Becker, C. D. Harris and B. D. Sales, 'Juveniles who commit sexual offenses: A critical review of research', in Donald Hall (ed.), *Sexual Aggression: Issues in aetiology, assessment and treatment* (chapter 12) (Taylor and Francis, 1993).

4. Waite et al., 'Juvenile Sex Offender Re-arrest Rates …', op. cit.

5. M. A. Alexander, 'Sexual offender treatment efficacy revisited', *Sexual Abuse: A Journal of Research and Treatment*, vol. 11 (1999), pp. 101–16.

6. Association of Therapists Treating Sexual Abuse (ATSA), 'Adolescents who have engaged in sexually abusive behaviors: Effective policies and practices' (30 October 2012); Australian Institute of Family Studies, NCPC Practice Brief no.1 (December 2006).

7. N. L. Papalia, S. Luebbers, J.P.R. Ogloff, M. Cutajar and P. E. Mullen, 'Exploring the longitudinal offending pathways of child sexual abuse victims: A preliminary analysis using variable modelling', *Child Abuse and Neglect*, vol. 66 (April 2017), pp. 84–100; J.P.R. Ogloff, M. Cutajar, E. Mann and P. Mullen, *Child sexual abuse and subsequent offending and victimisation: A 45-year follow-up study* (Australian Institute of Criminology, 2012).

8. *Age-appropriate sexual behaviours in children and young people: Information for carers, professionals and the general public*, 2nd ed. (South Easter Centre Against Sexual Assault, 2017).

9. Robert Prentky PhD and Sue Righthand PhD, Juvenile Sex Offender Assessment Protocol-II (J-SOAP-II) (2003); I. Hempel, N. Buck, M. Cima and H. van Marle, 'Review of risk assessment instruments for juvenile sex

offenders: what is next?', *International Journal of Offender Therapy and Comparative Criminology*, no. 57 (2) (February 2013), pp. 208–28; doi: 10.1177/0306624X11428315

9. Monsters or men?

1. Anthony Dowsley, 'Boy, 4, a "sex fiend"', *Herald Sun* (14 September 2006).
2. S. Napier, C. Dowling, A. Morgan, and D. Talbot, 'What impact do public sex offender registries have on community safety?', *Australian Institute of Criminology Trends and Issues,* no. 550 (2018); ISSN 0817-8542
3. A. Petrosino, C. Turpin-Petrosino, M. E. Hollis-Peel and J. G. Lavenberg, '"Scared straight" and other juvenile awareness programs for preventing delinquency', *Cochrane Review* (30 April 2013); NIJ (US) Practice Profiles, Juvenile Awareness Programs (Scared Straight).
4. S. A. Reid-MacNevin, 'Boot camps for young offenders: A politically acceptable punishment', *Journal of Contemporary Criminal Justice*, vol. 3, no. 2 (1997), pp. 155–71; National Criminal Justice Reference Service (UK) NCJ155437, *Boot camps for young offenders* (Penal Affairs Consortium, 1995); Dr Faith E. Lutz and Cortney A. Bell, 'Boot Camp Prisons as Masculine Organisations', *Journal of Offender Rehabilitation*, no. 40 (3–4) (2005), pp. 133–52.
5. John Braithwaite, *Re-integrative Shaming* (Australian National University); http://johnbraithwaite.com/wp-content/uploads/2016/05/2000_Reintegrative-Shaming.pdf
6. *World Prison Brief. World Prison Population List* (Institute for Criminal Policy Research, ICPR, at Birkbeck, University of London, November 2018); Seena Fazel and Achim Wolf, 'A Systematic Review of Criminal Recidivism Rates Worldwide: Current Difficulties and Recommendations for Best Practice', *PLOS One*, 10 (6) (2015), e0130390; doi: 10.1371/journal.pone.0130390
7. Michael Sheath, '"Confrontative" Work with Sex Offenders: Legitimised Nonce Bashing?', *Probation Journal*, vol. 37, issue 4 (1 December 1990), pp. 159–62.
8. W. L. Marshall, G. Serran, H. Moulden, R. Mulloy, Y. M. Fernandez, R. Mann and D. Thornton, 'Therapist features in sexual offender treatment: their reliable identification and influence on behaviour change', *Clinical Psychology and Psychotherapy*, vol. 9, issue 6 (November/December 2002), pp. 395–405.
9. Eileen Finnegan, 'Does Treatment of Sex Offenders Work?', *Irish Association of Humanistic and Integrative Psychotherapy*, issue 60 (Spring 2010).
10. Clare Feikert-Ahalt, 'Terror, Trial and Justice in Norway' (Law Library, Global Law, US Library of Congress, 26 September 2011).
11. 'Sex offender sentences hit record levels. Average sentence increased by 4.5 months and number of convictions reaches 10-year high', Ministry of Justice (13 August 2015).

12. Home Office, Ministry of Justice (2013); https://www.ons.gov.uk/people populationandcommunity/crimeandjustice/articles/sexualoffencesin englandandwales/yearendingmarch2017

13. Svenja Göbbels, Tony Ward, and Gwenda M. Willis, 'An integrative theory of desistance from sex offending, *Aggression and Violent Behavior*, vol. 17, issue 5 (September–October 2012), pp. 453–62; doi.org/10.1016/j. avb.2012.06.003; Tony Ward and D. Richard Laws, 'Desistance from Sex Offending: Motivating Change, Enriching Practice', *International Journal of Forensic Mental Health*, vol. 9, issue 1 (2010); https://doi. org/10.1080/14999011003791598; J. Carpentier, B. Leclerc and J. Proulx, 'Juvenile Sexual Offenders. Correlates of Onset, Variety, and Desistance', *Criminal Behavior*, vol. 38, issue 8 (1 August 2011), pp. 854–73; https:// doi.org/10.1177/0093854811407730

14. R. Karl Hanson, Andrew J. R. Harris and Leslie Helmus, 'High-Risk Sex Offenders May Not Be High Risk Forever', *Journal of Interpersonal Violence*, vol. 29, issue 15 (2014), pp. 2792–2813; https://doi.org/10.1177/ 0886260514526062.

15. Taylor (2015), 60 Cal. 4th 1019.

16. Don Thompson, Associated Press, 'California seeks solutions to homeless sex offender rate', *Washington Times* (29 July 2017).

17. California Sex Offender Management Board, annual report (2016).

18. S. Napier, C. Dowling, A. Morgan and D. Talbot, 'What impact do public sex offender registries have on community safety?', Australian Institute of Criminology, *Trends and Issues in Criminal Justice*, no. 550 (2018).

19. Napier et al., op. cit.

20. Emma Belton, 'Assessing the Risk: Protecting the child', Impact and Evidence briefing (NSPCC, January 2015); Association of Therapists Treating Sexual Abuse; http://www.atsa.com/risk-assessment

21. Anthony R. Beech, Dawn D. Fisher and David Thornton, 'Risk Assessment of Sex Offenders. Professional Psychology: Research and Practice', *American Psychological Association*, vol. 34, no. 4 (2003), pp. 339–52; 0735-7028/03/$12.00 doi: 10.1037/0735-7028.34.4.339

22. R. Karl Hanson, 'Will They Do It Again? Predicting Sex-Offense Recidivism', *Current Directions in Psychological Science*, vol. 9, issue 3 (2000), pp. 106–9.

23. UK Ministry of Justice. National Offender Management Service; https:// www.swmcrc.co.uk/wp-content/uploads/2010/06/what-works-sex-offender-treatment.pdf; Stop It Now (US); https://www.stopitnow.org/help-guidance/faqs/faqs-on-sex-offender-treatment

24. Ministry of Justice, *Impact evaluation of the prison-based Core Sex Offender Treatment Programme* (30 June 2017).

25. Committee on Assessing Juvenile Justice Reform, *Reforming Juvenile Justice: A Developmental Approach* (National Research Council at the National Academies, 2013); Richard J. Bonnie, Robert L. Johnson, Betty M. Chemers and Julie A. Schuck (eds), *Reforming Juvenile Justice. A Developmental*

Approach (2013), chapter: Appendix A: Costs and Benefits of Juvenile Justice Interventions, pp. 393–410.

26. F. Losel and M. Schmucker, 'The effectiveness of treatment for sexual offenders: A comprehensive meta-analysis', *Journal of Experimental Criminology*, vol. 1, issue 1 (April 2005), pp. 117–46; R. Karl Hanson, Guy Bourgon, Leslie Helmus and Shannon Hodgson, *A Meta-Analysis of the Effectiveness of Treatment for Sexual Offenders: Risk, Need, and Responsivity* (Public Safety Canada, 2009); Roger Przybylski, 'Effectiveness of Treatment for Adult Sex Offenders', chapter 7 of *Sex Offender Management Assessment and Planning Initiative* (US Department of Justice Programs, 2015); https://smart.gov/SOMAPI/sec1/ch7_treatment.html

27. James Bonta and D. A. Andrews, 'Risk-Need-Responsivity Model for Offender Assessment and Rehabilitation' (2007).

28. https://www.goodlivesmodel.com

29. M. Hoing, B. Vogelvang and S. Bogaerts, '"I am a different man now" – Sex offenders in Circles of Support and Accountability: A prospective study', *International Journal of Offender Therapy and Comparative Criminology*, vol. 61 (7) (2017), pp. 751–72; M. Clarke, L. Warwick and B. Vollm, 'Circles of support and accountability: The characteristics of core members in England and Wales', *Criminal Behaviour and Mental Health*, no 27 (2017), pp. 191–206.

30. https://mappa.justice.gov.uk/connect.ti/MAPPA/groupHome

10. The continuum

1. Report on the prevalence of sexual harassment (Stop Violence Against Women, a project of the Advocates for Human Rights, 2010).

2. Bianca Fileborn, 'Conceptual understandings and prevalence of sexual harassment and street harassment', ACSSA Resource Sheet no. 6 (July 2013).

3. Australian Bureau of Statistics (ABS), *Personal Safety Survey* (2005).

4. Australian Bureau of Statistics (ABS), *Personal Safety Survey* (2016).

5. Australian Institute of Family Studies (AIFS), 'The prevalence of child abuse and neglect', CFCA Resource Sheet (April 2017).

6. http://www.haut-conseil-egalite.gouv.fr/IMG/pdf/hcefh_avis_harcelement_transports-20150410.pdf; Henry Samuel, '100 per cent of Frenchwomen "victims of sexual harassment on public transport"', *Telegraph* (17 April 2015).

7. 'Reports of sexual assaults on London Underground soar', PA Media (23 September 2019).

8. https://tfl.gov.uk/travel-information/safety/report-it-to-stop-it

9. ABC TV, King's School, '*Me and My Girl*', (22 January 2005).

10. Nils Pratley, 'Shindig at the Dorchester erodes public trust in business', *Guardian* (25 January 2018).

11. J. B. Pryor, C. M. La Vite and L. M. Stoller, 'A social psychological analysis of sexual harassment: The person/situation interaction', *Journal of Vocational Behavior*, no. 42 (1993), pp. 68–83.

12. Nils Pratley, op. cit.

13. K. T. Schneider, S. Swan and L. F. Fitzgerald, 'Job-related and psychological effects of sexual harassment in the workplace: Empirical evidence from two organisations', *Journal of Applied Psychology*, vol. 82, no. 3 (1997), pp. 401–15.

14. Chai R. Feldblum and Victoria A. Lipnic, US Equal Employment Opportunity Commission Task Force Report (June 2016).

15. J. B. Pryor, C. M. La Vite and L. M. Stoller, op. cit.

16. Louise F. Fitzgerald, Fritz Hulin, Charles L. Drasgow, Michele J. Gelfand and Vicki J. Magley, 'Antecedents and consequences of sexual harassment in organisations: A test of an integrated model', *Journal of Applied Psychology*, vol. 82 (4) (August 1997), pp. 578–89; Barbara A. Gutek and Mary P. Koss, 'Changed Women and Changed Organisations: Consequences of and Coping with Sexual Harassment', *Journal of Vocational Behavior*, vol. 42, issue 1 (February 1993), pp. 28–48.

17. Victorian Human Rights and Equal Opportunity Commission, Independent review into sex discrimination and sexual harassment, including predatory behaviour in Victoria Police, Phase One report (2015).

18. J. A. Bargh, P. Raymond, J. B. Pryor and F. Strack, 'Attractiveness of the underling: An automatic power → sex association and its consequences for sexual harassment and aggression', *Journal of Personality and Social Psychology*, vol. 68, no. 5 (1995), pp. 768–81.

19. G. Abel et al., 'Self-Reported Sex Crimes of Nonincarcerated Paraphiliacs', *Journal of Interpersonal Violence*, vol. 2, issue 1 (1 March 1987), pp. 3–25; https://doi.org/10.1177/088626087002001001

20. Elizabeth Gilchrist, 'Implicit thinking about implicit theories in intimate partner violence', *Psychology, Crime and Law*, no. 15 (2–3) (2009), pp. 131–45; Sarah Weldon and Elizabeth Gilchrist, 'Implicit Theories in Intimate Partner Violence Offenders', *Journal of Family Violence* (published online 19 August 2012); doi: 10.1007/s10896-012-9465-x; Polaschek et al., 'Linking Violent Thinking', op. cit.; T. Ward and T. R. Keenan, 'Child Molesters' Implicit Theories', *Journal of Interpersonal Violence*, no. 14 (8) (1999), pp. 821–38; doi: 10.1177/088626099014008003; Polaschek et al., 'The Implicit Theories of Rapists', op. cit.; Emily Blake and Theresa A. Gannon, 'The Implicit Theories of Rape-prone men: An Information-Processing Investigation', *International Journal of Offender Therapy and Comparative Criminology*, no. 54 (6) (2010), pp. 895–914.

11. The Internet age

1. T. Krone, 'A typology of online child pornography offending', Australian Institute of Criminology, *Trends and Issues in Crime and Criminal Justice*, no. 279 (first published 2004; last modified 3 November 2017); ISSN:0817-8542.

2. M. C. Seto, C. Buckman, R. Gregg Dwyer and E. Quayle, 'Production and active trading of child sexual exploitation images depicting identified victims', National Centre for Missing and Exploited Children (March 2018).

3. IICSA 1st report, Huddersfield University, quoted by Owen Bowcott, *Guardian* (online 22 January 2018).

4. Kimberley Suiters, 'Stranger in the console: Predators lurking in your child's gaming devices', ABC-WJLA, Washington DC (2018); *Look both ways* – video blog by FBI Assistant Director Shawn Henry (23 May 2011); 'Virtual Depravity', *Economist*, Singapore edition (online 26 July 2014).

5. T. Martellozzo, D. Nehring and H. Taylor, 'Online child sexual abuse by female offenders: An exploratory study', *International Journal of Cyber Criminology*, vol. 4 (December 2010), pp. 592-604; Mary L. Pulldo, National Juvenile Online Victimisation study, quoted in *The Blog* (29 February 2016).

6. J. Wolak, D. Finkelhor and K. J. Mitchell, 'Child-pornography possessors arrested in internet-related crimes: Findings from the national juvenile online victimisation study', National Center for Missing and Exploited Children (2005); Public Safety Canada, *Child Pornography Offenders: A Review* (published online 1 May 2018); K. Sheldon, 'What we know about men who download child abuse images', *British Journal of Forensic Practice*, no. 13 (4) (2011), pp. 221-34.

7. Public Safety Canada, 'Internet Sexual Offenders', Research Summary vol. 16, no. 4 (July 2011); T. Krone and R. G. Smith, 'Trajectories in online child sexual exploitation offending in Australia', Australian Institute of Criminology, *Trends and Issues*, no. 524 (January 2017); ISSN 0817-8542; J. A. McCarthy, 'Internet sexual activity: A comparison between contact and non-contact child pornography offenders', *Journal of Sexual Aggression*, no. 16 (2) (2010), pp. 181-95.

8. Internet Watch Foundation, Annual Report (2016).

9. Andy Brown, 'Safe from harm: Tackling online child sexual abuse in the Philippines', UNICEF Newsline (19 October 2016); Melinda Tankard Reist, 'Why are Australian Telcos and ISPs enabling a child sexual abuse pandemic?', *Religion and Ethics*, Australian Broadcasting Commission (6 July 2017).

10. Murray Lee, Thomas Crofts, Alyce McGovern and Sanja Milivojevic, 'Sexting among young people: Perceptions and practices', Australian Institute of Criminology, *Trends and Issues in Crime and Criminal Justice*, no. 508 (last modified 10 January 2018).

11. J. Ringrose, L. Harvey, R. Gill, and S. Livingstone, 'Teen girls, sexual double standards and "sexting": gendered value in digital image exchange', *Feminist Theory* no. 14 (2013), p. 305.

12. Lee et al., op. cit.

13. Emily Dugan, 'Revenge porn: Are the police and courts taking the crime seriously?', *Independent* (25 August 2015).

14. M. Carmody, *Sex and Ethics* (2014); http://www.sexandethics.net

15. A. S. Dobson and J. Ringrose, 'Sext education: pedagogies of sex, gender and shame in the schoolyards of Tagged and Exposed', *Sexuality, Society and Learning*, vol. 16, 2016 – issue 1: Gender and Sexuality: Taking Up Space in Schooling (2015).

16. A. Powell and N. Henry, 'Policing technology-facilitated sexual violence against adult victims: police and service sector perspectives', *Policing and Society*, vol. 28, no. 3 (2018), pp. 291–307.

12. Pornography

1. Alexa, top 100 sites (published 23 March 2018).

2. *Fight the New Drug* Annual Report (2 April 2018), fightthenewdrug.org

3. Ibid.

4. *Huffington Post*, Communities/Women section (18 November 2013).

5. PornHub insights: 2017 year in review.

6. 'The Porn Factor' (2016), Risk and Reality Project; http://www.itstimewe talked.com.au/resources/the-porn-factor/

7. N. M. Malamuth, C. L. Heavey and D. Linz, 'The Confluence Model of Sexual Aggression: Combining Hostile Masculinity and Impersonal Sex, *Journal of Offender Rehabilitation*, vol. 23, 1996 – issues 3–4, pp. 13–37.

8. V. Vega and N. M. Malamuth, 'Predicting sexual aggression: The role of pornography in the context of general and specific risk factors', *Aggressive Behavior*, vol. 3 (2007), pp. 104–17.

9. J. G. Wheeler, W. H. George and B. J. Dahl, 'Sexually aggressive college males: Empathy as a moderator in the "Confluence Model" of Sexual Aggression', *Personality and Individual Differences*, vol. 33, issue 5 (2002), pp. 759–75.

10. L. P. Greene and K. C. Davis, 'Latent risk profiles among a community sample of men: Implications for sexual aggression', *Journal of Interpersonal Violence*, no. 26 (7) (2011), pp. 1463–77.

11. N. M. Malamuth, T. Adison and M. Koss, 'Pornography and sexual aggression: Are there reliable effects and can we understand them?', *Annual Review of Sex Research*, no. 11 (2000), pp. 26–91.

12. P. J. Wright, R. S. Tokunaga and A. Kraus, 'A meta-analysis of pornography consumption and actual acts of sexual aggression in general population studies', *Journal of Communication* (2015).

13. A. J. Bridges, R. Wosnitzer, E. Scharrer, C. Sun and R. Liberman, 'Aggression and sexual behavior in best-selling pornography videos: A content analysis update', *Violence Against Women*, no. 16 (10) (2010), pp. 1065-85.
14. 'The Porn Factor', op. cit.
15. Erika Lust, *Mums Make Porn*; https://www.imdb.com/title/tt10054588
16. Melinda Wenner Moyer, 'The Sunny Side of Smut', *Scientific American* (July 2011); https://www.scientificamerican.com/article/the-sunny-side-of-smut/
17. Joe Pinsker, 'The hidden economics of porn', *Atlantic* (4 April 2016).
18. Jennifer B. Johnston, 'Early exposure to pornography: Indirect and direct effects on sexual satisfaction in adulthood', Fielding Graduate University (ProQuest Dissertations Publishing, 2013).
19. H. Mouras et al., 'Activation of mirror-neuron system by erotic video clips predicts degree of induced erection: an fMRI study', *NeuroImage*, vol. 42, issue 3 (September 2008), pp. 1142-50.
20. Antonia Quadara, Alissar El-Murr and Joe Latham, *The effects of pornography on children and young people. An evidence scan*, Australian Institute of Family Studies, research report (December 2017).
21. Chiara Sabina, Janis Wolak and David Finkelhor, 'The Nature and Dynamics of Internet Pornography Exposure for Youth', *Cyber Psychology & Behavior*, vol. 11, no. 6 (published online 11 December 2008); https://doi.org/10.1089/cpb.2007.0179; Lotta Löfgren-Mårtenson and Sven-Axel Månsson, 'Lust, Love, and Life: A Qualitative Study of Swedish Adolescents' Perceptions and Experiences with Pornography', *Journal of Sex Research*, vol. 47, issue 6 (2010), pp. 568-79; https://doi.org/10.1080/00224490903151374
22. Jason S. Carroll, Laura M. Padilla-Walker, Larry J. Nelson, Chad D. Olson, Carolyn McNamara Barry and Stephanie D. Madsen, 'Generation XXX: Pornography Acceptance and Use Among Emerging Adults', *Journal of Adolescent Research*, vol. 23, issue 1 (1 January 2008), pp. 6-30.
23. Quadara, El-Murr and Latham, op. cit.; Löfgren-Mårtenson and Månsson, op. cit.
24. Jochen Peter and Patti M. Valkenburg, 'Adolescents and Pornography: A Review of 20 Years of Research', *Journal of Sex Research*, volume 53, issues 4-5 (2016), 'Annual Review of Sex Research'; Quadara, El-Murr and Latham, op. cit.
25. Gert Martin Hald and Neil M. Malamuth, 'Self-Perceived Effects of Pornography Consumption', *Archives of Sexual Behavior*, vol. 37, issue 4 (August 2008), pp. 614-25; Löfgren-Mårtenson and Sven-Axel Månsson, op. cit.
26. Carroll, Padilla-Walker et al., op. cit.; Hald and Malamuth, op. cit.
27. Gudrun Wallmyr and Catharina Welin, 'Young People, Pornography and Sexuality: Sources and Attitudes', *Journal of School Nursing*, vol. 22, issue 5 (2006), pp. 290-5; Quadara, El-Murr and Latham, op. cit; Hald and Malamuth, op. cit.; Löfgren-Mårtenson and Månsson, op. cit.

28. Louisa Allen, '"Say everything": Exploring young people's suggestions for improving sexuality education', *Sexuality, Society and Learning*, vol. 5, issue 4 (2005; published online 15 August 2006), pp. 389–404; https://doi.org/10.1080/14681810500278493

29. Nicholas Kristof, 'The Children of PornHub', *New York Times* (4 December 2020); Associated Press (Guardian report, Fri 11 December 2020), *Pornhub: Mastercard and Visa to block use of cards on site after child abuse allegations.*

Part III. Investigating sexual crime

1. Victorian Law Reform Commission, *Sexual Offences* report (2004).

2. Christine J. Eastwood, Sally M. Kift and Rachel Grace, 'Attrition in Child Sexual Assault Cases: Why Lord Chief Justice Hale Got It Wrong', *Journal of Judicial Administration*, no. 16 (2) (2006), pp. 81–91. In the UK, Kelly et al. (2005) found that between half and three-quarters of reported sexual assault incidents do not proceed beyond the police investigation stage. In New Zealand, Triggs, Mossman, Jordan and Kingi (2009) identified that police laid charges in 31 per cent of cases. The Bureau of Crime Statistics and Research (BOCSAR) in New South Wales found that of all sexual offences reported to police, criminal proceedings are initiated in only 15 per cent of incidents involving child victims and 19 per cent of incidents involving adult victims (Fitzgerald, 2006). Daly and Bouhours (2010) combined the results of seventy-five studies across five countries and identified that the rate of attrition (once a case enters the criminal justice system) is highest at the police investigation stage, with around 65 per cent of cases dropping off during the police investigation.

3. The Children's Society UK, report April 2018.

4. Crime Outcomes in England and Wales, year ending March 2019: Statistical Bulletin HOSB 12/19. Home Office (July 2019).

5. Elli Darwinkel, Martine Powell and Patrick Tidmarsh, 'Prosecutors' perceptions of the utility of "relationship" evidence in sexual abuse trials', *Australian and New Zealand Journal of Criminology*, vol. 47, issue 1 (2013), pp. 44–58.

6. Victorian Victim Support Agency Annual Report (2015).

13. Police

1. Victorian Human Rights and Equal Opportunity Commission (VHREOC), *Independent review into sex discrimination and sexual harassment, including predatory behaviour, in Victoria Police* (December 2015).

2. VHREOC, op. cit.

3. Victoria Police Sexual Offence and Child Abuse Investigation Teams reforms.

4. K. Rich and P. Seffrin, 'Birds of a feather or fish out of water? Policewomen taking rape reports', *Feminist Criminology*, no. 2 (2014), pp. 137–59; doi: 1557085113510551

5. VLRC (2004), pp. 111–2.

6. VicPol, *Options talk* booklet.

7. Caroline Taylor, 'Court-licensed Abuse: Patriarchal Lore and the Legal Response to Intrafamilial Sexual Abuse of Children (Peter Lang Publishing, 2004).

8. https://assets.publishing.service.gov.uk/government/uploads/system/uploads/attachment_data/file/575363/DVPO_guidance_FINAL_3.pdf

9. M. B. King, 'Male rape; victims need sensitive management', *British Medical Journal*, no. 301 (1990), pp. 1345–6; Samantha Hodge and David Canter, 'Victims and Perpetrators of Male Sexual Assault', *Journal of Interpersonal Violence*, vol. 13, issue 2 (1998), pp. 222–239; https://doi.org/10.1177/088626098013002004; J. A. Turchik and K. M. Edwards, 'Myths about male rape: A literature review', *Psychology of Men and Masculinity*, no. 13 (2) (2012), pp. 211–26.

10. Patrick Tidmarsh, 'Training sexual crime investigators to get the "Whole Story": Investigator qualities and field adherence to training principles', PhD thesis (2017), pp. 70–84.

11. Carolyn M. Burns, Jeff Morley, Richard Bradshaw, and José Domene, 'The Emotional Impact on and Coping Strategies Employed by Police Teams Investigating Internet Child Exploitation', *Traumatology*, vol. 14, issue 2 (2008), pp. 20–31; Victoria M. Follette, Melissa M. Polusny, and Kathleen Milbeck, 'Mental health and law enforcement professionals: Trauma history, psychological symptoms, and impact of providing services to child sexual abuse survivors', *Professional Psychology: Research and Practice*, vol. 25 (3) (August 1994), pp. 275–82.

14. Memory

1. A. Hardy, K. Young and E. A. Holmes, 'Does trauma memory play a role in the experience of reporting sexual assault during police interviews? An exploratory study', *Memory*, no. 17 (2009), pp. 783–8; doi: 10.1080/09658210903081835; K. S. LaBar and R. Cabeza, 'Cognitive neuroscience of emotional memory', *Nature Reviews Neuroscience*, 7 (2006), pp. 54–64; doi:10.1038/nrn1825

2. Christopher M. Heaps and Michael Nash (2001), 'Comparing recollective experience in true and false autobiographical memories', *Journal of Experimental Psychology: Learning, Memory, and Cognition*, vol. 27 (4) (July 2001), pp. 920–30; Robert F. Belli, 'Introduction: in the aftermath of the so-called memory wars', *Nebraska Symposium on Motivation* (2012); 58:1–13; doi: 10.1007/978-1-4614-1195-6_1

3. P. R. McHugh, *Try to Remember: Psychiatry's clash over meaning, memory, and mind* (Dana Press, 2008).

4. Richard J. McNally and Elke Geraerts, 'A New Solution to the Recovered Memory Debate', *Perspectives on Psychological Science*, vol. 4, no. 2 (2009).

5. Australian Law Reform Commission, *Seen and Heard: priority for children in the legal process* (ALRC Report 84), p. 14: 'Children's evidence. Children as reliable witnesses – Assumptions of unreliability'; https://www.alrc.gov.au/publications/14-childrens-evidence/children-reliable-witnesses; https://www.judicialcollege.vic.edu.au/eManuals/UEM/28982

6. J. Goodman-Delahunty, M. A. Nolan and E. L. Van Gijn-Grosvenor, *Empirical guidance on the effects of child sexual abuse on memory and complainants' evidence*, Report for the Royal Commission into Institutional Responses to Child Sexual Abuse (July 2017); M. R. Leippe, A. Romanczyk and A. P. Manion, 'Eyewitness memory for a touching experience: Accuracy differences between child and adult witnesses', *Journal of Applied Psychology*, no. 76 (3) (1991), pp. 367–79; http://dx.doi.org/10.1037/0021-9010.76.3.367

7. J. Ost, S. Foster, A. Costall and R. Bull, 'False reports of childhood events in appropriate interviews', *Memory*, no. 13 (2005), pp. 700–10; doi: 10.1080/09658210444000340; A. Cossins, 'Children, sexual abuse and suggestibility: What laypeople think they know and what the literature tells us', *Psychiatry, Psychology and Law*, no. 15 (2008), pp. 153–70; doi: 10.1080/13218710801886040

8. J. A. Quas, W. C. Thompson, and K. A. Clarke-Stewart, 'Do jurors "know" what isn't so about child witnesses?', *Law and Human Behavior*, no. 29 (2005), pp. 425–56; doi: 10.1007/s10979-005-5523-8

9. Clare Wilson and Martine Powell, *A Guide to Interviewing Children: Essential skills for counsellors, police, lawyers and social workers* (Allen & Unwin, 2001).

10. Cossins, op. cit.

11. Wilson and Powell, op. cit.

12. JCV, *Sexual Assault* manual, 6.4: 'Particularisation'.

13. JCV, *Sexual Assault* manual, 6.8: 'Course of conduct charges'.

14. Goodman-Delahunty et al., 'Empirical guidance …', op. cit.

15. Bessel A. van der Kolk MD, 'Trauma and memory', *Psychiatry and Clinical Neurosciences*, vol. 52, issue S1 (4 January 2002).

16. Evidence Act 2008, Part 2.1, 'Witnesses': 'Prior inconsistent statements of witnesses', p. 29; Judicial College of Victoria, Charge: Prior inconsistent statements 4.13.3; http://www.judicialcollege.vic.edu.au/eManuals/CCB/4282.htm

17. Bessel van der Kolk, *The Body Keeps the Score: Mind, Brain and Body in the Transformation of Trauma* (Penguin, 2014), p. 43.

18. J. M. Fawcett, E. J. Russell, K. A. Peace and J. Christie, 'Of guns and geese: A meta-analytic review of the "weapon focus" literature', *Psychology, Crime and Law*, no. 19 (2013), pp. 35–66; 10.1080/1068316X.2011.599325; N. M. Steblay, 'A meta-analytic review of the weapon focus effect', *Law and Human Behavior*, no. 16 (1992), pp. 413–24; doi: 10.1007/BF02352267

19. Shirley Henderson, 'Dissociation', *Information for survivors of sexual violence* (Rape Crisis Scotland, published online 2013); Bruce Perry and Maia Szalavitz, *The Boy Who Was Raised as a Dog*, chapter 'Raven' (Basic Books, 2006).
20. Peter A. Levine PhD, *Trauma and Memory: Brain and body in a search for the living past* (North Atlantic Books, 2015), p. 7.

15. Interviewing victims

1. M. B. Powell, R. P. Fisher and R. Wright, 'Investigative Interviewing', in N. Brewer and K. Williams (eds), *Psychology and Law: An empirical perspective* (Guilford Press, New York, 2005), pp. 11–42; D. Patterson, 'The impact of detectives' manner of questioning on rape victims' disclosure', *Violence Against Women*, no. 17 (2012), pp. 1349–73; doi: 1077801211434725
2. Michael S. Lewis-Beck, Alan Bryman and Tim Futing Liao, 'Open-Ended Questions', in *The SAGE Encyclopaedia of Social Science Research Methods* (2004); doi: http://dx.doi.org/10.4135/9781412950589.n665

16. Interviewing sexual offence suspects

1. G. Oxburgh, T. Myklebust, T. Grant and R. Milne, *Communication in Investigative and Legal Contexts: integrated approaches from forensic psychology, linguistics, and law enforcement* (John Wiley & Sons, London, 2015); E. Sanow, *The Reid technique of Interviewing and Interrogation*, Columbus (Law Enforcement Publications, 2011); I. A. Fahsing and A. Rachlew, 'Investigative interviewing in the Nordic region', in T. Williamson, R. Milne and S. P. Savage (eds), *International Developments in Investigative Interviewing* (Routledge, London, 2009), pp. 39–65; B. Snook, J. Eastwood, M. Stinson, J. Tedeschini and J. C. House, 'Reforming investigative interviewing in Canada', *Canadian Journal of Criminology and Criminal Justice*, no. 52 (2010), pp. 215–29; doi: 10.3138/cjccj.52.2.215
2. U. Holmberg and S. Å. Christianson, 'Murderers' and sexual offenders' experiences of police interviews and their inclination to admit or deny crimes', *Behavioral Sciences & the Law*, no. 20 (2002), pp. 31–45; doi: 0.1002/bsl.470
3. J. M. Read, M. B. Powell, M. R. Kebbell and R. Milne, 'Investigative interviewing of suspected sex offenders: A review of what constitutes best practice', *International Journal of Police Science & Management*, vol. 11 No. 4 (2009), pp. 442–459; doi: 10.1350/ijps.2009.11.4.143; I. Hershkowitz, D. Horowitz, M. E. Lamb, Y. Orbach and K. J. Sternberg, 'Interviewing youthful suspects in alleged sex crimes: A descriptive analysis', *Child Abuse and Neglect*, no. 28 (2004), pp. 423–38; doi: 10.1016/j.chiabu.2003.09.021
4. M. Kebbell, E. Hurren and P. Mazerolle, *An investigation into the effective and ethical interviewing of suspected sex offenders* (Australian Institute of Criminology, Canberra, 2006); Holmberg and Christianson, op. cit.

5. E. Shepherd, *Investigative Interviewing. The conversation management approach* (Oxford University Press, Oxford, 2007).
6. Tidmarsh, PhD Thesis, op. cit., pp. 46–57.
7. 'Bill Clinton asked by special prosecutor about using a cigar as a sexual aid on Monica Lewinsky', YouTube, posted by beebimbop.
8. Aldert Vrij, Ronald Fisher, Samantha Mann, and Sharon Leal, 'A Cognitive Load Approach to Lie Detection', *Journal of Investigative Psychology and Offender Profiling*, no. 5 (2008), pp. 39–43; Aldert Vrij, Samantha A. Mann, Ronald P. Fisher, Sharon Leal, Rebecca Milne and Ray Bull, 'Increasing Cognitive Load to Facilitate Lie Detection: The Benefit of Recalling an Event in Reverse Order', *Law and Human Behavior*, no. 32 (2007), pp. 253–65.
9. *Pretext Phone Calls in Sexual Assault Investigations*, International Association of Police Chiefs Training Key no. 574 (2004).

17. Getting the Whole Story

1. Daly and Bouhours, op. cit.
2. Judicial College of Victoria, Bench Notes: 4.7, 'Corroboration (General Principles)'.
3. J. C. Rideout, 'Storytelling, narrative rationality and legal persuasion', *Legal Writing: Justice Legal Writing Institution*, no. 14 (2008), pp. 53–69; N. Pennington and R. Hastie, 'Explaining the evidence: Tests of the Story Model for juror decision-making', *Journal of Personality and Social Psychology*, no. 62 (1992), 189206; doi: 10.1037/0022-3514.62.2.189; L. Feiner (1997), 'The whole truth: Restoring reality to children's narrative in long-term incest cases', *Journal of Criminal Law and Criminology*, no. 87, 13851429; doi: 10.2307/1144019
4. J. B. White, *Heracles' Bow: Essays on the Rhetoric and Poetics of the Law* (University of Wisconsin Press, Wisconsin, 1989).
5. Rideout, op. cit.
6. Feiner, op. cit.; H. L. Westcott and S. Kynan, 'The application of a "storytelling" framework to investigative interviews for suspected child sexual abuse', *Legal and Criminological Psychology*, no. 9 (2004), pp. 37–56; doi: 10.1348/135532504322776843
7. R. H. Conley and J. M. Conley, 'Stories from the jury room: how jurors use narrative to process evidence', *Studies in Law, Politics, and Society*, no. 49 (2009), pp. 25–56; doi: 10.1108/S1059-4337(2009)0000049005; T. A. Gannon, 'Social cognition in violent and sexual offending: An overview', *Psychology, Crime and Law*, no. 15 (2009), pp. 97–118; doi:10.1080/10683160802190822

Part IV. Justice and the courts

1. Helena Kennedy QC, *Eve Was Shamed: How British Justice is Failing Women* (Chatto and Windus, London, 2018).

2.   Crown Prosecution Service, *The Full Code Test* (gov.UK, 2017).
3.   Judicial College of Victoria, *Uniform Evidence Manual*, s55: 'Relevant evidence'.
4.   L. Frohmann, 'Discrediting victims' allegations of sexual assault: Prosecutorial accounts of case rejections', *Social Problems*, no. 38 (1991), pp. 213–26; doi: 10.2307/800530; L. Frohmann, 'Convictability and discordant locales: Reproducing race, class, and gender ideologies in prosecutorial decision-making', *Law and Society Review*, no. 31 (1997), pp. 531–56; doi: 0.2307/3054045
5.   April Pattavina, Melissa Morabito, and Linda Williams, 'Examining Connections between the Police and Prosecution in Sexual Assault Case Processing: Does the Use of Exceptional Clearance Facilitate a Downstream Orientation?', *Victims and Offenders. An International Journal of Evidence-based Research, Policy, and Practice*, no. 11:2 (2016), pp. 315–34.
6.   Royal Commission into Institutional Responses to Child Sexual Abuse, Criminal Justice Report recommendations: 'Police charging decisions' (2017), p. 95.
7.   Royal Commission into Institutional Responses to Child Sexual Abuse, Australia (2013–17).
8.   VLRC (2004), p. xviii.
9.   Alexandra Topping, 'Prosecutors urged to ditch "weak" rape cases to improve figures', *Guardian* (24 September 2018).

18. Reasonable

1.   Ray Finkelstein, 'The adversarial system and the search for the truth', *Monash University Law Review*, vol. 37, no. 1 (2011); Keith A. Findley, 'Adversarial inquisitions: Rethinking the search for the truth', *New York Law School Law Review*, vol. 56 (2011/12).
2.   M. P. Koss, 'Restoring Rape Survivors. Justice, Advocacy, and a Call to Action', *Annals of the New York Academy of Sciences*, no. 1087 (2006), pp. 206–34; doi: 10.1196/annals.1385.025
3.   Bursztajn H., 'More law and less protection: "critogenesis", "legal iatrogenesis" and medical decision making', *Journal of Geriatric Psychiatry*, 1985; 18(2):143–53. PMID: 4086735.
4.   Judith Lewis Herman, 'Justice from the Victim's Perspective', *Violence Against Women*, vol. 11, no. 5 (May 2005), pp. 571–602.
5.   'Child sex abuse commissioner hits out at lawyers who attack victim credibility', Australian Associated Press (2 March 2018).
6.   Crown Court Compendium (7 June 2016; updated November 2016); www.judiciary.uk/publications/crown-court-bench-book-directing-the-jury-2/lawreform.vic.gov.au/sites/default/files/VLRC_JuryDirections_FinalReport.pdf – VLRC (1 May 2009).
7.   *Judicial College of Victoria Manual*: 'Principles of evidence' and 'Jury directions, 19.2.3.

8. Jury Directions Act, 2015 (Vic.), s52 (4) (a), (b) and (c).

9. Australian Law Reform Commission (ALRC), Uniform Evidence Law (ALRC Report 102): 18. 'Comments, Warnings and Directions to the Jury'; Jane Goodman-Delahunty JD, PhD, Anne Cossins PhD and Kate O'Brien BSc. (Hons), 'Enhancing the credibility of complainants in child sexual assault trials: The effect of expert evidence and judicial directions', *Behavioral Sciences and the Law*, vol. 28, issue 6 (November/December 2010), pp. 769–83; https://doi.org/10.1002/bsl.936

10. Sarah Zydervelt, Rachel Zajac, Andy Kaladelfos and Nina Westera, 'Lawyers' strategies for cross-examining rape complainants: Have we moved beyond the 1950s?', *British Journal of Criminology*, no. 57 (2017), pp. 551–569.

11. Victorian Society for the Prevention of Child Abuse and Neglect (VICSPCAN).

12. New Zealand Ministerial Group on Family Violence and Sexual Violence, *Family Violence, Sexual Violence and Violence within Whanau* (2017).

13. S. J. Ko, J. D. Ford, N. Kassam-Adams, S. J. Berkowitz, C. Wilson, M. Wong and C. M. Layne, 'Creating trauma-informed systems: Child welfare, education, first responders, health care, juvenile justice', *Professional Psychology: Research and Practice*, no. 39 (4) (2008), pp. 396–404; http://dx.doi.org/10.1037/0735-7028.39.4.396; Denise E. Elliott, Paula Bjelajac, Roger D. Fallot, Laurie S. Markoff and Beth Glover Reed, 'Trauma-informed or trauma-denied: Principles and implementation of trauma-informed services for women', *Journal of Community Psychology* (27 May 2005); https://doi.org/10.1002/jcop.20063

14. E. Janssen, 'Integrating trauma-informed care into the treatment of adult male sex offenders: A systematic review', *Master of Social Work Clinical Research Papers* (2018), p. 826.

15. van Koppen, P. J., & Penrod, S. D. (eds) (2003), *Perspectives in law & psychology*, vol. 17, 'Adversarial versus inquisitorial justice: Psychological perspectives on criminal justice systems', Kluwer Academic/Plenum Publishers; https://doi.org/10.1007/978-1-4419-9196-6

16. Barbara Krahe and Jennifer Temkin, 'Addressing the attitude problem in rape trials: some proposals and methodological considerations', in Miranda Horvath and Jennifer Brown (eds), *Rape: Challenging Contemporary Thinking* (Routledge 2013).

17. Ellen M. Bublick, 'Comparative fault to the limits', *Vanderbilt Law Review*, vol. 56, no. 4 (May 2003).

18. 'George Pell's surviving victim reacts to the cardinal's appeal being dismissed', ABC news online (21 August 2019).

19. Mary Koss and Mary Achilles, 'Restorative Justice Responses to Sexual Assault', National Online Resource Center on Violence Against Women (February 2008); Kathleen Daly, *Conventional and innovative justice responses to sexual violence*, Australian Centre for the Study of Sexual Assault, ACSSA issue no. 12 (2011); M. P. Koss, 'Blame, shame, and community: Justice

responses to violence against women', *American Psychologist*, no. 55 (11) (2000), pp. 1332–43; http://dx.doi.org/10.1037/0003-066X.55.11.1332

20. John Braithwaite, 'Setting Standards for Restorative Justice', *British Journal of Criminology*, no. 42 (2002), pp. 563–77; Kathleen Daly, 'Restorative Justice. The real story', *Punishment and Society*, vol. 4 (1) (2002), pp. 55–79.

21. Centre for Justice and Reconciliation, Lesson 3: 'Programs – Group Conferencing' (2019); Judicial College of Victoria eManuals: 29.3.3, 'Group Conferencing Program' (2019).

22. Restorative Justice Council, 'Restorative justice and sexual harm': quote from 'Emma – rape survivor' (online 2016). *Restorative Justice in Australia*, Australian Institute of Criminology online resource (last updated November 2017).

23. Kathleen Daly, 'Conferencing in Australia and New Zealand: Variations, research findings, and prospects', in A. Morris and G. Maxwell (eds), *Restorative Justice for Juveniles: Conferencing, mediation, and circles* (Hart Publishing, Oxford, 2001), pp. 59–84; Tom R. Tyler, Robert J. Boeckmann, Heather J. Smith and Yuen J. Huo, *Social Justice in a Diverse Society* (Westview Press, Boulder, Co, 1997).

24. C. McGlynn and N. Westmarland, 'Kaleidoscopic justice: Sexual violence and victim-survivors' perceptions of justice', *Social and Legal Studies*, nos 1–23 (2018); doi: 10.1177/0964663918761200

19. Relevant

1. Evidence Act 2008, no. 47, part 3.1: 'Relevance', 55 (1), p. 42.

2. 'Truth, testimony, relevance: improving the quality of evidence in sexual offence cases', Australian Institute of Criminology, Melbourne Cricket Ground (15–16 May 2012).

3. Judicial College of Victoria eManuals, part 3.11: 'Discretionary and Mandatory Exclusions' (ss135 – 139) – (i), 'The concept of probative value' (2019); Andreas Glockner and Christoph Engel, 'Can We Trust Intuitive Jurors? Standards of Proof and Probative Value of Evidence in Coherence-based Reasoning', *Journal of Empirical Legal Studies*, vol. 10, issue 2 (June 2013), pp. 230–252.

4. The Criminal Procedure Rules, Part 21: 'Evidence of Bad Character', justice.gov.uk (October 2015, as amended April 2016).

5. Evidence Act 2008, op. cit., part 3.6, 'Tendency and coincidence', 101 (2), p. 77.

6. Evidence Act 2008, op. cit., part 3.1, 'Relevance', 55 (1), p. 42.

7. J. S. Hutton, 'Animal abuse as a diagnostic approach in social work: a pilot study', in R. Lockwood and F. R. Ascione (eds), *Cruelty to Animals and Interpersonal Violence: Readings in Research and Application* (Purdue University Press, Indiana, 1983, 1998), pp. 415–20; C. Ponder and R. Lockwood, 'Cruelty to animals and family violence', Training Key no. 526

(International Association of Chief of Police, 2000), pp.1–5; https://www.nspcc.org.uk/globalassets/documents/research-reports/understanding-links-child-abuse-animal-abuse-domestic-violence.pdf

8. Protecting Victoria's Vulnerable Children Inquiry report, tabled in the Victorian parliament (28 February 2018); https://www.soas.ac.uk/library/subjects/law/research/file70250.pdf

9. Victorian Supreme Court of Appeal, R&TC (November 2011).

10. Rideout, op. cit.

11. S. Dinos, N. Burrowes, K. Hammond and C. Cunliffe, 'A systematic review of juries' assessment of rape victims: Do rape myths impact on juror decision-making?', *International Journal of Law, Crime and Justice*, no. 43 (2015), pp. 36–49; doi: 10.1016/j.ijlcj.2014.07.001

12. W. R. Fisher, 'Human communication as narration: Toward a philosophy of reason, value, and action', *Philosophy and Rhetoric*, 22 (1) (1989), pp. 71–74.

13. L. Alison, L. Almond, P. Christiansen, S. Waring, N. Power and G. Villjoubert, 'When do we Believe Experts? The Power of the Unorthodox View', *Behavioral Sciences and the Law*, no. 30 (2012), pp. 729–48; doi: 10.1002/bsl.2030

20. Credible

1. SBS Insight (27 February 2018).

2. Denise Lievore, 'Victim credibility in adult sexual assault cases', *Australian Institute of Criminology Trends and Issues*, no. 288 (November 2004); J. M. Brown, C. Hamilton and D. O'Neill, 'Characteristics associated with rape attrition and the role played by scepticism or legal rationality by investigators and prosecutors', *Psychology, Crime and Law*, no. 13 (2007), pp. 355–70; doi: 0.1080/10683160601060507

3. Jennifer Temkin, 'Prosecuting and Defending Rape: Perspectives from the Bar', *Journal of Law and Society*, vol. 27, no. 2 (June 2000), pp. 219–48.

4. C. Spohn, D. Beichner and E. Davis-Frenzel, 'Prosecutorial justifications for sexual assault case rejection: Guarding the "gateway to justice"', *Social Problems*, no. 48 (2001), pp. 206–35; doi: 10.1525/sp.2001.48.2.206

5. E. N. O'Neal, K. Tellis and C. Spohn, 'Prosecuting intimate partner sexual assault: legal and extra-legal factors that influence charging decisions', *Violence Against Women*, no. 21 (2015), pp. 1237–58; doi: 10.1177/1077801215591630

6. Rideout, op. cit.; L. Ellison and V. E. Munro, 'Of "normal sex" and "real rape": Exploring the use of socio-sexual scripts in (mock) jury deliberation', *Social and Legal Studies*, no. 18 (2009), 291312; doi: 10.1177/0964663909339083; Dinos et al., op. cit.; L. Olsen-Fulero and S. M. Fulero, 'Common-sense rape judgments: An empathy-complexity theory of rape juror story-making', *Psychology, Public Policy, and Law*, no. 3 (1997), pp. 402–27; doi:10.1037/1076-8971.3.2-3.402

7. Ministry of Justice (UK), *Limiting the use of complainants' sexual history in sexual offence cases* (14 December 2017).

8. CPS (cps.gov.uk), *Disclosure of Previous Convictions of Prosecution Witnesses*; *The law and sexual offences against adults in Australia*, ACSSA issue no. 4 (June 2005).

9. 'Cardinal George Pell's lawyers seek access to complainants' medical records', ABC – Emma Younger (9 February 2018).

10. Hadley Freeman, 'What does the Belfast rape trial tell women? Make a complaint and you'll be vilified', *Guardian* (4 April 2018).

11. Bottoms et al., 'Explaining gender differences in jurors' reactions to child sexual assault cases', *Behavioral Sciences and the Law*, vol. 32, issue 6 (November 2014).

12. Suzanne Blackwell and Fred Seymour, 'Prediction of Jury Verdicts in Child Sexual Assault Trials', *Psychiatry, Psychology and Law*, no. 21:4 (2014), pp. 567–76.

13. Rose et al., 'Who Bought the Drinks? Juror Perceptions of Intoxication in a Rape Trial', *Journal of Interpersonal Violence* (August 2013).

14. Janice Du Mont, Karen-Lee Miller, and Terri L. Myhr, 'The Role of "Real Rape" and "Real Victim" Stereotypes in Police Reporting Practices of Sexually Assaulted Women', *Violence Against Women*, vol. 9, issue 4 (2003), pp. 446–86; Ellison and Munro, op. cit.; Eryb Nicole O'Neal, '"Victim is Not Credible": The Influence of Rape Culture on Police Perceptions of Sexual Assault Complainants', *Justice Quarterly*, 36: 1 (2019), pp. 127–60.

15. Wendy Larcombe, 'The Ideal Victim v Successful Rape Complainants: Not What You Might Expect', *Feminist Legal Studies*, no. 10 (2002), pp. 131–48.

16. M. C. Cutajar, P. E. Mullen, J. R. Ogloff, S. D. Thomas, D. L. Wells and J. Spataro, 'Schizophrenia and other psychotic disorders in a cohort of sexually abused children', *Archives of General Psychiatry*, no. 67 (2010), pp. 1114–9; doi: 10.1001/archgenpsychiatry.2010.147

17. Royal Commission into Institutional Responses to Child Sexual Abuse, Final Report (15 December 2017).

21. Consent

1. Bianca Fileborn, *Sexual assault laws in Australia*, Australian Institute of Family Studies, ACSSA Resource Sheet no. 1 (February 2011); Jennifer A. Bennice and Patricia A. Resick, 'Marital Rape: History, Research, and Practice', *Trauma, Violence and Abuse*, vol. 4, issue 1 (July 2003), pp. 228–46; https://doi.org/10.1177/1524838003004003003; J. E. Hasday, 'Contest and Consent: A legal history of marital rape', *California Law Review*, vol. 88, issue 5 (October 2000).

2. Sir Matthew Hale, *History of the Pleas to the Crown*, 1st edition (1736).

3. Adrian Williamson, 'The Law and Politics of Marital Rape in England, 1945–94', *Women's History Review*, no. 26:3 (2017), pp. 382–413.

4. Gov.UK, Criminal Law: 'Rape within marriage', Law Commission no. 205 (14 January 1992).

5. Sexual Offences Act (legislation.co.uk); (The National Archives, updated June 2018).

6. Victoria Ward, 'Remaining silent during a rape could be conceived as consent, DPP says', *Telegraph* (22 January 2018).

7. Paul Fontaine, 'Iceland unanimously passes landmark law on sexual consent', *Reykjavik Grapevine* (23 May 2018).

8. Paul Fontaine, 'Iceland Unanimously Passes Landmark Law on Sexual Consent', *The Good Men Project* (20 April 2018).

9. Christina Anderson, 'Swedish law now recognises sex without consent as rape', *New York Times* (23 May 2018); Government offices of Sweden (www.government.se), *Consent – the basic requirement of new sexual offence legislation* (26 April 2018; enacted into law 1 July 2018).

10. Anna Blus, 'Sex without consent is a crime, so why do only nine European countries recognise this?', *Amnesty* (23 April 2018).

11. Daniel Boffey, 'Finland under pressure to criminalise lack of consent in rape laws', *Guardian* (2 September 2019).

12. Government Offices of Sweden, Ministry of Justice fact sheet (April 2018).

13. JCV *Sexual Assault* manual, 1.4: 'Right of an accused person to a fair hearing'.

14. Jacqueline M. Gray, 'What constitutes a "reasonable belief" in consent to sex? A thematic analysis', *Journal of Sexual Aggression: An international, interdisciplinary forum for research, theory and practice*, vol. 21, issue 3 (2014), pp. 337–53; David Archard, '"A Nod's as Good as a Wink": Consent, Convention, and Reasonable Belief', *Legal Theory*, no. 3 (1997), pp. 273–90.

15. The Queen v Getachew (M139/2011); Court of Appeal of the Supreme Court of Victoria (2 June 2011).

16. The Queen and Thomas Getachew; On Appeal from the Court of Appeal Supreme Court of Victoria (28 March 2012).

17. Bianca Fileborn, op. cit.

18. Christopher P. Krebs PhD, Christine H. Lindquist PhD, Tara D. Warner MA, Bonnie S. Fisher PhD and Sandra L. Martin PhD, Campus Sexual Assault (CSA) Study, Final Report (National Institute of Justice, October 2007); Amy Young, Melissa Grey, Antonia Abbey and Carol J. Boyd, 'Alcohol-Related Sexual Assault Victimisation Among Adolescents: Prevalence, Characteristics and Correlates', *Journal of Studies on Alcohol and Drugs*, no. 69 (1) (2008), pp. 39–48.

19. Heather D. Flowe, Melanie K. T. Takarangi, Joyce E. Humphries and Deborah S. Wright, 'Alcohol and remembering a hypothetical sexual assault: Can people who were under the influence of alcohol during the event provide accurate testimony?', *Memory*, vol. 24, issue 8 (published online 17 August 2015), pp. 1042–61; https://doi.org/10.1080/09658211.2015.1064536; Ray

S.Bates ME, 'Acute alcohol effects on repetition priming and word recognition memory with equivalent memory cues', *Brain and Cognition*, 60 (2) (March 2006), pp. 118 –27.

20. Owen Bowcott and Kevin Rawlinson, 'Government "denying sexually abused children compensation"', *Guardian* (18 July 2017); Lizzie Dearden, 'Government agency apologises to man told he "consented" to sexual abuse aged thirteen', *Independent* (8 October 2017); Owen Bowcott, 'Child sexual abuse victims to be granted compensation following criticism', *Guardian* (31 October 2017).

21. Henry Samuel, 'France to set consent at age fifteen after outrage over cases of sex with eleven-year-old girls', *Telegraph* (6 March 2018); Scott Newman, 'France vows to make fifteen the legal age of consent for sex', NPR (6 March 2018).

22. 'Can an eleven-year-old consent to sex? A French court will address that question', *France 24* (with AFP, AP) (13 October 2018); 'French girl, 11, "not a child" say lawyers for man, 29, accused of sexual abuse', *Guardian/* AP (14 February 2018).

23. Chloe Farand, 'France votes against setting minimum age of sexual consent amid backlash', *Independent* (17 May 2018).

24. Australian Law Reform Commission, Report 102, Section 18: 'Comments, warnings and directions to the jury – Children's evidence'.

25. Triangle.org.uk – Children's services.

26. Penny Cooper and Michelle Mattison, 'Intermediaries, vulnerable people and the quality of evidence: An international comparison of three versions of the English intermediary model', *International Journal of Evidence and Proof*, vol. 21, issue 4 (2017), pp. 351–70.

27. ALRC, Report 102, Section 28, 'Other trial processes'.

28. ALRC, Report 102, Section 18, 'Warnings about unreliable evidence'.

29. Nina Funnell, https://www.news.com.au/lifestyle/real-life/news-life/letherspeak-nts-sexual-assault-gag-law-reformed

Part V. Where to from here?
23. Difficult conversations – prevention and change

1. M. Alexis Kennedy and Boris B. Gorzalka, 'Asian and Non-Asian Attitudes Toward Rape, Sexual Harassment, and Sexuality', *Sex Roles*, vol. 46, issues 7–8 (April 2002), pp. 227–38.

2. Klaus M. Beier MD, PhD, Dorit Grundmann MSc, Laura F. Kuhle MSc, Gerold Scherner MSc, Anna Konrad MSc and Till Amelung MD, 'The German Dunkelfeld Project: A Pilot Study to Prevent Child Sexual Abuse and the Use of Child Abusive Images', *Journal of Sexual Medicine* (4 December 2014); https://doi.org/10.1111/jsm.12785; Schaefer et al., 'Potential and Dunkenfeld offenders: Two neglected target groups for prevention of child

sexual abuse', *International Journal of Law and Psychiatry*, no. 33 (2010), pp. 154–63.

3. StopItNow.org.UK; https://www.stopitnow.org.uk/files/Helpline%20Report% 20Summary_13SEP15.pdf

4. Rebecca Russo, 'The state government has backed a program to help eliminate sexual assault at live music venues', *Time Out* (13 February 2017).

5. Kate B. Carey, Sarah E. Durney, Robyn L. Shepardson PhD and Michael P. Carey PhD, 'Incapacitated and Forcible Rape of College Women: Prevalence Across the First Year', *Journal of Adolescent Health*, vol. 56, issue 6 (June 2015), pp. 678–80; https://doi.org/10.1016/j.jadohealth.2015.02.018

6. Mythili Sampathkumar, 'Trump administration scraps Obama's campus sexual assault rules', *Independent*, New York (22 September 2017).

7. C. G. Boethius, 'Sex education in Swedish schools: the facts and the fiction', *Family Planning Perspectives*, no. 17 (6) (November–December 1985), pp. 276–9.

8. Pamela K. Kohler, Lisa E. Manhart, and William E. Lafferty, 'Abstinence-Only and Comprehensive Sex Education and the Initiation of Sexual Activity and Teen Pregnancy', *Journal of Adolescent Health*, vol. 42, issue 4 (April 2008), pp. 344–51; Trisha E. Mueller, Lorrie E. Gavin and Aniket Kulkarni, 'The Association Between Sex Education and Youth's Engagement in Sexual Intercourse, Age at First Intercourse, and Birth Control Use at First Sex', *Journal of Adolescent Health*, vol. 42, issue 1 (January 2008), pp. 89–96; Herman P. Schaal, Charles Abraham, Mary Rogers Gillmore and Gerjo Kok, 'Sex Education as Health Promotion: What Does It Take?', *Archives of Sexual Behavior*, vol. 33, issue 3 (June 2004), pp. 259–69.

9. UNESCO, *Why comprehensive sexuality education is important* (published online 15 February 2018); https://en.unesco.org/news/why-comprehensive-sexuality-education-important; Heather Weaver, Gary Smith and Susan Kippax, 'School-based sex education policies and indicators of sexual health among young people: a comparison of the Netherlands, France, Australia and the United States', *Sex Education: Sexuality, Society and Learning*, vol. 5, issue 2 (2005); https://doi.org/10.1080/14681810500038889; John Santelli, Mar A. Ott, Maureen Lyon, Jennifer Rogers, Daniel Summers and Rebecca Schleifer, 'Abstinence and abstinence-only education: A review of US policies and programs', *Journal of Adolescent Health*, vol. 38, issue 1 (January 2006), pp. 72–81.

10. Judith Herman, op. cit.

Acknowledgements

There are so many people to thank, I hardly know where to start. Over the course of more than thirty years, many people have helped and influenced me, so I'm going to start at the beginning.

I never would have started working in prisons if I hadn't met John Bergman and become part of starting the British Geese Theatre Company. I also learnt a great deal about sexual offenders from working with John. I must also thank Saul Hewish, an early colleague at Geese, who still works with prisoners all these years later. We all remain good friends, bonded by those times.

I'd like to thank Ray Wyre and Charles Fortt, who gave me a job, and the opportunity to be part of pioneering work with child molesters.

When I got to Australia, Priscilla Mulhern and Darren Eger helped establish the MAPPS programme and develop the work with adolescents. Thanks also to all the other staff members who worked with me over the fourteen years I was there.

I'd like to thank Tania Farha and Sue Clifford for the job at Victoria Police and, more importantly, for establishing the SOCIT project. It has been a ground-breaking initiative, changing the culture of policing and establishing the specialism of sexual crime investigation. Rena de Francesco and Rod Jouning carried on their work superbly, as Narelle Goodland and Sally Ruth do today.

The SOCIT training programme would never have been successful without my friend and colleague, Mark Barnett. Not only is he one of the finest trainers I know, but his quiet, steely determination guided us through a lot of challenges. Thanks also to Tony Breen, a passionate advocate for this work, who helped encourage his fellow officers to believe in the training, and in victim-centric work.

I have worked with many fine detectives whilst at Vic Pol, and the friendships of such investigator colleagues as Craig Gye, Marnie Johnstone, Darren Cooper, and Helen Chugg, along with a host of others, helped sustain me through the unique challenges of working in policing.

When it came to writing this book, it never would have happened without my dear friend, Chris Campbell. His early encouragement meant a lot, as did Ian Morse's, who read early drafts. I'd also like to thank Maree Crabbe and Mark Barnett for their help with the chapters on pornography and memory/interviewing respectively.

Sarah Ballard and Eli Keren, at United Agents, have been endlessly supportive, as has Bea Hemming at Jonathan Cape.

There are three final groups I would like to mention. Firstly, my wife and partner, Jacqui. I am so lucky to have you in my life. I would not have started, or finished, this huge project without your love, wisdom, and subject matter advice. Secondly, the girls and young women at the heart of my world, Asha, Natalia, Marina, and Madeleine, from whom I have learnt so much about love and connection.

Finally, I would like to thank all the survivors who have come forward to tell their stories. We continue to learn from you. I hope that soon we may have created communities where everyone can feel free to come forward, unafraid of us and our reactions.

Index

adolescent offenders, 61–2, 68,
    69, 78–85, 100
  identity, 78
  motivations, 80
  'tick the box' kids, 83–5
  pornography, use of, 101,
    110–11
  as victims, 80–81
adversarial justice system,
    xv–xvii, 28–9, 181, 182,
    193–233
  authorising cases, 195
  children and, xv–xvii, 144–5,
    153, 198, 200–201, 219, 231
  communications evidence,
    57, 182–3
  consent and, 222–33
  counter-intuitive behaviour
    and, 14, 19, 40, 63, 182
  credibility, 193, 194, 216–21
  criminal history and, 218, 220
  critogenic harm, 197
  cross-examination, xv–xvii,
    182, 199, 216, 220
  downstream orientation, 194,
    195, 217
  evidence, *see* evidence
  extra-judicial factors, 217
  interviews and, 152, 153, 155
  juries, *see* juries

memory and, xv–xvii, 144–5,
    147, 152, 154, 198, 200
  misconceptions and, 39, 40, 41,
    44, 126, 129, 197
  nature of harm and, 16
  police and, 194
  pre-trial meetings, 208
  pretext calls and, 178, 179
  re-traumatisation, 197
  reasonability, 34, 193, 197–206
  relevance, 193, 194, 207–15
  state and, 203
  storytelling and, 184–91,
    207–15
alcohol, 63, 116, 156
  abuse and, 11, 28, 55, 60, 63, 75,
    116, 220, 228, 247
  consent and, 28, 228–9
  victims and, 16, 25, 26, 220
anal penetration, 43, 57, 101, 118,
    154, 224
animals, killing of, 83, 209–14
anxiety, 14, 16, 140, 239
Armenia, 97
arousal, 42–3, 57
'asking for it', xiii, xvii, 1, 14
Australia
  false reporting narrative in,
    27, 29, 33–4
  family violence in, 12